What Readers Are Saying About
Practical Programming

Practical Programming is true to its name. The information it presents is organized around useful tasks rather than abstract constructs, and each chapter addresses a well-contained and important aspect of programming in Python. A student wondering "How do I make the computer do X?" would be able to find their answer very quickly with this book.

► **Christine Alvarado**
  Associate professor of computer science, Harvey Mudd College

Science is about learning by performing experiments. This book encourages computer science students to experiment with short, interactive Python scripts and in the process learn fundamental concepts such as data structures, sorting and searching algorithms, object-oriented programming, accessing databases, graphical user interfaces, and good program design. Clearly written text along with numerous compelling examples, diagrams, and images make this an excellent book for the beginning programmer.

► **Ronald Mak**
  Research staff member, IBM Almaden Research Center
  Lecturer, Department of Computer Science, San Jose State University

What, no compiler, no sample payroll application? What kind of programming book is this? A great one, that's what. It launches from a "You don't know anything yet" premise into a fearless romp through the concepts and techniques of relevant programming technology. And what fun students will have with the images and graphics in the exercises!

► **Laura Wingerd**
  Author, *Practical Perforce*

The debugging section is truly excellent. I know several practicing programmers who'd be rightfully offended by a suggestion to study the whole book but who could *really* do with brushing up on this section (and many others) once in a while.

▶ **Alex Martelli**
Author, *Python in a Nutshell*

This book succeeds in two different ways. It is both a science-focused CS1 text and a targeted Python reference. Even as it builds students' computational insights, it also empowers and encourages them to immediately apply their newfound programming skills in the lab or on projects of their own.

▶ **Zachary Dodds**
Associate professor of computer science, Harvey Mudd College

Practical Programming

An Introduction to Computer Science Using Python

Practical Programming

An Introduction to Computer Science Using Python

Jennifer Campbell

Paul Gries

Jason Montojo

Greg Wilson

The Pragmatic Bookshelf

Raleigh, North Carolina   Dallas, Texas

Many of the designations used by manufacturers and sellers to distinguish their products are claimed as trademarks. Where those designations appear in this book, and The Pragmatic Programmers, LLC was aware of a trademark claim, the designations have been printed in initial capital letters or in all capitals. The Pragmatic Starter Kit, The Pragmatic Programmer, Pragmatic Programming, Pragmatic Bookshelf and the linking *g* device are trademarks of The Pragmatic Programmers, LLC.

Every precaution was taken in the preparation of this book. However, the publisher assumes no responsibility for errors or omissions, or for damages that may result from the use of information (including program listings) contained herein.

Our Pragmatic courses, workshops, and other products can help you and your team create better software and have more fun. For more information, as well as the latest Pragmatic titles, please visit us at

http://www.pragprog.com

ISBN-10: 1-934356-27-1

ISBN-13: 978-1-934356-27-2

Printed on acid-free paper.

P2.0 printing, September 2009

Version: 2009-9-8

Contents

Chapter 1

Introduction

Take a look at the pictures in Figure 1.1, on the following page. The first one shows forest cover in the Amazon basin in 1975. The second one shows the same area 26 years later. Anyone can see that much of the rainforest has been destroyed, but how much is "much"?

Now look at Figure 1.2, on page 3.

Are these blood cells healthy? Do any of them show signs of leukemia? It would take an expert doctor a few minutes to tell. Multiply those minutes by the number of people who need to be screened. There simply aren't enough human doctors in the world to check everyone.

This is where computers come in. Computer programs can measure the differences between two pictures and count the number of oddly shaped platelets in a blood sample. Geneticists use programs to analyze gene sequences; statisticians, to analyze the spread of diseases; geologists, to predict the effects of earthquakes; economists, to analyze fluctuations in the stock market; and climatologists, to study global warming. More and more scientists are writing programs to help them do their work. In turn, those programs are making entirely new kinds of science possible.

Of course, computers are good for a lot more than just science. We used computers to write this book; you have probably used one today to chat with friends, find out where your lectures are, or look for a restaurant that serves pizza *and* Chinese food. Every day, someone figures out how to make a computer do something that has never been done before. Together, those "somethings" are changing the world.

This book will teach you how to make computers do what *you* want them to do. You may be planning to be a doctor, linguist, or physicist

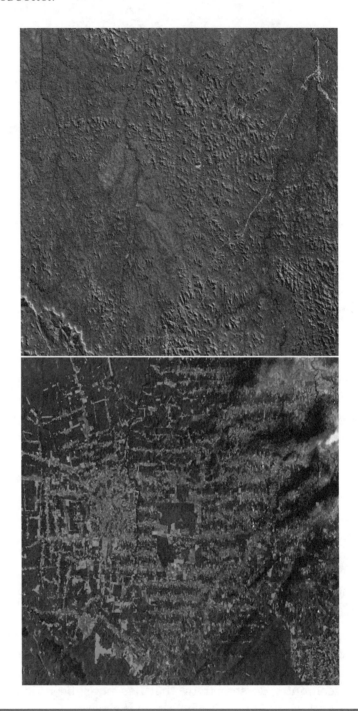

Figure 1.1: THE RAINFOREST RETREATS (PHOTO CREDIT: NASA/GODDARD SPACE FLIGHT CENTER SCIENTIFIC VISUALIZATION STUDIO)

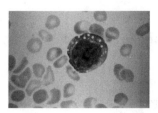

Figure 1.2: HEALTHY BLOOD CELLS—OR ARE THEY? (PHOTO CREDIT: CDC)

rather than a full-time programmer, but whatever you do, being able to program is as important as being able to write a letter or do basic arithmetic.

We begin in this chapter by explaining what programs and programming are. We then define a few terms and present a few boring-but-necessary bits of information for course instructors.

1.1 Programs and Programming

A *program* is a set of instructions. When you write down directions to your house for a friend, you are writing a program. Your friend "executes" that program by following each instruction in turn.

Every program is written in terms of a few basic operations that its reader already understands. For example, the set of operations that your friend can understand might include the following: "Turn left at Darwin Street," "Go forward three blocks," and "If you get to the gas station, turn around—you've gone too far."

Computers are similar but have a different set of operations. Some operations are mathematical, like "Add 10 to a number and take the square root," while others include "Read a line from the file named data.txt," "Make a pixel blue," or "Send email to the authors of this book."

The most important difference between a computer and an old-fashioned calculator is that you can "teach" a computer new operations by defining them in terms of old ones. For example, you can teach the computer that "Take the average" means "Add up the numbers in a set and divide by the set's size." You can then use the operations you have just defined to create still more operations, each layered on top of the ones that came before. It's a lot like creating life by putting atoms together to make proteins and then combining proteins to build cells and giraffes.

Defining new operations, and combining them to do useful things, is the heart and soul of programming. It is also a tremendously powerful way to think about other kinds of problems. As Prof. Jeannette Wing wrote [Win06], computational thinking is about the following:

- *Conceptualizing, not programming.* Computer science is not computer programming. Thinking like a computer scientist means more than being able to program a computer. It requires thinking at multiple levels of abstraction.
- *A way that humans, not computers, think.* Computational thinking is a way humans solve problems; it is not trying to get humans to think like computers. Computers are dull and boring; humans are clever and imaginative. We humans make computers exciting. Equipped with computing devices, we use our cleverness to tackle problems we would not dare take on before the age of computing and build systems with functionality limited only by our imaginations.
- *For everyone, everywhere.* Computational thinking will be a reality when it is so integral to human endeavors it disappears as an explicit philosophy.

We hope that by the time you have finished reading this book, you will see the world in a slightly different way.

1.2 A Few Definitions

One of the pieces of terminology that causes confusion is what to call certain characters. The Python style guide (and several dictionaries) use these names, so this book does too:

()   Parentheses
[]   Brackets
{}   Braces

1.3 What to Install

For current installation instructions, please download the code from the book website and open install/index.html in a browser. The book URL is http://pragprog.com/titles/gwpy/practical-programming.

1.4 For Instructors

This book uses the Python programming language to introduce standard CS1 topics and a handful of useful applications. We chose Python for several reasons:

- *It is free and well documented.* In fact, Python is one of the largest and best-organized open source projects going.
- *It runs everywhere.* The reference implementation, written in C, is used on everything from cell phones to supercomputers, and it's supported by professional-quality installers for Windows, Mac OS, and Linux.
- *It has a clean syntax.* Yes, every language makes this claim, but in the four years we have been using it at the University of Toronto, we have found that students make noticeably fewer "punctuation" mistakes with Python than with C-like languages.
- *It is relevant.* Thousands of companies use it every day; it is one of the three "official languages" at Google, and large portions of the game Civilization IV are written in Python. It is also widely used by academic research groups.
- *It is well supported by tools.* Legacy editors like Vi and Emacs all have Python editing modes, and several professional-quality IDEs are available. (We use a free-for-students version of one called Wing IDE.)

We use an "objects first, classes second" approach: students are shown how to *use* objects from the standard library early on but do not create their own classes until after they have learned about flow control and basic data structures. This compromise avoids the problem of explaining Java's public static void main(String[] args) to someone who has never programmed.

We have organized the book into two parts. The first covers fundamental programming ideas: elementary data types (numbers, strings, lists, sets, and dictionaries), modules, control flow, functions, testing, debugging, and algorithms. Depending on the audience, this material can be covered in nine or ten weeks.

The second part of the book consists of more or less independent chapters on more advanced topics that assume all the basic material has been covered. The first of these chapters shows students how to create their own classes and introduces encapsulation, inheritance, and polymorphism; courses for computer science majors will want to include this material. The other chapters cover application areas, such as 3D graphics, databases, GUI construction, and the basics of web programming; these will appeal to both computer science majors and students from the sciences and will allow the book to be used for both.

Lots of other good books on Python programming exist. Some are accessible to novices [Guz04, Zel03], and others are for anyone with any previous programming experience [DEM02, GL07, LA03]. You may also want to take a look at [Pyt], the special interest group for educators using Python.

1.5 Summary

In this book, we'll do the following:

- We will show you how to develop and use programs that solve real-world problems. Most of its examples will come from science and engineering, but the ideas can be applied to any domain.

- We start by teaching you the core features of a programming language called Python. These features are included in every modern programming language, so you can use what you learn no matter what you work on next.

- We will also teach you how to think methodically about programming. In particular, we will show you how to break complex problems into simple ones and how to combine the solutions to those simpler problems to create complete applications.

- Finally, we will introduce some tools that will help make your programming more productive, as well as some others that will help your applications cope with larger problems.

## Chapter 2

Hello, Python

Programs are made up of commands that a computer can understand. These commands are called *statements*, which the computer *executes*. This chapter describes the simplest of Python's statements and shows how they can be used to do basic arithmetic. It isn't very exciting in its own right, but it's the basis of almost everything that follows.

2.1 The Big Picture

In order to understand what happens when you're programming, you need to have a basic understanding of how a program gets executed on a computer. The computer itself is assembled from pieces of hardware, including a *processor* that can execute instructions and do arithmetic, a place to store data such as a *hard drive*, and various other pieces such as computer monitor, a keyboard, a card for connecting to a network, and so on.

To deal with all these pieces, every computer runs some kind of *operating system*, such as Microsoft Windows, Linux, or Mac OS X. An operating system, or OS, is a program; what makes it special is that it's the only program on the computer that's allowed direct access to the hardware. When any other program on the computer wants to draw on the screen, find out what key was just pressed on the keyboard, or fetch data from the hard drive, it sends a request to the OS (see Figure 2.1, on the following page).

This may seem a roundabout way of doing things, but it means that only the people writing the OS have to worry about the differences between one network card and another. Everyone else—everyone analyzing scientific data or creating 3D virtual chat rooms—only has to

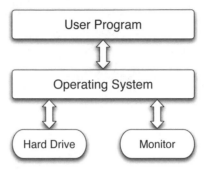

Figure 2.1: Talking to the operating system

learn their way around the OS, and their programs will then run on thousands of different kinds of hardware.

Twenty-five years ago, that's how most programmers worked. Today, though, it's common to add another layer between the programmer and the computer's hardware. When you write a program in Python, Java, or Visual Basic, it doesn't run directly on top of the OS. Instead, another program, called an *interpreter* or *virtual machine*, takes your program and runs it for you, translating your commands into a language the OS understands. It's a lot easier, more secure, and more portable across operating systems than writing programs directly on top of the OS.

But an interpreter alone isn't enough; it needs some way to interact with the world. One way to do this is to run a text-oriented program called a *shell* that reads commands from the keyboard, does what they ask, and shows their output as text, all in one window. Shells exist for various programming languages as well as for interacting with the OS; we will be exploring Python in this chapter using a Python shell.

The more modern way to interact with Python is to use an *integrated development environment*, or IDE. This is a full-blown graphical interface with menus and windows, much like a web browser, word processor, or drawing program.

Our favorite IDE for student-sized programs is the free Wing 101, a "lite" version of the professional tool.[1]

---

1. See http://www.wingware.com for details.

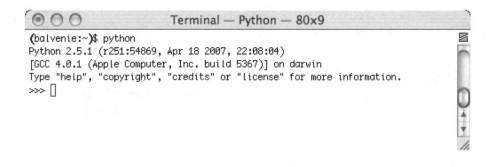

Figure 2.2: A PYTHON SHELL

Another fine IDE is IDLE, which comes bundled with Python. We prefer Wing 101 because it was designed specifically for beginning programmers, but IDLE is a capable development environment.

The Wing 101 interface is shown in Figure 2.3, on the next page. The top part is the editing pane where we will write Python programs. You can run the code you type there by clicking the Run button on the toolbar. You can also save the contents of that pane into a .py file. The bottom half of the IDE, labeled as Python Shell, is where we will experiment with snippets of Python programs. We'll use the top pane more when we get to Chapter 4, *Modules*, on page 41; for now we'll stick to the shell.

The >>> part is called a *prompt*, because it prompts us to type something.

2.2 Expressions

As we learned at the beginning of the chapter, Python commands are called *statements*. One kind of statement is an *expression statement*, or *expression* for short. You're familiar with mathematical expressions like 3 + 4 and 2 - 3 / 5; each expression is built out of *values* like 2 and 3 / 5 and *operators* like + and -, which combine their *operands* in different ways.

Like any programming language, Python can *evaluate* basic mathematical expressions. For example, the following expression adds 4 and 13:

```
basic/addition.cmd
```

```
>>> 4 + 13
```

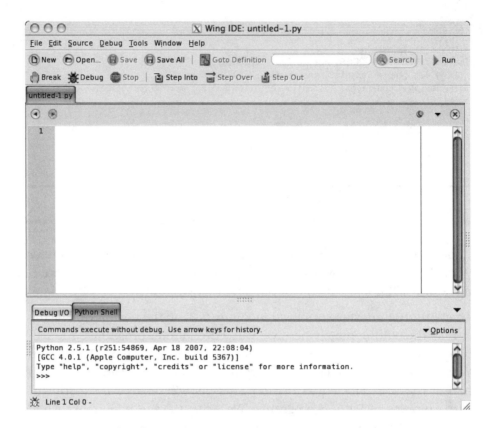

Figure 2.3: THE WING 101 INTERFACE

When an expression is evaluated, it produces a single result. In the previous expression, 4 + 13 produced the result 17.

Type int

It's not surprising that 4 + 13 is 17. However, computers do not always play by the rules you learned in primary school. For example, look at what happens when we divide 17 by 10:

`basic/int_div.cmd`

```
>>> 17 / 10
1
```

You would expect the result to be 1.7, but Python produces 1 instead. This is because every value in Python has a particular *type*, and the types of values determine how they behave when they're combined.

> **Division in Python 3.0**
>
> In the latest version of Python (Python 3.0), 5 / 2 is 2.5 rather than 2. Python 3.0 is currently less widely used than its predecessors, so the examples in this book use the "classic" behavior.

In Python, an expression involving values of a certain type produces a value of that same type. For example, 17 and 10 are integers—in Python, we say they are of type int. When we divide one by the other, the result is also an int.

Notice that Python doesn't round integer expressions. If it did, the result would have been 2. Instead, it takes the *floor* of the intermediate result. If you want the leftovers, you can use Python's modulo operator (%) to return the remainder:

`basic/int_mod.cmd`

```
>>> 17 % 10
7
```

Be careful about using % and / with negative operands. Since Python takes the floor of the result of an integer division, the result is one smaller than you might expect:

`basic/neg_int_div.cmd`

```
>>> -17 / 10
-2
```

When using modulo, the sign of the result matches the sign of the second operand:

`basic/neg_int_mod.cmd`

```
>>> -17 % 10
3
>>> 17 % -10
-3
```

Type float

Python has another type called float to represent numbers with fractional parts. The word *float* is short for *floating point*, which refers to the decimal point that moves around between digits of the number.

An expression involving two floats produces a float:

basic/float_div_intro.cmd

```
>>> 17.0 / 10.0
1.7
```

When an expression's operands are an int and a float, Python automatically converts the int to a float. This is why the following two expressions both return the same answer as the earlier one:

basic/float_division.cmd

```
>>> 17.0 / 10
1.7
>>> 17 / 10.0
1.7
```

If you want, you can omit the zero after the decimal point when writing a floating-point number:

basic/float_division2.cmd

```
>>> 17 / 10.
1.7
>>> 17. / 10
1.7
```

However, most people think this is bad style, since it makes your programs harder to read: it's very easy to miss a dot on the screen and see "17" instead of "17."

2.3 What *Is* a Type?

We've now seen two types of numbers, so we ought to explain exactly what we mean by a *type*. In computing, a type is a set of values, along with a set of operations that can be performed on those values. For example, the type int is the values ..., -3, -2, -1, 0, 1, 2, 3, ..., along with the operators +, -, *, /, and % (and a few others we haven't introduced yet). On the other hand, 84.2 is a member of the set of float values, but it is not in the set of int values.

Arithmetic was invented before Python, so the int and float types have exactly the same operators. We can see what happens when these are applied to various values in Figure 2.4, on the next page.

Operator	Symbol	Example	Result
-	Negation	-5	-5
*	Multiplication	8.5 * 3.5	29.75
/	Division	11 / 3	3
%	Remainder	8.5 % 3.5	1.5
+	Addition	11 + 3	14
-	Subtraction	{5 - 19}	-14
**	Exponentiation	2 ** 5	32

Figure 2.4: ARITHMETIC OPERATORS

Finite Precision

Floating-point numbers are not exactly the fractions you learned in grade school. For example, take a look at Python's version of the fraction $\frac{1}{3}$ (remember to include a decimal point so that the result isn't truncated):

basic/rate.cmd

```
>>> 1.0 / 3.0
0.33333333333333331
```

What's that 1 doing at the end? Shouldn't it be a 3? The problem is that real computers have a finite amount of memory, which limits how much information they can store about any single number. The number 0.33333333333333331 turns out to be the closest value to $\frac{1}{3}$ that the computer can actually store.

Operator Precedence

Let's put our knowledge of ints and floats to use to convert Fahrenheit to Celsius. To do this, we subtract 32 from the temperature in Fahrenheit and then multiply by $\frac{5}{9}$:

basic/precedence.cmd

```
>>> 212 - 32.0 * 5.0 / 9.0
194.22222222222223
```

Python claims the result is 194.22222222222223[2] degrees Celsius when in fact it should be 100. The problem is that * and / have higher

---

2. This is another floating-point approximation.

More on Numeric Precision

Computers use the same amount of memory to store an integer regardless of that integer's value, which means that -22984, -1, and 100000000 all take up the same amount of room. Because of this, computers can store int values only in a certain range. A modern desktop or laptop machine, for example, can store the numbers only from -2147483648 to 2147483647. (We'll take a closer look in the exercises at where these bounds come from.)

Computers can store only *approximations* to real numbers for the same reason. For example, $\frac{1}{4}$ can be stored exactly, but as we've already seen, $\frac{1}{3}$ cannot. Using more memory won't solve the problem, though it will make the approximation closer to the real value, just as writing a larger number of 3s after the 0 in 0.333... doesn't make it exactly equal to $\frac{1}{3}$.

The difference between $\frac{1}{3}$ and 0.33333333333333331 may look tiny. But if we use that value in a calculation, then the error may get compounded. For example, if we add the float to itself, the result ends in ...6662; that is a slightly worse approximation to $\frac{2}{3}$ than 0.666.... As we do more calculations, the rounding errors can get larger and larger, particularly if we're mixing very large and very small numbers. For example, suppose we add 10,000,000,000 and 0.00000000001. The result ought to have twenty zeroes between the first and last significant digit, but that's too many for the computer to store, so the result is just 10,000,000,000—it's as if the addition never took place. Adding lots of small numbers to a large one can therefore have no effect at all, which is *not* what a bank wants when it totals up the values of its customers' savings accounts.

It's important to be aware of the floating-point issue so that your programs don't bite you unexpectedly, but the solutions to this problem are beyond the scope of this text. In fact, *numerical analysis*, the study of algorithms to approximate continuous mathematics, is one of the largest subfields of computer science and mathematics.

Operator	Symbol
**	Exponentiation
-	Negation
*, /, %	Multiplication, division, and remainder
+-	Addition and subtraction

Figure 2.5: ARITHMETIC OPERATORS BY PRECEDENCE

precedence than -; in other words, when an expression contains a mix of operators, * and / are evaluated before - and +. This means that what we actually calculated was 212 - ((32.0 * 5.0) / 9.0).

We can alter the order of precedence by putting parentheses around parts of the expression, just as we did in Mrs. Singh's fourth-grade class:

basic/precedence_diff.cmd

```
>>> (212 - 32.0) * 5.0 / 9.0
100.0
```

The order of precedence for arithmetic operators is listed in Figure 2.5. It's a good rule to parenthesize complicated expressions even when you don't need to, since it helps the eye read things like 1+1.7+3.2*4.4-16/3.

2.4 Variables and the Assignment Statement

Most handheld calculators[3] have one or more memory buttons. These store a value so that it can be used later. In Python, we can do this with a *variable*, which is just a name that has a value associated with it. Variables' names can use letters, digits, and the underscore symbol. For example, X, species5618, and degrees_celsius are all allowed, but 777 isn't (it would be confused with a number), and neither is no-way! (it contains punctuation).

You create a new variable simply by giving it a value:

basic/assignment.cmd

```
>>> degrees_celsius = 26.0
```

---

3. And cell phones, and wristwatches, and...

$$\texttt{degrees\_celsius} \longrightarrow 26.0$$

Figure 2.6: Memory model for a variable and its associated value

---

This statement is called an *assignment statement*; we say that degrees_celsius is *assigned* the value 26.0. An assignment statement is executed as follows:

1. Evaluate the expression on the right of the = sign.
2. Store that value with the variable on the left of the = sign.

In Figure 2.6, we can see the *memory model* for the result of the assignment statement. It's pretty simple, but we will see more complicated memory models later.

Once a variable has been created, we can use its value in other calculations. For example, we can calculate the difference between the temperature stored in degrees_celsius and the boiling point of water like this:

`basic/variable.cmd`

```
>>> 100 - degrees_celsius
74.0
```

Whenever the variable's name is used in an expression, Python uses the variable's value in the calculation. This means that we can create new variables from old ones:

`basic/assignment2.cmd`

```
>>> difference = 100 - degrees_celsius
```

Typing in the name of a variable on its own makes Python display its value:

`basic/variable2.cmd`

```
>>> difference
74.0
```

What happened here is that we gave Python a very simple expression—one that had no operators at all—so Python evaluated it and showed us the result.

It's no more mysterious than asking Python what the value of 3 is:

basic/simplevalue.cmd

```
>>> 3
3
```

Variables are called variables because their values can change as the program executes. For example, we can assign difference a new value:

basic/variable3.cmd

```
>>> difference = 100 - 15.5
>>> difference
84.5
```

This does *not* change the results of any calculations done with that variable before its value was changed:

basic/variable4.cmd

```
>>> difference = 20
>>> double = 2 * difference
>>> double
40
>>> difference = 5
>>> double
40
```

As the memory models illustrate in Figure 2.7, on the following page, once a value is associated with double, it stays associated until the program explicitly overwrites it. Changes to other variables, like difference, have no effect.

We can even use a variable on both sides of an assignment statement:

basic/variable5.cmd

```
>>> number = 3
>>> number
3
>>> number = 2 * number
>>> number
6
>>> number = number * number
>>> number
36
```

This wouldn't make much sense in mathematics—a number cannot be equal to twice its own value—but = in Python doesn't mean "equals to." Instead, it means "assign a value to."

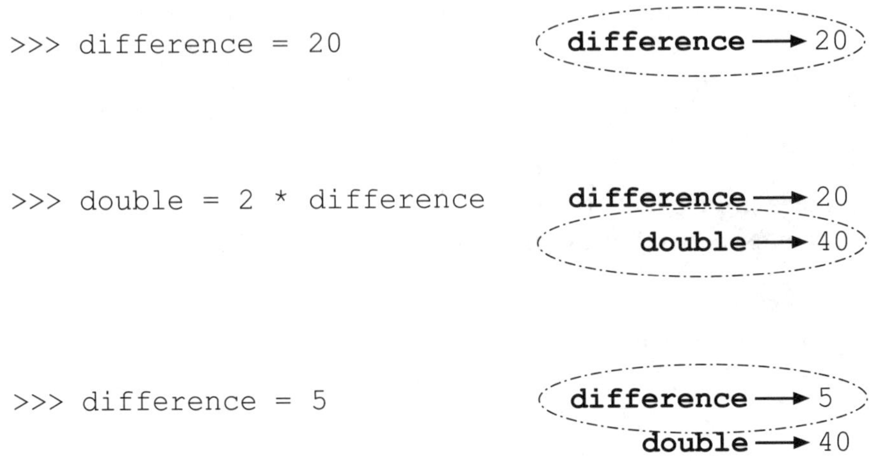

```
>>> difference = 20
```

difference ⟶ 20

```
>>> double = 2 * difference
```

difference ⟶ 20
double ⟶ 40

```
>>> difference = 5
```

difference ⟶ 5
double ⟶ 40

Figure 2.7: CHANGING A VARIABLE'S VALUE

When a statement like number = 2 * number is evaluated, Python does the following:

1. Gets the value currently associated with number
2. Multiplies it by 2 to create a new value
3. Assigns that value to number

Combined Operators

In the previous example, variable number appeared on both sides of the assignment statement. This is so common that Python provides a shorthand notation for this operation:

basic/variable6.cmd

```
>>> number = 100
>>> number -= 80
>>> number
20
```

Here is how a *combined operator* is evaluated:

1. Evaluate the expression to the right of the = sign.
2. Apply the operator attached to the = sign to the variable and the result of the expression.
3. Assign the result to the variable to the left of the = sign.

Note that the operator is applied *after* the expression on the right is evaluated:

basic/variable7.cmd

```
>>> d = 2
>>> d *= 3 + 4
>>> d
14
```

All the operators in Figure 2.5, on page 15, have shorthand versions. For example, we can square a number by multiplying it by itself:

basic/variable8.cmd

```
>>> number = 10
>>> number *= number
>>> number
100
```

which is equivalent to this:

basic/variable9.cmd

```
>>> number = 10
>>> number = number * number
>>> number
100
```

2.5 When Things Go Wrong

We said earlier that variables are created by assigning them values. What happens if we try to use a variable that hasn't been created yet?

basic/undefined_var.cmd

```
>>> 3 + something
Traceback (most recent call last):
  File "<stdin>", line 1, in <module>
NameError: name 'something' is not defined
```

This is pretty cryptic. In fact, Python's error messages are one of its few weaknesses from the point of view of novice programmers. The first two lines aren't much use right now, though they'll be indispensable when we start writing longer programs. The last line is the one that tells us what went wrong: the name something wasn't recognized.

Here's another error message you might sometimes see:

`basic/syntax_error.cmd`

```
>>> 2 +
  File "<stdin>", line 1
    2 +
      ^
SyntaxError: invalid syntax
```

The rules governing what is and isn't legal in a programming language (or any other language) are called its *syntax*. What this message is telling us is that we violated Python's syntax rules—in this case, by asking it to add something to 2 but not telling it what to add.

2.6 Function Basics

Earlier in this chapter, we converted 80 degrees Fahrenheit to Celsius. A mathematician would write this as $f(t) = \frac{5}{9}(t-32)$, where t is the temperature in Fahrenheit that we want to convert to Celsius. To find out what 80 degrees Fahrenheit is in Celsius, we replace t with 80, which gives us $f(80) = \frac{5}{9}(80-32)$, or $26\frac{2}{3}$.

We can write functions in Python, too. As in mathematics, they are used to define common formulas. Here is the conversion function in Python:

`basic/fahr_to_cel.cmd`

```
>>> def to_celsius(t):
...     return (t - 32.0) * 5.0 / 9.0
...
```

(Press enter to add a blank line so the Python interpreter knows you're done.) This has these major differences from its mathematical equivalent:

- A function definition is another kind of Python statement; it defines a new name whose value can be rather complicated but is still just a value.
- The *keyword* def is used to tell Python that we're defining a new function.
- We use a readable name like to_celsius for the function rather than something like f whose meaning will be hard to remember an hour later. (This isn't actually a requirement, but it's good style.)
- There is a colon instead of an equals sign.
- The actual formula for the function is defined on the next line. The line is indented four spaces and marked with the keyword return.

Python displays a triple-dot prompt automatically when you're in the middle of defining a new function; you do not type the dots any more than you type the greater-than signs in the usual >>> prompt. If you're using a smart editor, like the one in Wing 101, it will automatically indent the *body* of the function by the required amount. (This is another reason to use Wing 101 instead of a basic text editor like Notepad or Pico: it saves a lot of wear and tear on your spacebar and thumb.)

Here is what happens when we ask Python to evaluate to_celsius(80), to_celsius(78.8), and to_celsius(10.4):

`basic/fahr_to_cel_2.cmd`

```
>>> to_celsius(80)
26.666666666666668
>>> to_celsius(78.8)
26.0
>>> to_celsius(10.4)
-12.0
```

Each of these three statements is called a *function call*, because we're calling up the function to do some work for us. We have to define a function only once; we can call it any number of times.

The general form of a function definition is as follows:

```
def function_name(parameters):
    block
```

As we've already seen, the def keyword tells Python that we're defining a new function. The name of the function comes next, followed by zero or more *parameters* in parentheses and a colon. A *parameter* is a variable (like t in the function to_celsius) that is given a value when the function is called. For example, 80 was assigned to t in the function call to_celsius(80), and then 78.8 in to_celsius(78.8), and then 10.4 in to_celsius(10.4). Those actual values are called the *arguments* to the function.

What the function does is specified by the *block* of statements inside it. to_celsius's block consisted of just one statement, but as we'll see later, the blocks making up more complicated functions may be many statements long.

Finally, the return statement has this general form:

```
return expression
```

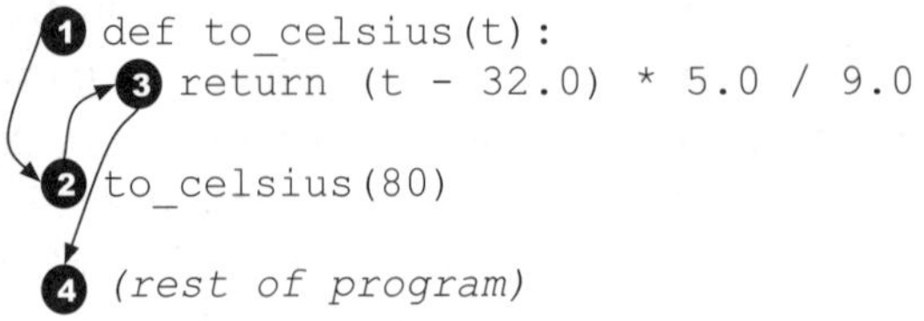

```
❶ def to_celsius(t):
   ❸ return (t - 32.0) * 5.0 / 9.0

❷ to_celsius(80)

❹ (rest of program)
```

Figure 2.8: FUNCTION CONTROL FLOW

---

and is executed as follows:

1. Evaluate the expression to the right of the keyword return.
2. Use that value as the result of the function.

It's important to be clear on the difference between a function *definition* and a function *call*. When a function is defined, Python records it but doesn't execute it. When the function is called, Python jumps to the first line of that function and starts running it (see Figure 2.8). When the function is finished, Python returns to the place where the function was originally called.

Local Variables

Some computations are complex, and breaking them down into separate steps can lead to clearer code. Here, we break down the evaluation of the polynomial $ax^2 + bx + c$ into several steps:

basic/multi_statement_block.cmd

```
>>> def polynomial(a, b, c, x):
...     first  = a * x * x
...     second = b * x
...     third  = c
...     return first + second + third
...
>>> polynomial(2, 3, 4, 0.5)
6.0
>>> polynomial(2, 3, 4, 1.5)
13.0
```

Variables like first, second, and third that are created within a function are called *local variables*. These variables exist only during function execution; when the function finishes executing, the variables no longer exist. This means that trying to access a local variable from outside the function is an error, just like trying to access a variable that has never been defined:

basic/local_variable.cmd

```
>>> polynomial(2, 3, 4, 1.3)
11.280000000000001
>>> first
Traceback (most recent call last):
  File "<stdin>", line 1, in <module>
NameError: name 'first' is not defined
>>> a
Traceback (most recent call last):
  File "<stdin>", line 1, in <module>
NameError: name 'a' is not defined
```

As you can see from this example, a function's parameters are also local variables. When a function is called, Python assigns the argument values given in the call to the function's parameters. As you might expect, if a function is defined to take a certain number of parameters, it must be passed the same number of arguments:[4]

basic/matching_args_params.cmd

```
>>> polynomial(1, 2, 3)
Traceback (most recent call last):
  File "<stdin>", line 1, in <module>
TypeError: polynomial() takes exactly 4 arguments (3 given)
```

The *scope* of a variable is the area of the program that can access it. For example, the scope of a local variable runs from the line on which it is first defined to the end of the function.

2.7 Built-in Functions

Python comes with many *built-in functions* that perform common operations. One example is abs, which produces the absolute value of a number:

basic/abs.cmd

```
>>> abs(-9)
9
```

---

4. We'll see later how to create functions that take any number of arguments.

Another is round, which rounds a floating-point number to the nearest integer:

basic/round.cmd

```
>>> round(3.8)
4.0
>>> round(3.3)
3.0
>>> round(3.5)
4.0
```

Just like user-defined functions, Python's built-in functions can take more than one argument. For example, we can calculate 2^4 using the power function pow:

basic/two_args.cmd

```
>>> pow(2, 4)
16
```

Some of the most useful built-in functions are ones that convert from one type to another. The type names int and float can be used as if they were functions:

basic/typeconvert.cmd

```
>>> int(34.6)
34
>>> float(21)
21.0
```

In this example, we see that when a floating-point number is converted to an integer, it is truncated—not rounded.

2.8 Style Notes

Psychologists have discovered that people can keep track of only a handful of things at any one time [Hoc04]. Since programs can get quite complicated, it's important that you choose names for your variables that will help you remember what they're for. X1, X2, and blah won't remind you of anything when you come back to look at your program next week; use names like celsius, average, and final_result instead.

Other studies have shown that your brain automatically notices differences between things—in fact, there's no way to stop it from doing this. As a result, the more inconsistencies there are in a piece of text, the longer it takes to read. (JuSt thInK a bout how long It w o u l d tAKE you to rEa d this cHaPTer iF IT wAs fORmaTTeD like thIs.) It's therefore also important to use consistent names for variables. If you call something maximum in one place, don't call it max_val in another; if you use the name max_val, don't also use the name maxVal, and so on.

These rules are so important that many programming teams require members to follow a style guide for whatever language they're using, just as newspapers and book publishers specify how to capitalize headings and whether to use a comma before the last item in a list. If you search the Internet for *programming style guide*, you'll discover links to hundreds of examples.

You will also discover that lots of people have wasted many hours arguing over what the "best" style for code is. Some of your classmates may have strong opinions about this as well. If they do, ask them what data they have to back up their beliefs, in other words, whether they know of any field studies that prove that spaces after commas make programs easier to read than no spaces. If they can't cite any studies, pat them on the back and send them on their deluded way.

2.9 Summary

In this chapter, we learned the following:

- An operating system is a program that manages your computer's hardware on behalf of other programs. An interpreter or virtual machine is a program that sits on top of the operating system and runs your programs for you. Building layers like this is the best way we have found so far for constructing complicated systems.

- Programs are made up of statements. These can be simple expressions (which are evaluated immediately), assignment statements (which create new variables or change the values of existing variables), and function definitions (which teach Python how to do new things).

- Every value in Python has a specific type, which determines what operations can be applied to it. The two types used to represent numbers are int and float.

- Expressions are evaluated in a particular order. However, you can change that order by putting parentheses around subexpressions.

- Variables must be given values before they are used.

- When a function is called, the values of its arguments are assigned to its parameters, the statements inside the function are executed, and a value is returned. The values assigned to the function's parameters, and the values of any local variables created inside the function, are forgotten after the function returns.

- Python comes with predefined functions called *built-ins*.

2.10 Exercises

Here are some exercises for you to try on your own:

1. For each of the following expressions, what value will the expression give? Verify your answers by typing the expressions into Python.

   a) 9 - 3

   b) 8 * 2.5

   c) 9 / 2

   d) 9 / -2

   e) 9 % 2

   f) 9 % -2

   g) -9 % 2

   h) 9 / -2.0

   i) 4 + 3 * 5

   j) (4 + 3) * 5

2. Unary minus negates a number. Unary plus exists as well; for example, Python understands +5. If x has the value -17, what do you think +x should do? Should it leave the sign of the number alone? Should it act like absolute value, removing any negation? Use the Python shell to find out its behavior.

3. a) Create a new variable temp, and assign it the value 24.

   b) Convert the value in temp from Celsius to Fahrenheit by multiplying by 1.8 and adding 32; associate the resulting value with temp. What is temp's new value?

4. a) Create a new variable x, and assign it the value 10.5.

b) Create a new variable y, and assign it the value 4.

c) Sum x and y, and associate the resulting value with x. What are x and y's new values?

5. Write a bullet list description of what happens when Python evaluates the statement x += x - x when x has the value 3.

6. The function name to_celsius is problematic: it doesn't mention the original unit, and it isn't a verb phrase. (Many function names are verb phrases because functions actively do things.) We also assumed the original unit was Fahrenheit, but Kelvin is a temperature scale too, and there are many others (see Section 6.5, *Exercises*, on page 120 for a discussion of them).

We could use a longer name such as fahrenheit_to_celsius or even convert_fahrenheit_to_celsius. We could abbreviate it as fahr_to_cel, make it much shorter and use f2c, or even just use f. Write a paragraph describing which name you think is best and why. Consider ease of remembering, ease of typing, and readability. Don't forget to consider people whose first language isn't English.

7. In the United States, a car's fuel efficiency is measured in miles per gallon. In the metric system, it is usually measured in liters per 100 kilometers.

a) Write a function called convert_mileage that converts from miles per gallon to liters per 100 kilometers.

b) Test that your functions returns the right values for 20 and 40 miles per gallon.

c) How did you figure out what the right value was? How closely do the computer's results match the ones you expected?

8. Explain the difference between a parameter and an argument.

9. a) Define a function called liters_needed that takes a value representing a distance in kilometers and a value representing gas mileage for a vehicle and returns the amount of gas needed in liters to travel that distance. Your definition should call the function convert_mileage that you defined as part of a previous exercise.

b) Verify that liters_needed(150, 30) returns 11.761938367442955 and liters_needed(100, 30) returns 7.84129224496197.

c) When liters_needed is called with arguments 100 and 30, what is the value of the argument to convert_mileage?

d) The function call liters_needed(100, 30) results in a call to convert_mileage. Which of those two functions finishes executing first?

10. We've seen built-in functions abs, round, pow, int, and float. Using these functions, write expressions that do the following:

a) Calculate 3 to the power of 7.

b) Convert 34.7 to an integer by truncating.

c) Convert 34.7 to an integer by rounding.

d) Take the absolute value of -86, then convert it to a floating-point number.

Chapter 3

Strings

Numbers are fundamental to computing—in fact, crunching numbers is what computers were invented to do—but there are many other kinds of data in the world as well, such as addresses, pictures, and music. Each of these can be represented as a data type, and knowing how to manipulate those data types is a big part of being able to program. This chapter introduces a non-numeric data type that represents text, such as the words in this sentence or a strand of DNA. Along the way, we will see how to make programs a little more interactive.

3.1 Strings

Computers may have been invented to do arithmetic, but these days, most of them spend a lot of their time processing text. From desktop chat programs to Google, computers create text, store it, search it, and move it from one place to another.

In Python, a piece of text is represented as a *string*, which is a sequence of *characters* (letters, numbers, and symbols). The simplest data type for storing sequences of characters is str; it can store characters from the Latin alphabet found on most North American keyboards. Another data type called unicode can store strings containing any characters at all, including Chinese ideograms, chemical symbols, and Klingon. We will use the simpler type, str, in our examples.

In Python, we indicate that a value is a string by putting either single or double quotes around it:

strings/string.cmd

```
>>> 'Aristotle'
'Aristotle'
>>> "Isaac Newton"
'Isaac Newton'
```

The quotes must match:

strings/mismatched_quotes.cmd

```
>>> 'Charles Darwin"
  File "<stdin>", line 1
    'Charles Darwin"
                    ^
SyntaxError: EOL while scanning single-quoted string
```

We can join two strings together by putting them side by side:

strings/concat.cmd

```
>>> 'Albert' 'Einstein'
'AlbertEinstein'
```

Notice that the words Albert and Einstein run together. If we want a space between the words, then we can add a space either to the end of Albert or to the beginning of Einstein:

strings/concat_space.cmd

```
>>> 'Albert ' 'Einstein'
'Albert Einstein'
>>> 'Albert' ' Einstein'
'Albert Einstein'
```

It's almost always clearer to join strings with +. When + has two string operands, then it is referred to as the *concatenation operator*:

strings/concat2.cmd

```
>>> 'Albert' + ' Einstein'
'Albert Einstein'
```

Since the + operator is used for both numeric addition and for string concatenation, we call this an *overloaded operator*. It performs different functions based on the type of operands that it is applied to.

The shortest string is the *empty string*, containing no characters at all.

As the following example shows, it's the textual equivalent of 0—adding it to another string has no effect:

strings/empty_string.cmd

```
>>> ''
''
>>> "Alan Turing" + ''
'Alan Turing'
>>> "" + 'Grace Hopper'
'Grace Hopper'
```

Here is an interesting question: can the + operator be applied to a string and numeric value? If so, what function would be applied, addition or concatenation? We'll give it a try:

strings/concat3.cmd

```
>>> 'NH' + 3
Traceback (most recent call last):
  File "<stdin>", line 1, in ?
TypeError: cannot concatenate 'str' and 'int' objects
>>> 9 + ' planets'
Traceback (most recent call last):
  File "<stdin>", line 1, in ?
TypeError: unsupported operand type(s) for +: 'int' and 'str'
```

This is the second time Python has told us that we have a type error. The first time, in Section 2.6, *Local Variables*, on page 22, the problem was not passing the right number of parameters to a function. Here, Python took exception to our attempts to add values of different data types, because it doesn't know which version of + we want: the one that adds numbers or the one that concatenates strings.

In this case, it's easy for a human being to see what the right answer is. But what about this example?

strings/concat4.cmd

```
>>> '123' + 4
```

Should Python produce the string '1234' or the integer 127? The answer is that it shouldn't do either: if it guesses what we want, it'll be wrong at least some of the time, and we will have to try to track down the problem without an error message to guide us.[1]

---

1. If you still aren't convinced, consider this: in JavaScript (a language used for web programming), '7'+0 is the string '70', but '7'-0 is 7.

If you want to put a number in the middle of a string, the easiest way is to convert it via the built-in str function and then do the concatenation:

strings/concat4.cmd

```
>>> '123' + 4
```

The fact that Python will not combine strings and numbers using + doesn't mean that other operators can't combine strings and integers. In particular, we can repeat a string using the * operator, like this:

strings/repeat.cmd

```
>>> 'AT' * 5
'ATATATATAT'
>>> 4 * '-'
'----'
```

If the integer is less than or equals to zero, then this operator yields the empty string (a string containing no characters):

strings/repeat2.cmd

```
>>> 'GC' * 0
''
>>> 'TATATATA' * -3
''
```

3.2 Escape Characters

Suppose you want to put a single quote inside a string. If you write it directly, Python will complain:

strings/single_in_single.cmd

```
>>> 'that's not going to work'
  File "<stdin>", line 1
    'that's not going to work'
         ^
SyntaxError: invalid syntax
```

The problem is that when Python sees the second quote—the one that you think of as being part of the string—it thinks the string is over. It then doesn't know what to do with all the stuff that comes after the second quote.

One simple way to fix this is to use double quotes around the string:

strings/single_in_double.cmd

```
>>> "that's better"
"that's better"
```

Escape Sequence	Description
\n	End of line
\\	Backslash
\'	Single quote
\"	Double quote
\t	Tab

Figure 3.1: ESCAPE SEQUENCES

If you need to put a double quote in a string, you can use single quotes around the string. But what if you want to put both kinds of quote in one string? You could do this:

strings/adding_quotes.cmd

```
>>> 'She said, "That' + "'" + 's hard to read."'
```

Luckily, there's a better way. If you type the previous expression into Python, the result is as follows:

strings/adding_quotes_output.cmd

```
'She said, "That\'s hard to read."'
```

The combination of the backslash and the single quote is called an *escape sequence*. The name comes from the fact that we're "escaping" from Python's usual syntax rules for a moment. When Python sees a backslash inside a string, it means that the next character represents something special—in this case, a single quote, rather than the end of the string. The backslash is called an *escape character*, since it signals the start of an escape sequence.

As shown in Figure 3.1, Python recognizes several escape sequences. In order to see how most are used, we will have to introduce two more ideas: multiline strings and printing.

3.3 Multiline Strings

If you create a string using single or double quotes, the whole string must fit onto a single line.

Here's what happens when you try to stretch a string across multiple lines:

strings/multi1.cmd

```
>>> 'one
Traceback (most recent call last):
  File "<string>", line 1, in <string>
Could not execute because an error occurred:
  EOL while scanning single-quoted string: <string>, line 1, pos 4:
  'one
```

EOL stands for "end of line," so in this error report, Python is saying that it reached the end of the line before it found the end of the string.

To span multiple lines, put three single quotes or three double quotes around the string instead of one of each. The string can then span as many lines as you want:

strings/multi2.cmd

```
>>> '''one
... two
... three'''
'one\ntwo\nthree'
```

Notice that the string Python creates contains a \n sequence everywhere our input started a new line. In reality, each of the three major operating systems uses a different set of characters to indicate the end of a line. This set of characters is called a *newline*. On Linux, a newline is one '\n' character; on Mac OS X, it is one '\r'; and on Windows, the ends of lines are marked with both characters as '\r\n'.

Python always uses a single \n to indicate a newline, even on operating systems like Windows that do things other ways. This is called *normalizing* the string; Python does this so that you can write exactly the same program no matter what kind of machine you're running on.

3.4 Print

So far, we have been able to display the value of only one variable or expression at a time. Real programs often want to display more information, such as the values of multiple variable values. This can be done using a print statement:

strings/print3.cmd

```
>>> print 1 + 1
2
```

```
>>> print "The Latin 'oryctolagus cuniculus' means 'domestic rabbit'."
The Latin 'Oryctolagus cuniculus' means 'domestic rabbit'.
```

The first statement does what you'd expect from the numeric examples we've seen previously, but the second does something slightly different from previous string examples: it strips off the quotes around the string and shows us the string's contents, rather than its representation. This example makes the difference between the two even clearer:

strings/print4.cmd

```
>>> print 'In 1859, Charles Darwin revolutionized biology'
In 1859, Charles Darwin revolutionized biology
>>> print 'and our understanding of ourselves'
and our understanding of ourselves
>>> print 'by publishing "On the Origin of Species".'
by publishing "On the Origin of Species".
```

And the following example shows that when Python prints a string, it prints the values of any escape sequences in the string, rather than their backslashed representations:

strings/print5.cmd

```
>>> print 'one\ttwo\nthree\tfour'
one     two
three   four
```

This example shows how the tab character \t can be used to lay values out in columns. A print statement takes a comma-separated list of items to print and displays them on a line of their own. If no values are given, print simply displays a blank line. You can use any mix of types in the list; Python always inserts a single space between each value:

strings/print_var.cmd

```
>>> area = 3.14159 * 5 * 5
>>> print "The area of the circle is", area, "sq cm."
The area of the circle is 78.539750 sq cm.
```

3.5 Formatted Printing

Sometimes, Python's default printing rules aren't what we want. In these cases, we can specify the exact format we want for our output by providing Python with a *format string*:

strings/print.cmd

```
>>> print "The area of the circle is %f sq cm." % area
The area of the circle is 78.539750 sq cm.
```

In the previous statement, %f is a *conversion specifier*. It indicates where the value of the variable area is to be inserted. Other markers that we might use are %s, to insert a string value, and %d, to insert an integer. The letter following the % is called the *conversion type*.

The % between the string and the value being inserted is another overloaded operator. We used % earlier for modulo; here, it is the *string formatting* operator. It does *not* modify the string on its left side, any more than the + in 3 + 5 changes the value of 3. Instead, the string formatting operator returns a new string.

We can use the string formatting operator to lay out several values at once. Here, for example, we are laying out a float and an int at the same time:

strings/print2.cmd

```
>>> rabbits = 17
>>> cage = 10
>>> print "%f rabbits are in cage #%d." % (rabbits, cage)
17.000000 rabbits are in cage #10.
```

As we said earlier, print automatically puts a newline at the end of a string. This isn't necessarily what we want; for example, we might want to print several pieces of data separately and have them all appear on one line. To prevent the newline from being added, put a comma at the end of the print statement:

strings/print_multiline2.cmd

```
>>> print rabbits,
17>>>
```

3.6 User Input

In an earlier chapter, we explored some built-in functions. Another built-in function that you will find useful is raw_input, which reads a single line of text from the keyboard. The "raw" part means that it returns whatever the user enters as a string, even if it looks like a number:

strings/user_input.cmd

```
>>> line = raw_input()
Galapagos Islands
>>> print line
Galapagos Islands
>>> line = raw_input()
123
```

```
>>> print line * 2
123123
```

If you are expecting the user to enter a number, you must use int or float to convert the string to the required type:

strings/user_input2.cmd
```
>>> value = raw_input()
123
>>> value = int(value)
>>> print value * 2
246
>>> value = float(raw_input())
Galapagos
Traceback (most recent call last):
  File "<stdin>", line 1, in <module>
ValueError: invalid literal for float(): Galapagos
```

Finally, raw_input can be given a string argument, which is used to prompt the user for input:

strings/raw_input_param.cmd
```
>>> name = raw_input("Please enter a name: ")
Please enter a name: Darwin
>>> print name
Darwin
```

3.7 Summary

In this chapter, we learned the following:

- Python uses the string type str to represent text as sequences of characters.

- Strings are usually created by placing pairs of single or double quotes around the text. Multiline strings can be created using matching pairs of triple quotes.

- Special characters like newline and tab are represented using escape sequences that begin with a backslash.

- Values can be displayed on the screen using a print statement and input can be provided by the user using raw_input.

3.8 Exercises

Here are some exercises for you to try on your own:

1. For each of the following expressions, what value will the expression give? Verify your answers by typing the expressions into the Python shell.

    a) 'Comp' 'Sci'

    b) 'Computer' + ' Science'

    c) 'H20' * 3

    d) 'C02' * 0

2. For each of the following phrases, express them as Python strings using the appropriate type of quotation marks (single, double or triple) and, if necessary, escape sequences:

    a) They'll hibernate during the winter.

    b) "Absolutely not," he said.

    c) "He said, 'Absolutely not,'" recalled Mel.

    d) hydrogen sulfide

    e) left\right

3. Rewrite the following string using single or double quotes instead of triple quotes:

    ```
    '''A
    B
    C'''
    ```

4. Use the built-in function len to find the length of the empty string.

5. Given variables x and y, which refer to values 3 and 12.5 respectively, use print to display the following messages. When numbers appear in the messages, the variables x and y should be used in the print statement.

    a) The rabbit is 3.

    b) The rabbit is 3 years old.

    c) 12.5 is average.

    d) 12.5 * 3

    e) 12.5 * 3 is 37.5.

6. Section 3.5, *Formatted Printing*, on page 35, introduced the use of the % operator to format strings for output. Explain what formats you would use to get the following outputs:

    a) "____" % 34.5 => "34.50"

    b) "____" % 34.5 => "3.45e+01"

    c) "____" % 8 => "0008"

    d) "____" % 8 => "8 "

7. Use raw_input to prompt the user for a number and store the number entered as a float in a variable named num, and then print the contents of num.

8. If you enter two strings side by side in Python, it automatically concatenates them:

```
>>> 'abc' 'def'
'abcdef'
```

If those same strings are stored in variables, though, putting them side by side is a syntax error:

```
>>> left = 'abc'
>>> right = 'def'
>>> left right
  File "<stdin>", line 1
left right
  ^
SyntaxError: invalid syntax
```

Why do you think Python doesn't let you do this?

9. Some people believe that multiplying a string by a negative number ought to produce an error, rather than an empty string. Explain why they might think this. If you agree, explain why; if you don't, explain why not.

Chapter 4

Modules

Mathematicians don't prove every theorem from scratch. Instead, they build their proofs on the truths their predecessors have already established. In the same way, it's vanishingly rare for someone to write all of a program herself; it's much more common—and productive—to make use of the millions of lines of code that other programmers have written before.

A *module* is a collection of functions that are grouped together in a single file. Functions in a module are usually related to each other in some way; for example, the math module contains mathematical functions such as cos (cosine) and sqrt (square root). This chapter shows you how to use some of the hundreds of modules that come with Python and how to create new modules of your own. You will also see how you can use Python to explore and view images.

4.1 Importing Modules

When you want to refer to someone else's work in a scientific paper, you have to cite it in your bibliography. When you want to use a function from a module, you have to *import* it. To tell Python that you want to use functions in the math module, for example, you use this import statement:

modules/import.cmd

```
>>> import math
```

Once you have imported a module, you can use the built-in help function to see what it contains:[1]

modules/help_math.cmd

```
>>> help(math)
Help on built-in module math:

NAME
    math

FILE
    (built-in)

DESCRIPTION
    This module is always available.  It provides access to the
    mathematical functions defined by the C standard.

FUNCTIONS
    acos(...)
        acos(x)

        Return the arc cosine (measured in radians) of x.

    asin(...)
        asin(x)

        Return the arc sine (measured in radians) of x.
...
```

Great—our program can now use all the standard mathematical functions. When we try to calculate a square root, though, we get an error telling us that Python is still unable to find the function sqrt:

modules/sqrt.cmd

```
>>> sqrt(9)
Traceback (most recent call last):
  File "<string>", line 1, in <string>
NameError: name 'sqrt' is not defined
```

The solution is to tell Python explicitly to look for the function in the math module by combining the module's name with the function's name using a dot:

modules/sqrt2.cmd

```
>>> math.sqrt(9)
3.0
```

---

1. When you do this interactively, Python displays only a screenful of information at a time. Press the spacebar when you see the "More" prompt to go to the next page.

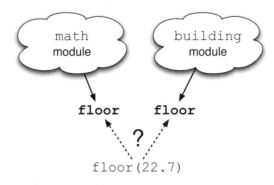

Figure 4.1: HOW IMPORT WORKS

The reason we have to join the function's name with the module's name is that several modules might contain functions with the same name. For example, does the following call to floor refer to the function from the math module that rounds a number down or the function from the (completely fictional) building module that calculates a price given an area (see Figure 4.1)?

modules/import_ambiguity.cmd

```
>>> import math
>>> import building
>>> floor(22.7)
```

Once a module has been imported, it stays in memory until the program ends. There are ways to "unimport" a module (in other words, to erase it from memory) or to reimport a module that has changed while the program is running, but they are rarely used. In practice, it's almost always simpler to stop the program and restart it.

Modules can contain more than just functions. The math module, for example, also defines some variables like pi. Once the module has been imported, you can use these variables like any others:

modules/pi.cmd

```
>>> math.pi
3.1415926535897931
>>> radius = 5
>>> print 'area is %6f' % (math.pi * radius ** 2)
area is 78.539816
```

You can even assign to variables imported from modules:

modules/pi_change.cmd

```
>>> import math
>>> math.pi = 3 # would turn circles into hexagons
>>> radius = 5
>>> print 'circumference is', 2 * math.pi * radius
circumference is 30
```

Don't do this! Changing the value of π is not a good idea. In fact, it's such a bad idea that many languages allow programmers to define unchangeable *constants* as well as variables. As the name suggests, the value of a constant cannot be changed after it has been defined: π is always 3.14159 and a little bit, while SECONDS_PER_DAY is always 86,400. The fact that Python doesn't allow programmers to "freeze" values like this is one of the language's few significant flaws.

Combining the module's name with the names of the things it contains is safe, but it isn't always convenient. For this reason, Python lets you specify exactly what you want to import from a module, like this:

modules/from.cmd

```
>>> from math import sqrt, pi
>>> sqrt(9)
3.0
>>> radius = 5
>>> print 'circumference is %6f' % (2 * pi * radius)
circumference is 31.415927
```

This can lead to problems when different modules provide functions that have the same name. If you import a function called spell from a module called magic and then you import another function called spell from the module grammar, the second replaces the first. It's exactly like assigning one value to a variable, then another: the most recent assignment or import wins.

This is why it's usually *not* a good idea to use import *, which brings in everything from the module at once. It saves some typing:

modules/from2.cmd

```
>>> from math import *
>>> '%6f' % sqrt(8)
'2.828427'
```

but using it means that every time you add anything to a module, you run the risk of breaking every program that uses it.

The standard Python library contains several hundred modules to do everything from figuring out what day of the week it is to fetching data from a website. The full list is online at http://docs.python.org/modindex. html; although it's far too much to absorb in one sitting (or even one course), knowing how to use the library well is one of the things that distinguishes good programmers from poor ones.

4.2 Defining Your Own Modules

Section 2.1, *The Big Picture*, on page 7 explained that in order to save code for later use, you can put it in a file with a .py extension. You can then tell Python to run the code in that file, rather than typing commands in at the interactive prompt. What we didn't tell you then is that every Python file can be used as a module. The name of the module is the same as the name of the file, but without the .py extension.

For example, the following function is taken from Section 2.6, *Function Basics*, on page 20:

modules/convert.py
```
def to_celsius(t):
    return (t - 32.0) * 5.0 / 9.0
```

Put this function definition in a file called temperature.py, and then add another function called above_freezing that returns True if its argument's value is above freezing (in Celsius), and False otherwise:

modules/freezing.py
```
def above_freezing(t):
    return t > 0
```

Congratulations—you have now created a module called temperature:

modules/temperature.py
```
def to_celsius(t):
    return (t - 32.0) * 5.0 / 9.0

def above_freezing(t):
    return t > 0
```

Now that you've created this file, you can now import it like any other module:

modules/import_temp.cmd
```
>>> import temperature
>>> temperature.above_freezing(temperature.to_celsius(33.3))
True
```

The __builtins__ Module

Python's built-in functions are actually in a module named __builtins__. The double underscores before and after the name signal that it's part of Python; we'll see this convention used again later for other things. You can see what's in the module using help(__builtins__), or if you just want a directory, you can use dir instead (which works on other modules as well):

modules/dir1.cmd

```
>>> dir(__builtins__)
['ArithmeticError', 'AssertionError', 'AttributeError',
'BaseException', 'DeprecationWarning', 'EOFError', 'Ellipsis',
'EnvironmentError', 'Exception', 'False', 'FloatingPointError',
'FutureWarning', 'GeneratorExit', 'IOError', 'ImportError',
'ImportWarning', 'IndentationError', 'IndexError', 'KeyError',
'KeyboardInterrupt', 'LookupError', 'MemoryError', 'NameError',
'None', 'NotImplemented', 'NotImplementedError', 'OSError',
'OverflowError', 'PendingDeprecationWarning', 'ReferenceError',
'RuntimeError', 'RuntimeWarning', 'StandardError',
'StopIteration', 'SyntaxError', 'SyntaxWarning', 'SystemError',
'SystemExit', 'TabError', 'True', 'TypeError',
'UnboundLocalError', 'UnicodeDecodeError', 'UnicodeEncodeError',
'UnicodeError', 'UnicodeTranslateError', 'UnicodeWarning',
'UserWarning', 'ValueError', 'Warning', 'ZeroDivisionError', '_',
'__debug__', '__doc__', '__import__', '__name__', 'abs', 'all',
'any', 'apply', 'basestring', 'bool', 'buffer', 'callable',
'chr', 'classmethod', 'cmp', 'coerce', 'compile', 'complex',
'copyright', 'credits', 'delattr', 'dict', 'dir', 'divmod',
'enumerate', 'eval', 'execfile', 'exit', 'file', 'filter',
'float', 'frozenset', 'getattr', 'globals', 'hasattr', 'hash',
'help', 'hex', 'id', 'input', 'int', 'intern', 'isinstance',
'issubclass', 'iter', 'len', 'license', 'list', 'locals', 'long',
'map', 'max', 'min', 'object', 'oct', 'open', 'ord', 'pow',
'property', 'quit', 'range', 'raw_input', 'reduce', 'reload',
'repr', 'reversed', 'round', 'set', 'setattr', 'slice', 'sorted',
'staticmethod', 'str', 'sum', 'super', 'tuple', 'type', 'unichr',
'unicode', 'vars', 'xrange', 'zip']
```

As of Python 2.5, 32 of the 135 things in __builtins__ are used to signal errors of particular kinds, such as SyntaxError and ZeroDivisionError. There are also functions called copyright, which tells you who holds the copyright on Python, and license, which displays Python's rather complicated license. We'll meet some of this module's other members in later chapters.

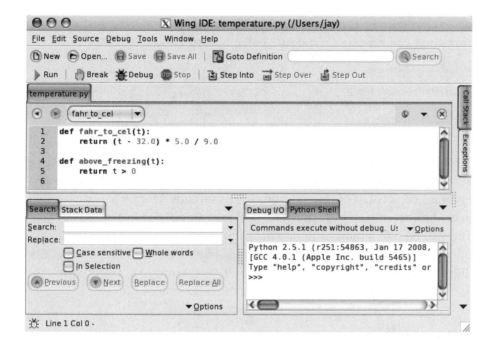

Figure 4.2: THE TEMPERATURE MODULE IN WING 101

What Happens During Import

Let's try another experiment. Put the following in a file called experiment.py:

modules/experiment.py

```
print "The panda's scientific name is 'Ailuropoda melanoleuca'"
```

and then import it (or click Wing 101's Run button):

modules/import_experiment.cmd

```
>>> import experiment
The panda's scientific name is 'Ailuropoda melanoleuca'
```

What this shows is that *Python executes modules as it imports them.* You can do anything in a module you would do in any other program, because as far as Python is concerned, it's just another bunch of statements to be run.

Let's try another experiment. Start a fresh Python session, and try importing the experiment module twice in a row:

modules/import_twice.cmd

```
>>> import experiment
The panda's scientific name is 'Ailuropoda melanoleuca'
>>> import experiment
>>>
```

Notice that the message wasn't printed the second time. That's because Python loads modules only the first time they are imported. Internally, Python keeps track of the modules it has already seen; when it is asked to load one that's already in that list, it just skips over it. This saves time and will be particularly important when you start writing modules that import other modules, which in turn import other modules—if Python didn't keep track of what was already in memory, it could wind up loading commonly used modules like math dozens of times.

Using __main__

As we've now seen, every Python file can be run directly from the command line or IDE or can be imported and used by another program. It's sometimes useful to be able to tell inside a module which is happening, in other words, whether the module is the main program that the user asked to execute or whether some other module has that honor.

Python defines a special variable called __name__ in every module to help us figure this out. Suppose we put the following into echo.py:

modules/echo.py

```
print "echo: __name__ is", __name__
```

If we run this file, its output is as follows:

modules/echo.out

```
echo: __name__ is __main__
```

As promised, Python has created the variable __name__. Its value is "__main__", meaning, "This module is the main program."

But look at what happens when we import echo.py, instead of running it directly:

modules/echo.cmd

```
>>> import echo
echo: __name__ is echo
```

The same thing happens if we write a program that does nothing but import our echoing module:

`modules/import_echo.py`

```
import echo
print "After import, __name__ is", __name__, "and echo.__name__ is", echo.__name__
```

which, when run from the command line, produces this:

`modules/import_echo.out`

```
echo: __name__ is echo
After import, __name__ is __main__ and echo.__name__ is echo
```

What's happening here is that when Python imports a module, it sets that module's __name__ variable to be the name of the module, rather than the special string "__main__". This means that a module can tell whether it is the main program:

`modules/test_main.py`

```
if __name__ == "__main__":
    print "I am the main program"
else:
    print "Someone is importing me"
```

Try it, and see what happens when you run it directly and when you import it.

Knowing whether a module is being imported or not turns out to allow a few handy programming tricks. One is to provide help on the command line whenever someone tries to run a module that's meant to be used as a library. For example, think about what happens when you run the following on the command line vs. importing it into another program:

`modules/main_help.py`

```
'''
This module guesses whether something is a dinosaur or not.
'''

def is_dinosaur(name):
    '''
    Return True if the named create is recognized as a dinosaur,
    and False otherwise.
    '''
    return name in ['Tyrannosaurus', 'Triceratops']

if __name__ == '__main__':
    help(__name__)
```

We will see other uses in the following sections and in later chapters.

Providing Help

Let's return to the temperature module for a moment and modify it to round temperatures off. We'll put the result in temp_round.py:

modules/temp_round.py

```
def to_celsius(t):
    return round((t - 32.0) * 5.0 / 9.0)

def above_freezing(t):
    return t > 0
```

What happens if we ask for help on the function to_celsius?

modules/help_temp.cmd

```
>>> import temp_round
>>> help(temp_round)
Help on module temp_round:

NAME
    temp_round

FILE
    /home/pybook/modules/temp_round.py

FUNCTIONS
    above_freezing(t)

    to_celsius(t)
```

That's not much use: we know the names of the functions and how many parameters they need, but not much else. To provide something more useful, we should add *docstrings* to the module and the functions it contains and save the result in temp_with_doc.py:

modules/temp_with_doc.py

```
'''Functions for working with temperatures.'''

def to_celsius(t):
    '''Convert Fahrenheit to Celsius.'''
    return round((t - 32.0) * 5.0 / 9.0)

def above_freezing(t):
    '''True if temperature in Celsius is above freezing, False otherwise.'''
    return t > 0
```

Asking for help on this module produces a much more useful result.

```
modules/help_temp_with_doc.cmd
```

```
>>> import temp_with_doc
>>> help(temp_with_doc)
Help on module temp_with_doc:

NAME
    temp_with_doc - Functions for working with temperatures.

FILE
    /home/pybook/modules/temp_with_doc.py

FUNCTIONS
    above_freezing(t)
        True if temperature in Celsius is above freezing, False otherwise.

    to_celsius(t)
        Convert Fahrenheit to Celsius.
```

The term *docstring* is short for "documentation string." Docstrings are easy to create: if the first thing in a file or a function is a string that isn't assigned to anything, Python saves it so that help can print it later.

You might think that a module this small doesn't need much documentation. After all, it has only two functions, and their names are pretty descriptive of what they do. But writing documentation is more than a way to earn a few extra marks—it's essential to making software usable. Small programs have a way of turning into larger and more complicated ones. If you don't document as you go along and keep the documentation in the same file as the program itself, you will quickly lose track of what does what.

4.3 Objects and Methods

Numbers and strings may have been enough to keep programmers happy back in the twentieth century, but these days, people expect to work with images, sound, and video as well. A Python module called media provides functions for manipulating and viewing pictures; it isn't in the standard library, but it can be downloaded for free from http://www.pragprog.com/titles/gwpy/source_code. (One of the exercises discusses why it needs a separate download.)

In order to understand how media works, we first have to introduce two concepts that are fundamental to modern program design. And to do *that*, we have to back up and take another look at strings.

So far, we have seen two operators that work on strings: concatenation (+), which "adds" strings, and formatting (%), which gives you control over how values are displayed. There are dozens of other things we might want to do to strings, such as capitalize them, strip off any leading or trailing blanks, or find out whether one string is contained inside another. Having single-character operators such as + and - for all of these is impractical, because we would quickly run out of letters and have to start using two- and three-character combinations that would be impossible to remember.

We could put all the functions that work on strings in a module and ask users to load that module, but there's a simpler way to solve the problem. Python strings "own" a set of special functions called *methods*. These are called just like the functions inside a module. If we have a string like 'hogwarts', we can capitalize it by calling 'hogwarts'.capitalize(), which returns 'Hogwarts'. Similarly, if the variable villain has been assigned the string 'malfoy', the expression villain.capitalize() will return the string 'Malfoy'.

Every string we create automatically shares all the methods that belong to the string data type. The most commonly used ones are listed in Figure 4.3, on the next page; you can find the complete list in Python's online documentation or type help(str) into the command prompt.

Using methods is almost the same as using functions, though a method almost always does something to or with the thing that owns it. For example, let's call the startswith method on the string 'species':

`modules/startswith.cmd`

```
>>> 'species'.startswith('a')
False
>>> 'species'.startswith('s')
True
```

The method startswith takes a string argument and returns a bool to tell us whether the string whose method was called—the one on the left of the dot—starts with the string that is given as an argument. String also has an endswith method:

`modules/endswith.cmd`

```
>>> 'species'.endswith('a')
False
>>> 'species'.endswith('s')
True
```

Method	Description
capitalize()	Returns a copy of the string with the first letter capitalized
find(s)	Returns the index of the first occurrence of s in the string, or -1 if s is not in the string
find(s, beg)	Returns the index of the first occurrence of s after index beg in the string, or -1 if s is not in the string after index beg
find(s, beg, end)	Returns the index of the first occurrence of s between indices beg and end in the string, or -1 if s is not in the string between indices beg and end
islower()	Tests that all characters are lowercase
isupper()	Tests that all characters are uppercase
lower()	Returns a copy of the string with all characters converted to lowercase
replace(old, new)	Returns a copy of the string with all occurrences of the substring old replaced with new
split()	Returns the space-separated words as a list
split(del)	Returns the del-separated words as a list
strip()	Returns a copy of the string with leading and trailing whitespace removed
strip(s)	Returns a copy of the string with the characters in s removed
upper()	Returns a copy of the string with all characters converted to uppercase

Figure 4.3: Common string methods

We can chain multiple method calls together in a single line by calling a method of the value returned by another method call. To show how this works, let's start by calling swapcase to change lowercase letters to uppercase and uppercase to lowercase:

`modules/swap.cmd`

```
>>> 'Computer Science'.swapcase()
'cOMPUTER sCIENCE'
```

Since the result of this method is a string, we can immediately call the result's endswith method to check that the first call did the right thing to the last few letters of the original string.

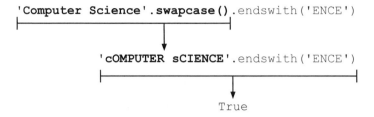

Figure 4.4: CHAINING METHOD CALLS

modules/swap_endswith.cmd

```
>>> 'Computer Science'.swapcase().endswith('ENCE')
True
```

In Figure 4.4, we can see what's going on when we do this. Note that Python automatically creates a temporary variable to hold the value of the swapcase method call long enough for it to call that value's endswith method.

Something that has methods is called an *object*. It turns out that *everything* in Python is an object, even the number zero:

modules/int_help.cmd

```
>>> help(0)
Help on int object:

class int(object)
 |  int(x[, base]) -> integer
 |
 |  Convert a string or number to an integer, if possible.  A floating point
 |  argument will be truncated towards zero (this does not include a string
 |  representation of a floating point number!)  When converting a string, use
 |  the optional base.  It is an error to supply a base when converting a
 |  non-string. If the argument is outside the integer range a long object
 |  will be returned instead.
 |
 |  Methods defined here:
 |
 |  __abs__(...)
 |      x.__abs__() <==> abs(x)
 |
 |  __add__(...)
 |      x.__add__(y) <==> x+y
...
```

Most modern programming languages are structured this way: the "things" in the program are objects, and most of the code in the program consists of methods that use the data stored in those objects. Chapter 13, *Object-Oriented Programming*, on page 267 will show you how to create new kinds of objects; for now, let's take a look at the objects Python uses to store and manipulate images.

Images

Now that we have seen the basic features of modules, objects, and methods, let's look at how they can solve real-world problems. For our running example, we will write some programs that display and manipulate pictures and other images.

Suppose you have a file called pic207.jpg on your hard drive and want to display it on your screen. You could double-click to open it, but what does that actually *do*? To start to answer that question, type the following into a Python prompt:

`modules/open_pic.cmd`

```
>>> import media
>>> f = media.choose_file()
>>> pic = media.load_picture(f)
>>> media.show(pic)
```

When the file dialog box opens, navigate to pic207.jpg. The result should be the awesomely cute photo shown in Figure 4.5, on the following page. Here's what the commands shown earlier actually did:

1. Import the functions from the media module.

2. Call that module's choose_file function to open a file-choosing dialog box. This call returns a string that contains the path to the picture file.

3. Call the module's load_picture function to read the contents of the picture file into memory. This creates a Python object, which is assigned to the variable pic.

4. Call that module's show function, which launches another program to display the picture. Python has to launch another program because it can't print the picture out at the command line.

Double-clicking would definitely have been easier.

Figure 4.5: MADELEINE

But let's see your mouse do this:

`modules/pic_props.cmd`

```
>>> pic.get_width()
500
>>> pic.get_height()
375
>>> pic.title
'modules/pic207.jpg'
```

The first two commands tell us how wide and high the picture is in pixels. The third tells us the path to the file containing the picture.

Now try this:

`modules/pic_crop.cmd`

```
>>> media.crop_picture(pic, 150, 50, 450, 300)
>>> media.show(pic)
>>> media.save_as(pic, 'pic207cropped.jpg')
```

Figure 4.6: MADELEINE CROPPED

As you can guess from the name, crop crops the picture. The upper-left corner is (150, 50), and the lower-right corner is (450, 300); the resulting picture is shown in Figure 4.6.

The code also shows the new picture and then writes it to a new file. This file is saved in the *current working directory*, which by default is the directory in which the program is running. On our system this happens to be '/Users/pgries/'.

Now let's put Madeleine's name on her hat. To do that, we use picture's add_text function; the result is shown in Figure 4.7, on the following page.

modules/pic_text.cmd

```
>>> media.add_text(pic, 115, 40, 'Madeleine', media.magenta)
>>> media.show(pic)
```

Figure 4.7: MADELEINE NAMED

Function choose_file is useful for writing interactive programs, but when we know exactly which files we want or we want more than one file, it's often easier to skip that navigation step. As an example, let's open up all three pictures of Madeleine in a single program:

modules/show_madeleine.py

```
import media

pic1 = media.load_picture('pic207.jpg')
media.show(pic1)
pic2 = media.load_picture('pic207cropped.jpg')
media.show(pic2)
pic3 = media.load_picture('pic207named.jpg')
media.show(pic3)
```

Since we haven't specified what directory to find the files in, the program looks for them in the current working directory. If the program can't find them there, it reports an error.

Color	Value
black	Color(0, 0, 0)
white	Color(255, 255, 255)
red	Color(255, 0, 0)
green	Color(0, 255, 0)
blue	Color(0, 0, 255)
magenta	Color(255, 0, 255)
yellow	Color(255, 255, 0)
aqua	Color(0, 255, 255)
pink	Color(255, 192, 203)
purple	Color(128, 0, 128)

Figure 4.8: EXAMPLE COLOR VALUES

4.4 Pixels and Colors

Most people want to do a lot more to pictures than just display them and crop them. If you do a lot of digital photography, you may want to remove the "red-eye" caused by your camera flash. You might also want to convert pictures to black and white for printing, highlight certain objects, and so on.

To do these things, you must work with the individual *pixels* that make up the image. The media module represents pixels using the *RGB color model* discussed in the sidebar on page 63. Module media provides a Color type and more than 100 predefined Color values. Several of them are listed in Figure 4.8; black is represented as "no blue, no green, no red," white is the maximum possible amount of all three, and other colors lie somewhere in between.

The media module provides functions for getting and changing the colors in pixels (see Figure 4.9, on the following page) and for manipulating colors themselves (see Figure 4.10, on page 61).

To see how these functions are used, let's go through all the pixels in Madeleine's cropped and named picture and make it look like it was taken at sunset. To do this, we're going to remove some of the blue and some of the green from each pixel, making the picture darker and redder.[2]

---

2. We're not actually adding any red, but reducing the amount of blue and green will fool the eye into thinking we have.

Function	Description
get_red(pixel)	Gets the red component of pixel
set_red(pixel, value)	Sets the red component of pixel to value
get_blue(pixel)	Gets the red component of pixel
set_blue(pixel, value)	Sets the blue component of pixel to value
get_green(pixel)	Gets the red component of pixel
set_green(pixel, value)	Sets the green component of pixel to value
get_color(pixel)	Gets the color of pixel
set_color(pixel, color)	Sets the color of pixel to color

Figure 4.9: PIXEL-MANIPULATION FUNCTIONS

modules/sunset.py

```
import media

pic = media.load_picture('pic207.jpg')
media.show(pic)
for p in media.get_pixels(pic):
    new_blue = int(0.7 * media.get_blue(p))
    new_green = int(0.7 * media.get_green(p))
    media.set_blue(p, new_blue)
    media.set_green(p, new_green)

media.show(pic)
```

Some things to note:

- Color values are integers, so we need to convert the result of multiplying the blue and green by 0.7 using the function int.

- The for loop does something to each pixel in the picture. We will talk about for loops in detail in Section 5.4, *Processing List Items*, on page 81, but just reading the code aloud will give you the idea that it associates each pixel in turn with the variable p, extracts the blue and green components, calculates new values for them, and then resets the values in the pixel.

Try this code on a picture of your own, and see how convincing the result is.

Function	Description
darken(color)	Returns a color slightly darker than color
lighten(color)	Returns a color slightly darker than color
create_color(red, green, blue)	Returns color (red, green, blue)
distance(c1, c2)	Returns how far apart colors c1 and c2 are

Figure 4.10: COLOR FUNCTIONS

4.5 Testing

Another use for modules in real-world Python programming is to make sure that programs don't just run but also produce the right answers. In science, for example, the programs you use to analyze experimental data must be at least as reliable as the lab equipment you used to collect that data, or there's no point running the experiment. The programs that run CAT scanners and other medical equipment must be even more reliable, since lives depend on them. As it happens, the tools used to make sure that these programs are behaving correctly can also be used by instructors to grade students' assignments and by students to check their programs before submitting them.

Checking that software is doing the right thing is called *quality assurance*, or QA. Over the last fifty years, programmers have learned that quality isn't some kind of magic pixie dust that you can sprinkle on a program after it has been written. Quality has to be designed in, and software must be tested and retested to check that it meets standards.

The good news is that putting effort into QA actually makes you more productive overall. The reason can be seen in Boehm's curve in Figure 4.11, on the following page. The later you find a bug, the more expensive it is to fix, so catching bugs early reduces overall effort.

Most good programmers today don't just test their software while writing it; they build their tests so that other people can rerun them months later and a dozen time zones away. This takes a little more time up front but makes programmers more productive overall, since every hour invested in preventing bugs saves two, three, or ten frustrating hours tracking bugs down.

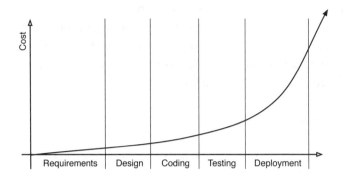

Figure 4.11: BOEHM'S CURVE

One popular testing library for Python is called Nose, which can be downloaded for free at http://code.google.com/p/python-nose/. To show how it works, we will use it to test our temperature module. To start, create a new Python file called test_temperature.py. The name is important: when Nose runs, it automatically looks for files whose names start with the letters test_. The second part of the name is up to us—we could call it test_hagrid.py if we wanted to—but a sensible name will make it easier for other people to find things in our code.

Every Nose test module should contain the following:

- Statements to import Nose and the module to be tested
- Functions that actually test our module
- A function call to trigger execution of those test functions

Like the name of the test module, the names of the test functions must start with test_. Using the structure outlined earlier, our first sketch of a testing module looks like this:

`modules/structure.py`

```python
import nose
import temperature

def test_to_celsius():
    '''Test function for to_celsius'''
    pass # we'll fill this in later

def test_above_freezing():
    '''Test function for above_freezing.'''
    pass # we'll fill this in too

if __name__ == '__main__':
    nose.runmodule()
```

RGB and Hexadecimal

In the red-green-blue (or RGB) color system, each pixel in a picture has a certain amount of the three primary colors in it, and each color component is specified by a number in the range 0–255 (which is the range of numbers that can be represented in a single 8-bit byte).

By tradition, RGB values are represented in *hexadecimal*, or base-16, rather than in the usual base-10 decimal system. The "digits" in hexadecimal are the usual 0–9, plus the letters A–F (or a–f). This means that the number after 9_{16} is not 10_{16}, but A_{16}; the number after A_{16} is B_{16}, and so on, up to F_{16}, which is followed by 10_{16}. Counting continues to $1F_{16}$, which is followed by 20_{16}, and so on, up to FF_{16} (which is $15_{10} \times 16_{10} + 15_{10}$, or 255_{10}).

An RGB color is therefore six hexadecimal digits: two for red, two for green, and two for blue. Black is therefore #000000 (no color of any kind), while white is #FFFFFF (all colors saturated), and #008080 is a bluish-green (no red, half-strength green, half-strength blue).

For now, each test function contains nothing except a docstring and a pass statement. As the name suggests, this does nothing—it's just a placeholder to remind ourselves that we need to come back and write some more code.

If you run the test module, the output starts with two dots to say that two tests have run successfully. (If a test fails, Nose prints an "F" instead to attract attention to the problem.) The summary after the dashed line tells us that Nose found and ran two tests, that it took less than a millisecond to do so, and that everything was OK:

`modules/structure.out`

```
..
----------------------------------------------------------------------
Ran 2 tests in 0.000s

OK
```

Two successful tests isn't surprising, since our functions don't actually test anything yet. The next step is to fill them in so that they actually do something useful. The goal of testing is to confirm that our code works properly; for to_celsius, this means that given a value in Fahrenheit, the function produces the corresponding value in Celsius.

It's clearly not practical to try every possible value—after all, there are a lot of real numbers. Instead, we select a few representative values and make sure the function does the right thing for them.

For example, let's make sure that the round-off version of to_celsius from Section 4.2, *Providing Help*, on page 50 returns the right result for two reference values: 32 Fahrenheit (0 Celsius) and 212 Fahrenheit (100 Celsius). Just to be on the safe side, we should also check a value that doesn't translate so neatly. For example, 100 Fahrenheit is 37.777... Celsius, so our function should return 38 (since it's rounding off).

We can execute each test by comparing the *actual value* returned by the function with the *expected value* that it's supposed to return. In this case, we use an assert statement to let Nose know that to_celsius(100) should be 38:

`modules/assert.py`
```python
import nose
from temp_with_doc import to_celsius

def test_freezing():
    '''Test freezing point.'''
    assert to_celsius(32) == 0

def test_boiling():
    '''Test boiling point.'''
    assert to_celsius(212) == 100

def test_roundoff():
    '''Test that roundoff works.'''
    assert to_celsius(100) == 38 # NOT 37.777...

if __name__ == '__main__':
    nose.runmodule()
```

When the code is executed, each test will have one of three outcomes:

- *Pass.* The actual value matches the expected value.

- *Fail.* The actual value is different from the expected value.

- *Error.* Something went wrong inside the test itself; in other words, the test code contains a bug. In this case, the test doesn't tell us anything about the system being tested.

Run the test module; the output should be as follows:

```
modules/outcome.out
...
----------------------------------------------------------------------
Ran 3 tests in 0.002s

OK
```

As before, the dots tell us that the tests are passing.

Just to prove that Nose is doing the right thing, let's compare to_celsius's result with 37.8 instead:

```
modules/assert2.py
import nose
from temp_with_doc import to_celsius

def test_to_celsius():
    '''Test function for to_celsius'''
    assert to_celsius(100) == 37.8

if __name__ == '__main__':
    nose.runmodule()
```

This causes the test case to fail, so the dot corresponding to it is replaced by an "F," an error message is printed, and the number of failures is listed in place of OK:

```
modules/fail.out
F
======================================================================
FAIL: Test function for to_celsius
----------------------------------------------------------------------
Traceback (most recent call last):
  File "/python25/lib/site-packages/nose/case.py", line 202, in runTest
    self.test(*self.arg)
  File "assert2.py", line 6, in test_to_celsius
    assert to_celsius(100) == 37.8
AssertionError

----------------------------------------------------------------------
Ran 1 test in 0.000s

FAILED (failures=1)
```

The error message tells us that the failure happened in test_to_celsius on line 6. That is helpful, but the reason for failure can be made even clearer by adding a description of what is being tested to each assert statement.

modules/assert3.py

```python
import nose
from temp_with_doc import to_celsius

def test_to_celsius():
    '''Test function for to_celsius'''
    assert to_celsius(100) == 37.8, 'Returning an unrounded result'

if __name__ == '__main__':
    nose.runmodule()
```

That message is then included in the output:

modules/fail_comment.out

```
F
======================================================================
FAIL: Test function for to_celsius
----------------------------------------------------------------------
Traceback (most recent call last):
  File "c:\Python25\Lib\site-packages\nose\case.py", line 202, in runTest
    self.test(*self.arg)
  File "assert3.py", line 6, in test_to_celsius
    assert to_celsius(100) == 37.8, 'Returning an unrounded result'
AssertionError: Returning an unrounded result


----------------------------------------------------------------------
Ran 1 test in 0.000s

FAILED (failures=1)
```

Having tested test_to_celsius with one value, we need to decide whether any other test cases are needed. The description of that test case states that it is a positive value, which implies that we may also want to test our code with a value of 0 or a negative value. The real question is whether our code will behave differently for those values. Since all we're doing is some simple arithmetic, we probably don't need to bother; in future chapters, though, we will see functions that are complicated enough to need several tests each.

Let's move on to test_above_freezing. The function it is supposed to test, above_freezing, is supposed to return True for any temperature above freezing, so let's make sure it does the right thing for 89.4. We should also check that it does the right thing for a temperature below freezing, so we'll add a check for -42.

Finally, we should also test that the function does the right thing for the dividing case, when the temperature is exactly freezing. Values like this are often called *boundary cases*, since they lie on the boundary between two different possible behaviors of the function. Experience shows that boundary cases are much more likely to contain bugs than other cases, so it's always worth figuring out what they are and testing them.

The test module, including comments, is now complete:

`modules/test_freezing.py`

```python
import nose
from temp_with_doc import above_freezing

def test_above_freezing():
    '''Test function for above_freezing.'''
    assert above_freezing(89.4), 'A temperature above freezing.'
    assert not above_freezing(-42), 'A temperature below freezing.'
    assert not above_freezing(0), 'A temperature at freezing.'

if __name__ == '__main__':
    nose.runmodule()
```

When we run it, its output is as follows:

`modules/test_freezing.out`

```
.
----------------------------------------------------------------------
Ran 1 test in 0.000s

OK
```

Whoops—Nose believes that only one test was run, even though there are three assert statements in the file. The reason is that as far as Nose is concerned, each function is one test. If some of those functions want to check several things, that's their business. The problem with this is that as soon as one assertion fails, Python stops executing the function it's in. As a result, if the first check in test_above_freezing failed, we wouldn't get any information from the ones after it. It is therefore generally a good idea to write lots of small test functions, each of which only checks a small number of things, rather than putting dozens of assertions in each function.

4.6 Style Notes

Anything that can go in a Python program can go in a module, but that doesn't mean that anything *should*. If you have functions and variables that logically belong together, you should put them in the same module. If there isn't some logical connection—for example, if one of the functions calculates how much carbon monoxide different kinds of cars produce, while another figures out how strong bones are given their diameter and density—then you shouldn't put them in one module just because you happen to be the author of both.

Of course, people often have different opinions about what is logical and what isn't. Take Python's math module, for example; should functions to multiply matrices go in there too or in a separate linear algebra module? What about basic statistical functions? Going back to the previous paragraph, should a function that calculates gas mileage go in the same module as one that calculates carbon monoxide emissions? You can always find a reason why two functions should *not* be in the same module, but 1,000 modules with one function each are going to be hard for people (including you) to find their way around.

As a rule of thumb, if a module has less than half a dozen things in it, it's probably too small, and if you can't sum up the contents and purpose of a module in a one- or two-sentence docstring, it's probably too large. These are just guidelines, though; in the end, you will have to decide based on how more experienced programmers have organized modules like the ones in the Python standard library and eventually on your own sense of style.

4.7 Summary

In this chapter, we learned the following:

- A module is a collection of functions and variables grouped together in a file. To use a module, you must first import it. After it has been imported, you refer to its contents using modulename. thingname.

- Put docstrings at the start of modules or functions to describe their contents and use.

- Every "thing" in a Python program is an object. Objects have methods, which work just like functions but are associated with the object's type. Methods are called using object.methodname, just like the functions in a module.

- You can manipulate images using the picture module, which has functions for loading, displaying, and manipulating entire images, as well as inspecting and modifying individual pixels and colors.

- Programs have to do more than just run to be useful; they have to run correctly. One way to ensure that they do is to test them, which you can do in Python using the Nose module. Since you usually can't test every possible case, you should focus your testing on boundary cases.

4.8 Exercises

Here are some exercises for you to try on your own:

1. Import module math, and use its functions to complete the following exercises:

   a) Write a single expression that rounds the value of -4.3 and then takes the absolute value of that result.

   b) Write an expression that takes the ceiling of sine of 34.5.

2. In the following exercises, you will work with Python's calendar module:

   a) Visit the Python documentation website at http://docs.python. org/modindex.html, and look at the documentation on the calendar module.

   b) Import the calendar module.

   c) Read the description of the function isleap. Use isleap to determine the next leap year.

   d) Find and use a function in module calendar to determine how many leap years there will be between the years 2000 and 2050, inclusive.

   e) Find and use a function in module calendar to determine which day of the week July 29, 2016 will be.

3. Using string methods, write expressions that do the following:

   a) Capitalize 'boolean'.

   b) Find the first occurrence of '2' in 'C02 H20'.

   c) Find the second occurrence of "2" in 'C02 H20'.

   d) Determine whether 'Boolean' begins with a lowercase.

  e) Convert "MoNDaY" to lowercase letters and then capitalize the result.

  f) Remove the leading whitespace from " Monday".

4. The example used to explain import * was as follows:

modules/from2.cmd

```
>>> from math import *
>>> '%6f' % sqrt(8)
'2.828427'
```

Explain why there are quotes around the value 2.828427.

5. Why do you think the media module mentioned in Section 4.3, *Objects and Methods*, on page 51 isn't part of the standard Python library? How do you think Python's developers decide what should be in the standard library and what shouldn't? If you need something that isn't in the standard library, where and how can you find it?

6. Write a program that allows the user to choose a file and then shows the picture twice.

7. Write a program that allows the user to choose a file, sets the red value of each pixel in the picture to 0, and shows the picture.

8. Write a program that allows the user to pick a file, halves the green value of each pixel in the picture, and shows the picture.

9. Write a program that allows the user to pick a file and makes it grayscale; it should calculate the average of red, green, and blue values of each pixel and then set the red, green, and blue values to that average.

10. Write a program that allows the user to pick a file, doubles the red value of each pixel in the picture, and shows the picture. What happens when a value larger than 255 is calculated?

11. Media outlets such as newspapers and TV stations sometimes "enhance" photographs by recoloring them or digitally combine pictures of two people to make them appear together. Do you think they should be allowed to use only unmodified images? Given that almost all pictures and TV footage are now digital and have to be processed somehow for display, what would that rule actually mean in practice?

12. Suppose we want to test a function that calculates the distance between two XY points:

modules/distance.py

```python
import math

def distance(x0, y0, x1, y1):
    '''Calculate the distance between (x0, y0) and (x1, y1).'''

    return math.sqrt((x1 - x0) ** 2 + (y1 - y0) ** 2)
```

a) Unlike the rounding-off version of to_celsius, this returns a floating-point number. Explain why this makes testing more difficult.

b) A friend of yours suggests testing the function like this:

modules/test_distance.py

```python
import nose
from distance import distance

def close(left, right):
    '''Test if two floating-point values are close enough.'''

    return abs(left - right) < 1.0e-6

def test_distance():
    '''Test whether the distance function works correctly.'''

    assert close(distance(1.0, 0.0, 1.0, 0.0), 0.0), 'Identical points fail.'
    assert close(distance(0.0, 0.0, 1.0, 0.0), 1.0), 'Unit distance fails.'

if __name__ == '__main__':
    nose.runmodule()
```

Explain what your friend is trying to do. As gently as you can, point out two flaws in his approach.

Chapter 5

Lists

Up to this point, each variable we have created has referred to a single number or string. In this chapter, we will work with collections of data and use a Python type named list. Lists contain 0 or more objects, and they allow us to store data such as 90 experiment measurements or 10,000 student IDs. We'll also see how to access files and represent their contents using lists.

5.1   Lists and Indices

Figure 5.1, on the next page, taken from http://www.acschannelislands. org/2008CountDaily.pdf, shows the number of gray whales counted near the Coal Oil Point Natural Reserve in a two-week period in the spring of 2008.

Using what we have seen so far, we would have to create fourteen variables to keep track of these numbers (see Figure 5.2, on the following page). If we wanted to track an entire year's worth of observations, we'd need 366 (just in case it was a leap year). Even worse, if we didn't know in advance how long we wanted to watch the whales, we wouldn't know how many variables to create.

The solution is to store all the values together in a *list*. Lists show up everywhere in the real world: students in a class, the kinds of birds native to New Guinea, and so on. To create a list in Python, we put the values, separated by commas, inside square brackets:

`lists/whalelist.py`

```
# Number of whales seen per day
[5, 4, 7, 3, 2, 3, 2, 6, 4, 2, 1, 7, 1, 3]
```

Day	Number of Whales
1	5
2	4
3	7
4	3
5	2
6	3
7	2
8	6
9	4
10	2
11	1
12	7
13	1
14	3

Figure 5.1: GRAY WHALE CENSUS

Figure 5.2: LIFE WITHOUT LISTS

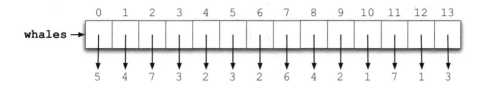

Figure 5.3: List example

A list is an object; like any other object, it can be assigned to a variable:

lists/whales1.cmd

```
>>> whales = [5, 4, 7, 3, 2, 3, 2, 6, 4, 2, 1, 7, 1, 3]
>>> whales
[5, 4, 7, 3, 2, 3, 2, 6, 4, 2, 1, 7, 1, 3]
```

In Figure 5.3, we can see a memory model of whales after this assignment. It's important to keep in mind that the list itself is one object but may contain references to other objects (shown by the arrows).

So, how do we get at the objects in a list? By providing an *index* that specifies the one we want. The first item in a list is at index 0, the second at index 1, and so on.[1] To refer to a particular item, we put the index in square brackets after a reference to the list (such as the name of a variable):

lists/whales2.cmd

```
>>> whales = [5, 4, 7, 3, 2, 3, 2, 6, 4, 2, 1, 7, 1, 3]
>>> whales[0]
5
>>> whales[1]
4
>>> whales[12]
1
>>> whales[13]
3
```

We can use only those indices that are in the range from zero up to one less than the length of the list. In a fourteen-item list, the legal indices are 0, 1, 2, and so on, up to 13. Trying to use an out-of-range index is an error, just like trying to divide by zero.

---

1. Yes, it would be more natural to use 1 as the first index, as human languages do. Python, however, uses the same convention as languages like C and Java and starts counting at zero.

```
lists/whales3.cmd
>>> whales = [5, 4, 7, 3, 2, 3, 2, 6, 4, 2, 1, 7, 1, 3]
>>> whales[1001]
Traceback (most recent call last):
  File "<stdin>", line 1, in ?
IndexError: list index out of range
```

Unlike most programming languages, Python also lets us index backward from the end of a list. The last item is at index -1, the one before it at index -2, and so on:

```
lists/whales4.cmd
>>> whales = [5, 4, 7, 3, 2, 3, 2, 6, 4, 2, 1, 7, 1, 3]
>>> whales[-1]
3
>>> whales[-2]
1
>>> whales[-14]
5
```

We can assign the values in a list to other variables:

```
lists/whales5.cmd
>>> whales = [5, 4, 7, 3, 2, 3, 2, 6, 4, 2, 1, 7, 1, 3]
>>> third = whales[2]
>>> print 'Third day:', third
Third day: 7
```

The Empty List

Zero is a useful number, and as we saw in Chapter 3, *Strings*, on page 29, the empty string is often useful as well. There is also an *empty list*, in other words, a list with no items in it. As you might guess, it is written []. Trying to index an empty list always results in an error:

```
lists/whales6.cmd
>>> whales = []
>>> whales[0]
Traceback (most recent call last):
  File "<stdin>", line 1, in <module>
IndexError: list index out of range
>>> whales[-1]
Traceback (most recent call last):
  File "<stdin>", line 1, in <module>
IndexError: list index out of range
```

This follows from the definition of legal index:

- Legal indices for a list of N items are the integers in the set $\{i: 0 \leq i < N\}$.
- The length of the empty list is 0.
- Legal indices for the empty list are therefore the elements of the set $\{i: 0 \leq i < -1\}$.
- Since this set is empty, there are no legal indices for the empty list.

Lists Are Heterogeneous

Lists can contain any type of data, including integers, strings, and even other lists. Here is a list of information about the element Krypton, including its name, symbol, melting point (in degrees Celsius), and boiling point (also in degrees Celsius). Using a list to aggregate related information is somewhat prone to error; a better, but more advanced, way to do this is described in Chapter 13, *Object-Oriented Programming*, on page 267.

lists/krypton1.cmd

```
>>> krypton = ['Krypton', 'Kr', -157.2, -153.4]
>>> krypton[1]
'Kr'
>>> krypton[2]
-157.19999999999999
```

5.2 Modifying Lists

Suppose we're typing in a list of the noble gases[2] and our fingers slip:

lists/nobles1.cmd

```
>>> nobles = ['helium', 'none', 'argon', 'krypton', 'xenon', 'radon']
```

The error here is that we typed 'none' instead of 'neon'. Rather than retyping the whole list, we can assign a new value to a specific element of the list:

lists/nobles2.cmd

```
>>> nobles = ['helium', 'none', 'argon', 'krypton', 'xenon', 'radon']
>>> nobles[1] = 'neon'
>>> nobles
['helium', 'neon', 'argon', 'krypton', 'xenon', 'radon']
```

---

2. A *noble gas* is one whose outermost electron shell is completely full, which makes it chemically inert.

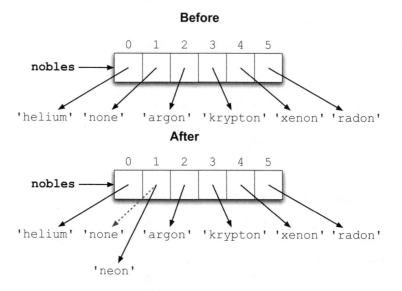

Figure 5.4: LIST MUTATION

In Figure 5.4, we show what the assignment to nobles[1] did. It also shows that lists are *mutable*, in other words, that their contents can be changed after they have been created. In contrast, numbers and strings are *immutable*. You cannot, for example, change a letter in a string after you have created it. Methods that appear to, like upper, actually create new strings:

lists/strings_immutable.cmd

```
>>> name = 'Darwin'
>>> capitalized = name.upper()
>>> print capitalized
'DARWIN'
>>> print name
'Darwin'
```

The expression L[i] behaves just like a simple variable (see Section 2.4, *Variables and the Assignment Statement*, on page 15). If it's on the right, it means "Get the value of the item at location i in the list L." If it's on the left, it means "Figure out where item i in the list L is located so that we can overwrite it."

Function	Description
len(L)	Returns the number of items in list L
max(L)	Returns the maximum value in list L
min(L)	Returns the minimum value in list L
sum(L)	Returns the sum of the values in list L

Figure 5.5: LIST FUNCTIONS

5.3 Built-in Functions on Lists

Section 2.6, *Function Basics*, on page 20 introduced a few of Python's built-in functions. Some of these, such as len, can be applied to lists as well, as can others that we haven't seen before (see Figure 5.5). Here they are in action working on a list of the half-lives[3] of our plutonium isotopes:

lists/plu4.cmd
```
>>> half_lives = [87.74, 24110.0, 6537.0, 14.4, 376000.0]
>>> len(half_lives)
5
>>> max(half_lives)
376000.0
>>> min(half_lives)
14.4
>>> sum(half_lives)
406749.14000000001
```

We can use the results of the built-in functions in expressions; for example, the following code demonstrates that we can check whether an index is in range:

lists/plu5.cmd
```
>>> half_lives = [87.74, 24110.0, 6537.0, 14.4, 376000.0]
>>> i = 2
>>> 0 <= i < len(half_lives)
True
>>> half_lives[i]
6537.0
>>> i = 5
>>> 0 <= i < len(half_lives)
False
```

---

3. The half-life of a radioactive substance is the time taken for half of it to decay. After twice this time has gone by, three quarters of the material will have decayed; after three times, seven eighths, and so on.

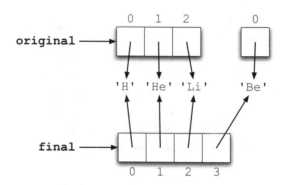

Figure 5.6: LIST CONCATENATION

```
>>> half_lives[i]
Traceback (most recent call last):
  File "<stdin>", line 1, in ?
IndexError: list index out of range
```

Like all other objects, lists have a particular type, and Python complains
if you try to combine types in inappropriate ways. Here's what happens
if you try to "add" a list and a string:

lists/add_list_str.cmd

```
>>> ['H', 'He', 'Li'] + 'Be'
Traceback (most recent call last):
  File "<stdin>", line 1, in <module>
TypeError: can only concatenate list (not "str") to list
```

That error report is interesting. It hints that we might be able to con-
catenate lists with lists to create new lists, just as we concatenated
strings to create new strings. A little experimentation shows that this
does in fact work:

lists/concat_lists.cmd

```
>>> original = ['H', 'He', 'Li']
>>> final = original + ['Be']
>>> final
['H', 'He', 'Li', 'Be']
```

As shown in Figure 5.6, this doesn't modify either of the original lists.
Instead, it creates a new list whose entries refer to the entries of the
original lists.

So if + works on lists, will sum work on lists of strings? After all, if sum([1, 2, 3]) is the same as 1 + 2 + 3, shouldn't sum('a', 'b', 'c') be the same as 'a' + 'b' + 'c', or 'abc'? The following code shows that the analogy can't be pushed that far:

`lists/sum_of_str.cmd`

```
>>> sum(['a', 'b', 'c'])
Traceback (most recent call last):
  File "<stdin>", line 1, in <module>
TypeError: unsupported operand type(s) for +: 'int' and 'str'
```

On the other hand, you *can* multiply a list by an integer to get a new list containing the elements from the original list repeated a certain number of times:

`lists/mult_lists.cmd`

```
>>> metals = 'Fe Ni'.split()
>>> metals * 3
['Fe', 'Ni', 'Fe', 'Ni', 'Fe', 'Ni']
```

As with concatenation, the original list isn't modified; instead, a new list is created. Notice, by the way, how we use string.split to turn the string 'Fe Ni' into a two-element list ['Fe', 'Ni']. This is a common trick in Python programs.

5.4 Processing List Items

Lists were invented so that we wouldn't have to create 1,000 variables to store a thousand values. For the same reason, Python has a *for loop* that lets us process each element in a list in turn, without having to write one statement per element. The general form of a for loop is as follows:

```
for variable in list:
    block
```

As we saw in Section 2.6, *Function Basics*, on page 20, a block is just a sequence of one or more statements. variable and list are just a variable and a list.

When Python encounters a loop, it executes the loop's block once for each value in the list. Each pass through the block is called an *iteration*, and at the start of each iteration, Python assigns the next value in the list to the specified variable. In this way, the program can do something with each value in turn.

For example, this code prints every velocity of a falling object in metric and imperial units:

lists/velocity_loop.cmd

```
>>> velocities = [0.0, 9.81, 19.62, 29.43]
>>> for v in velocities:
...     print "Metric:", v, "m/sec;",
...     print "Imperial:", v * 3.28, "ft/sec"
...
Metric: 0.0 m/sec; Imperial: 0.0 ft/sec
Metric: 9.81 m/sec; Imperial: 32.1768 ft/sec
Metric: 19.62 m/sec; Imperial: 64.3536 ft/sec
Metric: 29.43 m/sec; Imperial: 96.5304 ft/sec
```

Here are two other things to notice about this loop:

- In English we would say "for each velocity in the list, print the metric value, and then print the imperial value." In Python, we said roughly the same thing.
- As with function definitions, the statements in the loop block are indented. (We use four spaces in this book; check with your instructors to find out whether they prefer something else.)

In this case, we created a new variable v to store the current value taken from the list inside the loop. We could equally well have used an existing variable. If we do this, the loop still starts with the first element of the list—whatever value the variable had before the loop is lost:

lists/velocity_recycle.cmd

```
>>> speed = 2
>>> velocities = [0.0, 9.81, 19.62, 29.43]
>>> for speed in velocities:
...     print "Metric:", speed, "m/sec;",
...
Metric: 0.0 m/sec
Metric: 9.81 m/sec
Metric: 19.62 m/sec
Metric: 29.43 m/sec
>>> print "Final:", speed
Final: 29.43
```

Either way, the variable is left holding its last value when the loop finishes. Notice, by the way, that the last print statement in this program is not indented, so it is not part of the for loop. It is executed after the for loop has finished and is executed only once.

Nested Loops

We said earlier that the block of statements inside a loop could contain anything. This means that it can also contain another loop.

This program, for example, loops over the list inner once for each element of the list outer:

lists/nested_loops.cmd

```
>>> outer = ['Li', 'Na', 'K']
>>> inner = ['F', 'Cl', 'Br']
>>> for metal in outer:
...     for gas in inner:
...         print metal + gas
...
...
LiF
LiCl
LiBr
NaF
NaCl
NaBr
KF
KCl
KBr
```

If the outer loop has N_o iterations and the inner loop executes N_i times for each of them, the inner loop will execute a total of $N_o N_i$ times. One special case of this is when the inner and outer loops are running over the same list of length N, in which case the inner loop executes N^2 times. This can be used to generate a multiplication table; after printing the header row, we use a nested loop to print each row of the table in turn, using tabs to make the columns line up:

lists/multiplication_table.py

```
def print_table():
    '''Print the multiplication table for numbers 1 through 5.'''

    numbers = [1, 2, 3, 4, 5]

    # Print the header row.
    for i in numbers:
        print '\t' + str(i),

    print # End the header row.

    # Print the column number and the contents of the table.
    for i in numbers:
        print i,
        for j in numbers:
            print '\t' + str(i * j),
        print # End the current row.
```

Here is print_table's output:

```
lists/multiplication_out.txt
>>> from multiplication_table import *
>>> print_table()
        1       2       3       4       5
1       1       2       3       4       5
2       2       4       6       8       10
3       3       6       9       12      15
4       4       8       12      16      20
5       5       10      15      20      25
```

Notice when the two different kinds of formatting are done: the print statement at the bottom of the program prints a new line when outer loop advances, while the inner loop includes a tab in front of each item.

5.5 Slicing

Geneticists describe *C. elegans* (nematodes, or microscopic worms) using three-letter short-form markers. Examples include Emb (embryonic lethality), Him (High incidence of males), Unc (Uncoordinated), Dpy (dumpy: short and fat), Sma (small), and Lon (long). We can thus keep a list:

```
lists/celegans.cmd
>>> celegans_markers = ['Emb', 'Him', 'Unc', 'Lon', 'Dpy', 'Sma']
>>> celegans_markers
['Emb', 'Him', 'Unc', 'Lon', 'Dpy', 'Sma']
```

It turns out that Dpy worms and Sma worms are difficult to distinguish from each other, so they are not as useful as markers in complex strains. We can produce a new list based on celegans_markers, but without Dpy or Sma, by taking a *slice* of the list:

```
lists/celegans1.cmd
>>> celegans_markers = ['Emb', 'Him', 'Unc', 'Lon', 'Dpy', 'Sma']
>>> useful_markers = celegans_markers[0:4]
```

This creates a new list consisting of only the four distinguishable markers (see Figure 5.7, on the facing page).

The first index in the slice is the starting point. The second index is *one more than* the index of the last item we want to include. More rigorously,

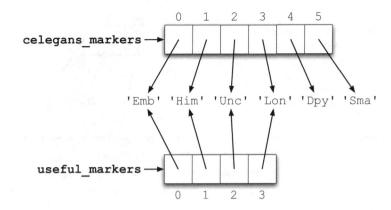

Figure 5.7: SLICING DOESN'T MODIFY LISTS.

list[i:j] is a slice of the original list from index i (inclusive) up to, but not including, index j (exclusive).[4]

The first index can be omitted if we want to slice from the beginning of the list, and the last index can be omitted if we want to slice to the end:

```
lists/celegans2.cmd
```

```
>>> celegans_markers = ['Emb', 'Him', 'Unc', 'Lon', 'Dpy', 'Sma']
>>> celegans_markers[:4]
['Emb', 'Him', 'Unc', 'Lon']
>>> celegans_markers[4:]
['Dpy', 'Sma']
```

To create a copy of the entire list, we just omit both indices so that the "slice" runs from the start of the list to its end:

```
lists/celegans3.cmd
```

```
>>> celegans_markers = ['Emb', 'Him', 'Unc', 'Lon', 'Dpy', 'Sma']
>>> celegans_copy = celegans_markers[:]
>>> celegans_markers[5] = 'Lvl'
>>> celegans_markers
['Emb', 'Him', 'Unc', 'Lon', 'Dpy', 'Lvl']
>>> celegans_copy
['Emb', 'Him', 'Unc', 'Lon', 'Dpy', 'Sma']
```

---

4. Python uses this convention to be consistent with the rule that the legal indices for a list go from 0 up to one less than the list's length.

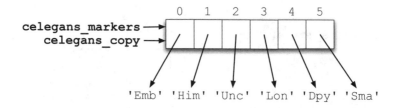

Figure 5.8: ALIASING LISTS

5.6 Aliasing

An *alias* is an alternative name for something. In Python, two variables are said to be aliases when they refer to the same value. For example, the following code creates two variables, both of which refer to a single list (see Figure 5.8). When we modify the list using one of the variables, references through the other variable show the change as well:

```
lists/celegans4.cmd
>>> celegans_markers = ['Emb', 'Him', 'Unc', 'Lon', 'Dpy', 'Sma']
>>> celegans_copy = celegans_markers
>>> celegans_markers[5] = 'Lvl'
>>> celegans_markers
['Emb', 'Him', 'Unc', 'Lon', 'Dpy', 'Lvl']
>>> celegans_copy
['Emb', 'Him', 'Unc', 'Lon', 'Dpy', 'Lvl']
```

Aliasing is one of the reasons why the notion of mutability is important. For example, if x and y refer to the same list, then any changes you make to the list through x will be "seen" by y, and vice versa. This can lead to all sorts of hard-to-find errors in which a list's value changes as if by magic, even though your program doesn't appear to assign anything to it. This can't happen with immutable values like strings. Since a string can't be changed after it has been created, it's safe to have aliases for it.

Aliasing in Function Calls

Aliasing occurs when we use list parameters as well, since parameters are variables.

Method	Description
L.append(v)	Appends value v to list L
L.insert(i, v)	Inserts value v at index i in list L, shifting following items to make room
L.remove(v)	Removes the first occurrence of value v from list L
L.reverse()	Reverses the order of the values in list L
L.sort()	Sorts the values in list L in ascending order (for strings, alphabetical order)
L.pop()	Removes and returns the last element of L (which must be nonempty)

Figure 5.9: LIST METHODS

Here is a simple function that takes a list, sorts it, and then reverses it:

`lists/alias_parameters.cmd`

```
>>> def sort_and_reverse(L):
...        '''Return list L sorted and reversed.'''
...        L.sort()
...        L.reverse()
...        return L
...
>>> celegans_markers = ['Emb', 'Him', 'Unc', 'Lon', 'Dpy', 'Lvl']
>>> sort_and_reverse(celegans_markers)
['Unc', 'Lvl', 'Lon', 'Him', 'Emb', 'Dpy']
>>> celegans_markers
['Unc', 'Lvl', 'Lon', 'Him', 'Emb', 'Dpy']
```

This function modifies list L, and since L is an alias of celegans_markers, that list is modified as well.

5.7 List Methods

Lists are objects and thus have methods. Some of the most commonly used are listed in Figure 5.9. Here is a sample interaction showing how we can use these methods to construct a list containing all the colors of the rainbow:

`lists/colors.cmd`

```
>>> colors = 'red orange green black blue'.split()
>>> colors.append('purple')
>>> colors
['red', 'orange', 'green', 'black', 'blue', 'purple']
```

> ### Where Did My List Go?
>
> Beginning programmers often forget that many list methods return None rather than creating and returning a new list. (Experienced programmers sometimes forget too.) As a result, their lists sometimes seem to disappear:
>
> lists/colors2.cmd
>
> ```
> >>> colors = 'red orange yellow green blue purple'.split()
> >>> colors
> ['blue', 'green', 'orange', 'purple', 'red', 'yellow']
> >>> sorted_colors = colors.sort()
> >>> print sorted_colors
> None
> ```
>
> As we'll discuss in Section 4.5, *Testing*, on page 61, mistakes like these can quickly be caught by writing and running a few tests.

```
>>> colors.insert(2, 'yellow')
>>> colors
['red', 'orange', 'yellow', 'green', 'black', 'blue', 'black', 'purple']
>>> colors.remove('black')
>>> colors
['red', 'orange', 'yellow', 'green', 'blue', 'purple']
```

It is important to note that all these methods modify the list instead of creating a new list. They do this because lists can grow very, very large—a million patient records, for example, or a billion measurements of a magnetic field. Creating a new list every time someone wanted to make a change to such a list would slow Python down so much that it would no longer be useful; having Python guess when it should make a copy, and when it should operate on the list in place, would make it impossible to figure out.

It's just as important to remember that all of these methods except pop return the special value None, which means "There is no useful information" or "There's nothing here." Python doesn't display anything when asked to display the value None. Printing it, on the other hand, shows us that it's there:

lists/none.cmd

```
>>> x = None
>>> x
>>> print x
None
```

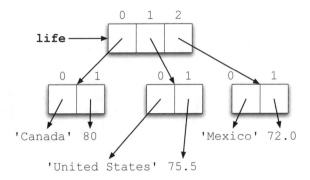

Figure 5.10: NESTED LISTS

Finally, a call to append is not the same as using +. First, append appends a single value, while + expects two lists as operands. Second, append modifies the list rather than creating a new one.

5.8 Nested Lists

We said in Section 5.1, *Lists Are Heterogeneous*, on page 77 that lists can contain any type of data. That means that they can contain other lists, just as the body of a loop can contain another loop. For example, the following nested list describes life expectancies in different countries:

`lists/lifelist.py`

```
[['Canada', 76.5], ['United States', 75.5], ['Mexico', 72.0]]
```

As shown in Figure 5.10, each element of the outer list is itself a list of two items. We use the standard notation to access the items in the outer list:

`lists/life0.cmd`

```
>>> life = [['Canada', 76.5], ['United States', 75.5], ['Mexico', 72.0]]
>>> life[0]
['Canada', 76.5]
>>> life[1]
['United States', 75.5]
>>> life[2]
['Mexico', 72.0]
```

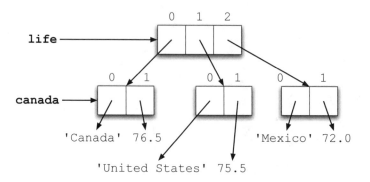

Figure 5.11: ALIASING SUBLISTS

Since each of these items is also a list, we can immediately index it again, just as we can chain together method calls or pass the result of one function call as an argument to another function:

`lists/life1.cmd`

```
>>> life = [['Canada', 76.5], ['United States', 75.5], ['Mexico', 72.0]]
>>> life[1]
['United States', 75.5]
>>> life[1][0]
'United States'
>>> life[1][1]
75.5
```

We can also assign sublists to variables:

`lists/life2.cmd`

```
>>> life = [['Canada', 76.5], ['United States', 75.5], ['Mexico', 72.0]]
>>> canada = life[0]
>>> canada
['Canada', 76.5]
>>> canada[0]
'Canada'
>>> canada[1]
76.5
```

Assigning a sublist to a variable creates an alias for that sublist (see Figure 5.11). As before, any change we make through the sublist reference will show up when we access the main list, and vice versa:

`lists/life3.cmd`

```
>>> life = [['Canada', 76.5], ['United States', 75.5], ['Mexico', 72.0]]
>>> canada = life[0]
```

```
>>> canada[1] = 80.0
>>> canada
['Canada', 80.0]
>>> life
[['Canada', 80.0], ['United States', 75.5], ['Mexico', 72.0]]
```

5.9 Other Kinds of Sequences

Lists aren't the only kind of sequence in Python. You've already met one of the others: strings. Formally, a string is an immutable sequence of characters. The "sequence" part of this definition means that it can be indexed and sliced like a list to create new strings:

lists/string_seq.cmd

```
>>> rock = 'anthracite'
>>> rock[9]
'e'
>>> rock[0:3]
'ant'
>>> rock[-5:]
'acite'
>>> for character in rock[:5]:
...     print character
...
a
n
t
h
r
```

Python also has an immutable sequence type called a *tuple*. Tuples are written using parentheses instead of square brackets; like strings and lists, they can be subscripted, sliced, and looped over:

lists/tuples1.cmd

```
>>> bases = ('A', 'C', 'G', 'T')
... for b in bases:
...     print b
A
C
G
T
```

There is one small catch: although () represents the empty tuple, a tuple with one element is *not* written as (x) but instead as (x,) (with a trailing comma). This has to be done to avoid ambiguity. If the trailing comma weren't required, (5 + 3) could mean either 8 (under the normal rules of arithmetic) or the tuple containing only the value 8. This is one of the few places where Python's syntax leaves something to be desired....

Once a tuple is created, it cannot be changed:

`lists/life4.cmd`

```
>>> life = (['Canada', 76.5], ['United States', 75.5], ['Mexico', 72.0])
>>> life[0] = life[1]
Traceback (most recent call last):
  File "<stdin>", line 1, in ?
TypeError: object does not support item assignment
```

However, the objects inside it *can* still be changed:

`lists/life5.cmd`

```
>>> life = (['Canada', 76.5], ['United States', 75.5], ['Mexico', 72.0])
>>> life[0][1] = 80.0
>>> life
(['Canada', 80.0], ['United States', 75.5], ['Mexico', 72.0])
```

This is because it's actually sloppy English to say that something is "inside" a tuple. It would be more accurate to say this: "The references contained in a tuple cannot be changed after the tuple has been created, though the objects referred to may themselves change."

Newcomers to Python often ask why tuples exist. The answer is that they make some operations more efficient and others safer. We won't get far enough in this book to explain the former, but we will explore the latter in Chapter 9, *Sets and Dictionaries*, on page 179.

5.10   Files as Lists

Most data is stored in files, which are just ordered sequences of bytes. Those bytes may represent characters, pixels, or postal codes; the important thing is that they're in a particular order, which means that lists are usually a natural way to work with them.

In order to read data from a file, we must first open it using Python's built-in function open:

`lists/open_basic.cmd`

```
>>> file = open("data.txt", "r")
```

The first argument to open is a string containing the name of the file. The second argument indicates a *mode*. The three options are "r" for reading, "w" for writing, and "a" for appending. (The difference between writing and appending is that writing a file erases anything that was already in it, while appending adds new data to the end.)

The result of open is *not* the contents of the file. Instead, open returns a *file object* whose methods allow the program to access the contents of the file.

The most fundamental of these methods is read. When it is called without any arguments, it reads all the data in the file and returns it as a string of characters. If we give read a positive integer argument, it reads only up to that many characters; this is useful when we are working with very large files. In either case, if there's no more data in the file, the method returns an empty string.

Although read gives us access to the bytes in a file, we usually use higher-level methods to do our work. If the file contains text, for example, we will probably want to process it one line at a time. To do this, we can use the file object's readline method, which reads the next line of text from the file. A line is defined as being all the characters up to and including the next end-of-line marker (see Section 3.3, *Multiline Strings*, on page 33). Like read, readline returns an empty string when there's no more data in the file.

The neatest thing about readline is that Python calls it for us automatically when a file object is used in a for loop. Assume this data is in a file called data.txt:

`lists/data.txt`

```
Mercury
Venus
Earth
Mars
```

This program opens that file and prints the length of each line:

`lists/fileinputloop.cmd`

```
>>> data = open('data.txt', 'r')
>>> for line in data:
...     print len(line)
...
8
6
6
5
```

Take a close look at the last line of output. There are only four characters in the word *Mars*, but our program is reporting that the line is five characters long. The reason for this is that each of the lines we read from the file has an end-of-line character at the end. We can get rid of it using string.strip, which returns a copy of a string that has leading and trailing whitespace characters (spaces, tabs, and newlines) stripped away:

lists/fileinputloop2.cmd
```
>>> data = open('data.txt', 'r')
>>> for line in data:
...     print len(line.strip())
...
7
5
5
4
```

This example shows the result of applying strip to a string with leading and trailing whitespace:

lists/strip_basic.cmd
```
>>> compound = "      \n  Methyl butanol    \n"
>>> print compound

  Methyl butanol


>>> print compound.strip()
Methyl butanol
```

Note that the space inside the string is unaffected: string.strip takes whitespace only off the front and end of the string.

Using string.strip, we can now produce the correct output when reading from our file:

lists/fileinputloop_strip.cmd
```
>>> file = open('data.txt', 'r')
>>> for line in file:
...     line = line.strip()
...     print len(line)
...
7
5
5
4
```

Command-Line Arguments

We said earlier that the file data.txt contains the name of planets. To finish the example, let's go back to reading that file but display only a certain range of the lines. We'll provide the start and end line numbers when we run the program. For example, we might want to read the first three lines one time and lines 2 to 4 another time.

We can do this using *command-line arguments*. When we run a program, we can send arguments to it, much like when we call a function or method. These values end up in a special variable of the system module sys called argv, which is just a list of the arguments (as strings).

sys.argv[0] always contains the name of the Python program being run. In this case, it is read_lines_range.py. The rest of the command-line arguments are in sys.argv[1], sys.argv[2], and so on.

Here, then, is a program that reads all the data from a file and displays lines with line numbers within the start and end line range:

`lists/read_lines_range.py`

```python
''' Display the lines of data.txt from the given starting line number to the
given end line number.

Usage: read_lines_range.py start_line end_line '''

import sys

if __name__ == '__main__':

    # get the start and end line numbers
    start_line = int(sys.argv[1])
    end_line = int(sys.argv[2])

    # read the lines of the file and store them in a list
    data = open('data.txt', 'r')
    data_list = data.readlines()
    data.close()

    # display lines within start to end range
    for line in data_list[start_line:end_line]:
        print line.strip()
```

5.11 Comments

The previous line-reading program is one of the longest we have seen to date—so long, in fact, that we have added comments as well as a docstring. The docstring is primarily for people who want to use the program; it describes *what* the program does but not *how*.

Comments, on the other hand, are written for the benefit of future developers.[5] Each comment starts with the # character and runs to the end of the line. We can put whatever we want in comments, because Python ignores them completely.

Here are a few rules for good commenting:

- Assume your readers know as much Python as you do (for example, don't explain what strings are or what an assignment statement does).

- Don't comment the obvious—the following comment is *not* useful:

  ```
  count = count + 1  # add one to count
  ```

- Many programmers leave comments beginning with "TODO" or "FIXME" in code to remind themselves of things that need to be written or tidied up.

- If you needed to think hard when you wrote a piece of software, you should write a comment so that the next person doesn't have to do the same thinking all over again. In particular, if you develop a program or function by writing a simple point-form description in English, then making the points more and more specific until they turn into code, you should keep the original points as comments. (We will discuss this style of development further in Chapter 10, *Algorithms*, on page 197.)

- Similarly, if a bug was difficult to find or if the fix is complicated, you should write a comment to explain it. If you don't, the next programmer to work on that part of the program might think that the code is needlessly complicated and undo your hard work.

- On the other hand, if you need lots of comments to explain what a piece of code does, you should clean up the code. For example, if you have to keep reminding readers what each of the fifteen lists in a function are for, you should break the function into smaller pieces, each of which works only with a few of those lists.

---

5. Including future versions of ourselves, who might have forgotten the details of this program by the time a change needs to be made or a bug needs to be fixed.

And here's one more rule:

- An out-of-date comment is worse than no comment at all, so if you change a piece of software, read the comments carefully and fix any that are no longer accurate.

5.12 Summary

In this chapter, we learned the following:

- Lists are used to keep track of zero or more objects. We call the objects in a list its elements and refer to them by position using indices ranging from zero to one less than the length of the list.

- Lists are mutable, which means that their contents can be modified. Lists can contain any type of data, including other lists.

- Slicing is used to create new lists that have the same values or a subset of the values of the originals.

- When two variables refer to the same object, we call them aliases.

- Tuples are another kind of Python sequence. Tuples are similar to lists, except they are immutable.

- When files are opened and read, their contents are commonly stored in lists of strings.

5.13 Exercises

Here are some exercises for you to try on your own:

1. Assign a list that contains the atomic numbers of the six alkaline earth metals—beryllium (4), magnesium (12), calcium (20), strontium (38), barium (56), and radium (88)—to a variable called alkaline_earth_metals.

2. Which index contains radium's atomic number? Write the answer in two ways, one using a positive index and one using a negative index.

3. Which function tells you how many items there are in alkaline_ earth_metals?

4. Write code that returns the highest atomic number in alkaline_ earth_metals. (Hint: use one of the functions from Figure 5.5, on page 79.)

5. What is the difference between print 'a' and print 'a',?

6. Write a for loop to print all the values in list celegans_markers from Section 5.5, *Slicing*, on page 84, one per line.

7. Write a for loop to print all the values in list half_lives from Section 5.5, *Slicing*, on page 84, all on a single line.

8. Consider the following statement, which creates a list of populations of countries in eastern Asia (China, DPR Korea, Hong Kong, Mongolia, Republic of Korea, and Taiwan), in millions: country_populations = [1295, 23, 7, 3, 47, 21]. Write a for loop that adds up all the values and stores them in variable total. (Hint: give total an initial value of zero, and, inside the loop body, add the population of the current country to total.)

9. Create a list of temperatures in degrees Celsius with the values 25.2, 16.8, 31.4, 23.9, 28, 22.5, and 19.6, and assign it to a variable called temps.

10. Using one of the list methods, sort temps in ascending order.

11. Using slicing, create two new lists, cool_temps and warm_temps, which contain the temperatures below and above 20 degrees celsius, respectively.

12. Using list arithmetic, recombine cool_temps and warm_temps in into a new list called temps_in_celsius.

13. Write a for loop to convert all the values from temps_in_celsius into Fahrenheit, and store the converted values in a new list temps_in_fahrenheit. The list temps_in_celsius should remain unchanged.

14. Create a nested list where each element of the outer list contains the atomic number and atomic weight for an alkaline earth metal. The values are beryllium (4 and 9.012), magnesium (12 and 24.305), calcium (20 and 40.078), strontium (38 and 87.62), barium (56 and 137.327), and radium (88 and 226). Assign the list to a variable alkaline_earth_metals.

15. Write a for loop to print all the values in alkaline_earth_metals, with the atomic number and atomic weight for each alkaline earth metal on a different line.

16. Write a for loop to create a new list called number_and_weight that contains the elements of alkaline_earth_metals in the same order but not nested.

17. Suppose the file alkaline_metals.txt contains this:

```
4 9.012
12 24.305
20 20.078
38 87.62
56 137.327
88 226
```

Write a for loop to read the contents of alkaline_metals.txt, and store it in a nested list with each element of the list contains the atomic number and atomic weight for an element. (Hint: use string.split.)

18. Draw a memory model showing the effect of the following statements:

```
values = [0, 1, 2]
values[1] = values
```

19. The following function does not have a docstring or comments. Write enough of both to make it easy for the next person to understand what the function does, and how, and then compare your solution with those of at least two other people. How similar are they? Why do they differ?

```
def mystery_function(values):
    result = []
    for i in range(len(values[0])):
        result.append([values[0][i]])
        for j in range(1, len(values)):
            result[-1].append(values[j][i])
    return result
```

20. Section 5.2, *Modifying Lists*, on page 77 said that strings are immutable. Why might mutable strings be useful? Why do you think Python made them immutable?

21. What happens when you sort a list that contains a mix of numbers and strings, such as [1, 'a', 2, 'b']? Is this consistent with the rules given in Chapter 3, *Strings*, on page 29 and Chapter 6, *Making Choices*, on page 101 for how comparison operators like < work on numbers and strings? Is this the "right" thing for Python to do, or would some other behavior be more useful?

Chapter 6

Making Choices

This chapter introduces another fundamental concepts of programming: making choices. We have to do this whenever we want to have our program behave differently depending on the data it's working with. For example, we might want to do different things depending on whether a solution is acidic or basic.

The statements we'll meet in this chapter for making choices are called *control flow* statements, because they control the way the computer executes programs. We have already met one control flow statement—the loops introduced in Section 5.4, *Processing List Items*, on page 81—and we will meet others in future chapters as well. Together, they are what give programs their "personalities."

Before we can explore control flow statements, we must introduce a Python type that is used to represent truth and falsehood. Unlike the integers, floating-point numbers, and strings we have already seen, this type has only two values and three operators, but it is extremely powerful.

6.1 Boolean Logic

In the 1840s, the mathematician George Boole showed that the classical rules of logic could be expressed in purely mathematical form using only the two values "true" and "false." A century later, Claude Shannon (later the inventor of information theory) realized that Boole's work could be used to optimize the design of electromechanical telephone switches. His work led directly to the use of *Boolean logic* to design computer circuits.

In honor of Boole's work, most modern programming languages use a type named after him to keep track of what's true and what isn't.

In Python, that type is called bool (without an "e"). Unlike int and float, which have billions of possible values, bool has only two: True and False. True and False are values, just as much as the numbers 0 and -43.7. It feels a little strange at first to think of them this way, since "true" and "false" in normal speech are adjectives that we apply to other statements. As we'll see, though, treating True and False as nouns is natural in programs.

Boolean Operators

There are only three basic Boolean operators: and, or, and not. not has the highest precedence, followed by and, followed by or.

not is a unary operator; in other words, it is applied to just one value, like the negation in the expression -(3 + 2). An expression involving not produces True if the original value is False, and it produces False if the original value is True:

cond/boolean_not_examples.cmd

```
>>> not True
False
>>> not False
True
```

In the previous example, instead of not True, we could simply use False; and instead of not False, we could use True. Rather than apply not directly to a Boolean value, we would typically apply not to a Boolean variable or a more complex Boolean expression. The same goes for the following examples of Boolean operators and and or, so although we apply them to Boolean constants in the following examples, we'll give an example of how they are typically used at the end of this section.

and is a binary operator; the expression left and right is True if both left and right are True, and it's False otherwise:

cond/boolean_and_examples.cmd

```
>>> True and True
True
>>> False and False
False
>>> True and False
False
>>> False and True
False
```

cold	windy	(not cold) and windy	not (cold and windy)
True	True	False	False
True	False	False	True
False	True	True	True
False	False	False	True

Figure 6.1: RELATIONAL AND EQUALITY OPERATORS

or is also a binary operator. It produces True if *either* operand is True, and it produces False only if both are False:

```
cond/boolean_or_examples.cmd
```
```
>>> True or True
True
>>> False or False
False
>>> True or False
True
>>> False or True
True
```

This definition is called *inclusive or*, since it allows both possibilities as well as either. In English, the word *or* is also sometimes an *exclusive or*. For example, if someone says, "You can have pizza or tandoori chicken," they probably don't mean that you can have both. Like most programming languages, Python always interprets or as inclusive. We will see in the exercises how to create an exclusive or.

We mentioned earlier that Boolean operators are usually applied to Boolean expressions, rather than Boolean constants. If we want to express "It is not cold and windy" using two variables cold and windy that contain Boolean values, we first have to decide what the ambiguous English expression means: is it not cold but at the same time windy, or is it not both cold and windy? A *truth table* for each alternative is shown in Figure 6.1, and the following code snippet shows what they look like translated into Python:

```
cond/boolean_expression.cmd
```
```
>>> (not cold) and windy
>>> not (cold and windy)
```

Symbol	Operation
>	Greater than
<	Less than
>=	Greater than or equal to
<=	Less than or equal to
==	Equal to
!=	Not equal to

Figure 6.2: RELATIONAL AND EQUALITY OPERATORS

Relational Operators

We said earlier that True and False are values. The most common way to produce them in programs is not to write them down directly but rather to create them in expressions. The most common way to do that is to do a comparison using a *relational operator*. For example, 3<5 is a comparison using the relational operator < whose value is True, while 13≥77 uses ≥ and has the value False.

As shown in Figure 6.2, Python has all the operators you're used to using. Some of them are represented using two characters instead of one, like <= instead of ≤.

The most important representation rule is that Python uses == for equality instead of just =, because = is used for assignment. Beginners often mix the two up and type x = 3 when they meant to check whether the variable x was equal to three. This always produces a syntax error, but if you don't know what to look for, it can be hard to spot the reason.

All relational operators are binary operators: they compare two values and produce True or False, as appropriate. The "greater than" > and "less than" < operators work as expected:

```
cond/relational_1.cmd

>>> 45 > 34
True
>>> 45 > 79
False
>>> 45 < 79
True
>>> 45 < 34
False
```

We can compare integers to floating-point numbers with any of the relational operators. Integers are automatically converted to floating point when we do this, just as they are when we add 14 to 23.3:

cond/relational_2.cmd
```
>>> 23.1 >= 23
True
>>> 23.1 >= 23.1
True
>>> 23.1 <= 23.1
True
>>> 23.1 <= 23
False
```

The same holds for "equal to" and "not equal to":

cond/relational_3.cmd
```
>>> 67.3 == 87
False
>>> 67.3 == 67
False
>>> 67.0 == 67
True
>>> 67.0 != 67
False
>>> 67.0 != 23
True
```

Of course, it doesn't make much sense to compare two numbers that you know in advance, since you would also know the result of the comparison. Relational operators therefore almost always involve variables, like this:

cond/relational_var.cmd
```
>>> def positive(x):
...     return x > 0
...
>>> positive(3)
True
>>> positive(-2)
False
>>> positive(0)
False
```

Combining Comparisons

We have now seen three types of operators: arithmetic, Boolean, and relational.

Here are the rules for combining them:

- Arithmetic operators have higher precedence than relational operators. For example, + and / are evaluated before < or >.

- Relational operators have higher precedence than Boolean operators. For example, comparisons are evaluated before and, or, and not.

- All relational operators have the same precedence.

These rules mean that the expression 1 + 3 > 7 is evaluated as (1 + 3) > 7, not as 1 + (3 > 7). These rules also mean that you can often skip the parentheses in complicated expressions:

cond/skipping_parens.cmd

```
>>> x = 2
>>> y = 5
>>> z = 7
>>> x < y and y < z
True
```

It's usually a good idea to put the parentheses in, though, since it helps the eye find the subexpressions and clearly communicates the order to anyone reading your code:

cond/parens_included.cmd

```
>>> (x < y) and (y < z)
True
```

It's very common in mathematics to check whether a value lies in a certain range, in other words, that it is between two other values. You can do this in Python by combining the comparisons with and:

cond/compare_range.cmd

```
>>> x = 3
>>> (1 < x) and (x <= 5)
True
>>> x = 7
>>> (1 < x) and (x <= 5)
False
```

This comes up so often, however, that Python lets you *chain* the comparisons:

cond/chain1.cmd

```
>>> x = 3
>>> 1 < x <= 5
True
```

Most combinations work as you would expect, but there are cases that may startle you:

`cond/chain2.cmd`

```
>>> 3 < 5 != True
True
>>> 3 < 5 != False
True
```

It seems impossible for both of these expressions to be True. However, the first one is equivalent to this:

```
(3 < 5) and (5 != True)
```

while the second is equivalent to this:

```
(3 < 5) and (5 != False)
```

Since 5 is not True or False, the second half of each expression is True, so the expression as a whole is True as well.

This kind of expression is an example of something that is a bad idea even though it is legal.[1] We strongly recommend that you only chain comparisons in ways that would seem natural to a mathematician, in other words, that you use < and <= together, or > and >= together, and nothing else. If you're tempted to do something else, resist. Use simple comparisons and combine them with and in order to keep your code readable. It's also a good idea to use parentheses whenever you think the expression you are writing may not be entirely clear.

Applying Boolean Operators to Integers, Floats, and Strings

We have already seen that Python converts ints to floats in mixed expressions. It also converts numbers to bools, which means that the three Boolean operators can be applied directly to numbers. When this happens, Python treats 0 and 0.0 as False and treats all other numbers as True:

`cond/not.cmd`

```
>>> not 0
True
>>> not 1
False
>>> not 5
False
```

---

1. Sort of like going on a roller coaster right after eating two extra large ice cream sundaes back to back on a dare.

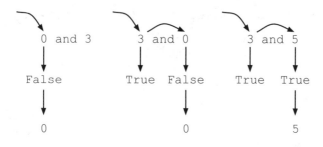

Figure 6.3: SHORT-CIRCUIT EVALUATION

```
>>> not 34.2
False
>>> not -87
False
```

Things are more complicated with and and or. When Python evaluates an expression containing either of these operators, it always does so from left to right. As soon as it knows enough to stop evaluating, it stops, even if some operands haven't been looked at yet. The result is the last thing that was evaluated, which is *not* necessarily either True or False.

This is much easier to demonstrate than explain. Here are three expressions involving and:

cond/and.cmd

```
>>> 0 and 3
0
>>> 3 and 0
0
>>> 3 and 5
5
```

In the first expression, Python sees a 0, which is equivalent to False, and immediately stops evaluating. It doesn't need to look at the 3 to know that the expression as a whole is going to be false, since and is true only if both operands are true (see Figure 6.3).

In the second expression, though, Python has to check both operands, since knowing that the first one (the 3) isn't false is not enough to know what the value of the whole expression will be. Python also checks both operands in the third expression; as you can see, it takes the value of the last thing it checked as the value of the expression as a whole (in this case, 5).

With or, if the first operand is considered to be true, or evaluates to that value *immediately*, without even checking the second operand. The reason for this is that Python already knows the answer: True or X is True, regardless of the value of X.

If the first operand is equivalent to False, though, or has to check the second operand. Its result is then that operand's value:

`cond/or.cmd`

```
>>> 1 or 0
1
>>> 0 or 1
1
>>> True or 0
True
>>> 0 or False
False
>>> False or 0
0
>>> False or 18.2
18.199999999999999
```

(Remember, computers can't represent all fractions exactly: the last value in the previous code fragment is as close as it can get to 18.2.)

We claimed that if the first operand to the or operator is true, then or evaluates to that value immediately without evaluating the second operand. In order to show that this is what happens, try an expression that divides by zero:

`cond/div_zero.cmd`

```
>>> 1 / 0
Traceback (most recent call last):
  File "<string>", line 1, in <string>
ZeroDivisionError: integer division or modulo by zero
```

Now use that expression as the second operand to or:

`cond/or_lazy.cmd`

```
>>> True or 1 / 0
True
```

Since the first operand is true, the second operand is not evaluated, so the computer never actually tries to divide anything by zero.

> ### There's Such a Thing as Being Too Clever
>
> An expression like y = x and 1/x works, but that doesn't mean you should use it, any more than you should use this:
>
> ```
> result = test and first or second
> ```
>
> as a shorthand for the following:
>
> ```
> if test:
>     result = first
> else:
>     result = second
> ```
>
> Programs are meant to be readable. If you have to puzzle over a line of code or if there's a high likelihood that someone seeing it for the first time will misunderstand it, it's bad code, even if it runs correctly.

It's possible to compare strings with each other, just as you would compare numbers. The characters in strings are represented by integers: a capital *A*, for example, is represented by 65, while a space is 32, and a lowercase *z* is 172.[2] Python decides which string is greater than which by comparing corresponding characters from left to right. If the character from one string is greater than the character from the other, the first string is greater than the second. If all the characters are the same, the two strings are equal; if one string runs out of characters while the comparison is being done (in other words, is shorter than the other), then it is less. The following code fragment shows a few comparisons in action:

cond/string_compare.cmd

```
>>> 'A' < 'a'
True
>>> 'A' > 'z'
False
>>> 'abc' < 'abd'
True
>>> 'abc' < 'abcd'
True
```

---

2. This encoding is called *ASCII*, which stands for "American Standard Code for Information Interchange." One of its quirks is that all the uppercase letters come before all the lowercase letters, so a capital *Z* is less than a small *a*.

Like zero, the empty string is equivalent to False; all other strings are equivalent to True:

`cond/empty_false.cmd`

```
>>> '' and False
''
>>> 'salmon' or True
'salmon'
```

Python can also convert Booleans to numbers: True becomes 1, while False becomes 0:

`cond/truefalse.cmd`

```
>>> False == 0
True
>>> True == 1
True
>>> True == 2
False
>>> False < True
True
```

This means that you can add, subtract, multiply, and divide using Boolean values:

`cond/bool_math.cmd`

```
>>> 5 + True
6
>>> 7 - False
7
```

But "can" isn't the same as "should": adding True to 5, or multiplying the temperature by current_time<NOON, will make your code much harder to read. In practice, programmers routinely rely on conversion *to* Booleans but rarely if ever use conversions in the other direction.

6.2 if Statements

The basic form of an if statement is as follows:

```
if condition:
    block
```

The *condition* is an expression, such as name != " or x < y. Note that this doesn't have to be a Boolean expression. As we discussed in Section 6.1, *Applying Boolean Operators to Integers, Floats, and Strings*, on page 107, non-Boolean values are automatically converted to True or False when required.

In particular, 0, None, the empty string ", and the empty list [] all are considered to false, while all other values that we have encountered are considered to be true.

If the condition is true, then the statements in the block are executed; otherwise, they are not. As with loops and functions, the block of statements must be indented to show that it belongs to the if statement. If you don't indent properly, Python might raise an error, or worse, might happily execute the code that you wrote but, because some statements were not indented properly, do something you didn't intend. We'll briefly explore both problems in this chapter.

Here is a table of solution categories based on pH level:

pH Level	Solution Category
0–4	Strong acid
5–6	Weak acid
7	Neutral
8–9	Weak base
10–14	Strong base

We can use an if statement to print a message only when the pH level given by the program's user is acidic:

cond/if_basictrue.cmd

```
>>> ph = float(raw_input())
6.0
>>> if ph < 7.0:
...     print "%s is acidic." % (ph)
...
6.0 is acidic.
```

(Recall from Section 3.6, *User Input*, on page 36 that we have to convert user input from a string to a float before doing the comparison.)

If the condition is false, the statements in the block are not executed:

cond/if_basicfalse.cmd

```
>>> ph = float(raw_input())
8.0
>>> if ph < 7.0:
...     print "%s is acidic." % (ph)
...
>>>
```

If we don't indent the block, Python lets us know:

`cond/if_indenterror.cmd`

```
>>> ph = float(raw_input())
6.0
>>> if ph < 7.0:
... print "%s is acidic." % (ph)
  File "<stdin>", line 2
    print "%s is acidic." % (ph)
        ^
IndentationError: expected an indented block
```

Since we're using a block, we can have multiple statements, which are executed only if the condition is true:

`cond/if_multilinetrue.cmd`

```
>>> ph = float(raw_input())
6.0
>>> if ph < 7.0:
...     print "%s is acidic." % (ph)
...     print "You should be careful with that!"
...
6.0 is acidic.
You should be careful with that!
```

When we indent the first line of the block, the Python interpreter changes its prompt to ... until the end of the block, which is signaled by a blank line:

`cond/if_multiline_indent_error.cmd`

```
>>> ph = float(raw_input())
8.0
>>> if ph < 7.0:
...     print "%s is acidic." % (ph)
...
>>> print "You should be careful with that!"
You should be careful with that!
```

If we don't indent the code that's in the block, the interpreter complains:

`cond/if_multiline_indent_error2.cmd`

```
>>> ph = float(raw_input())
8.0
>>> if ph < 7.0:
...     print "%s is acidic." % (ph)
... print "You should be careful with that!"
  File "<stdin>", line 3
    print "You should be careful with that!"
        ^
SyntaxError: invalid syntax
```

If the program is in a file, then no blank line is needed. As soon as the indentation ends, Python assumes that the block has ended as well. This is therefore legal:

cond/if_multiline_indent_error3.cmd

```
ph = 8.0
if ph < 7.0:
    print "%s is acidic." % (ph)
print "You should be careful with that!"
```

In practice, this slight inconsistency is never a problem, and most people never even notice it.

Of course, sometimes there are situations where a single decision isn't sufficient. If there are multiple criteria to examine, there are a couple of ways to handle it. One way is to use multiple if statements. For example, we might print different messages depending on whether a pH level is acidic or basic:

cond/multi_if.cmd

```
>>> ph = float(raw_input())
8.5
>>> if ph < 7.0:
...     print "%s is acidic." % (ph)
...
>>> if ph > 7.0:
...     print "%s is basic." % (ph)
...
8.5 is basic.
>>>
```

In Figure 6.4, on the facing page, we see that both conditions are always evaluated, even though we know that only one of the blocks can be executed. We can merge both cases by adding another condition/block pair using the elif keyword (which stands for "else if"); each condition/block pair is called a *clause*:

cond/elif_basic.cmd

```
>>> ph = float(raw_input())
8.5
>>> if ph < 7.0:
...     print "%s is acidic." % (ph)
... elif ph > 7.0:
...     print "%s is basic." % (ph)
...
8.5 is basic.
>>>
```

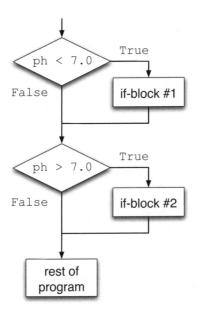

Figure 6.4: IF STATEMENT

The difference between the two is that the elif is checked only when the if above it was false. In Figure 6.5, on the next page, we can see the difference pictorially, with conditions drawn as diamonds, other statements as rectangles, and arrows to show the flow of control.

An if statement can be followed by multiple elif clauses. This longer example translates a chemical formula into English:

cond/elif_longer.cmd

```
>>> compound = raw_input()
CH3
>>> if compound == "H2O":
...     print "Water"
... elif compound == "NH3":
...     print "Ammonia"
... elif compound == "CH3":
...     print "Methane"
...
Methane
>>>
```

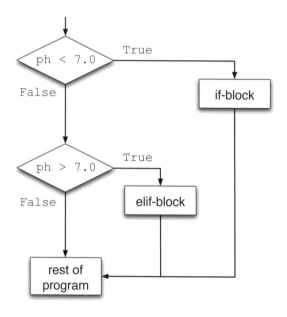

Figure 6.5: ELIF STATEMENT

If none of the conditions in a chain of if/elif statements are satisfied, Python does not execute any of the associated blocks. This isn't always what we'd like, though. In our translation example, we probably want our program to print something even if it doesn't recognize the compound. To do this, we add an else clause at the end of the chain:

cond/else_basic.cmd

```
>>> compound = raw_input()
H2SO4
>>> if compound == "H2O":
...     print "Water"
... elif compound == "NH3":
...     print "Ammonia"
... elif compound == "CH3":
...     print "Methane"
... else:
...     print "Unknown compound"
...
Unknown compound
>>>
```

An if statement can have at most one else clause, and it has to be the final clause in the statement. Notice there is no condition associated with the else; logically, the following statement:

```
if condition:
    if-block
else:
    else-block
```

is the same as this:

```
if condition:
    if-block
if not condition:
    else-block
```

Nested if Statements

An if statement's block can contain any type of Python statement, which means that it can include other if statements. An if statement inside another is called a *nested* if statement.

cond/nested_if.cmd

```
input = raw_input()
if len(input) > 0:
    ph = float(input)
    if ph < 7.0:
        print "%s is acidic." % (ph)
    elif ph > 7.0:
        print "%s is basic." % (ph)
    else:
        print "%s is neutral." % (ph)
else:
    print "No pH value was given!"
```

In this case, we ask the user to provide a pH value, which we'll initially receive as a string. The first, or *outer*, if statement checks whether the user typed something, which determines whether we examine the value of pH with the *inner* if statement.

Nested if statements are sometimes necessary, but they can get complicated and difficult to understand. To describe when a statement is executed, we have to mentally combine conditions; for example, print "That's acidic!" is executed only if the length of the string input is greater than 0 *and* pH < 7.0 also evaluates to true.

6.3 Storing Conditionals

Take a look at the following line of code and guess what value is stored in x:

`cond/assign_bool.cmd`

```
>>> x = 15 > 5
```

If you said "True", you were right: 15 is greater than 5, so the comparison produces True, and since that's a value like any other, it can be assigned to a variable.

The most common situation in which you would want to do this comes up when translating decision tables into software. For example, suppose you want to calculate someone's risk of heart disease using the following rules based on age and body mass index (BMI):

		Age	
		<45	≥45
BMI	<22.0	Low	Medium
	≥22.0	Medium	High

One way to implement this would be to use nested if statements:

```
if age < 45:
    if bmi < 22.0:
        risk = 'low'
    else:
        risk = 'medium'
else:
    if bmi < 22.0:
        risk = 'medium'
    else:
        risk = 'high'
```

The problem with this is that it's hard to see that we're testing exactly the same condition in several places. If there were four thresholds each for age and BMI, for example, we'd have sixteen inner conditions, and it wouldn't be obvious that they were all identical.

Here's a better way to do this:

```
young = age < 45
slim = bmi < 22.0
if young:
    if slim:
        risk = 'low'
    else
        risk = 'medium'
```

```
else:
    if slim:
        risk = 'medium'
    else:
        risk = 'high'
```

We could also write this as follows:

```
young = age < 45
slim = bmi < 22.0
if young and slim:
    risk = 'low'
elif young and not slim:
    risk = 'medium'
elif not young and slim:
    risk = 'medium'
elif not young and not slim:
    risk = 'high'
```

We can even take advantage of the fact that False has the value 0 when converted to an integer and that True has the value 1:

```
table = [['medium', 'high'],
         ['low',    'medium']]
young = age < 45
heavy = bmi >= 22.0
risk = table[young][heavy]
```

6.4 Summary

In this chapter, we learned the following:

- Python uses the Boolean values True and False to represent what is true and what isn't. Programs can combine these values using three operators: not, and, and or.

- Boolean operators can also be applied to numeric values. 0 and 0.0 are equivalent to False; all other numeric values are equivalent to True. When Boolean values are converted to numbers, False becomes 0, and True becomes 1.

- Relational operators such as "equals" and "less than" compare values and produce a Boolean result.

- When different operators are combined in an expression, the order of precedence from highest to lowest is arithmetic, relational, and then Boolean.

6.5 Exercises

Here are some exercises for you to try on your own:

1. For each of the following expressions, what value will the expression give? Verify your answers by typing the expressions into Python.

   a) True and not False

   b) True or True and False

   c) not True or not False

   d) True and not 0

   e) 52 < 52.3

   f) 1 + 52 < 52.3

   g) 4 != 4.0

2. Here is a possible definition of how and works:

   If both operands are true, and's result is its second value. If either is false, and's result is its first value.

   Is this the rule that Python actually uses? If not, provide a counter example.

3. You are given variables x and y.

   a) Write an expression that evaluates to True if both variables are True and that evaluates to False otherwise.

   b) Write an expression that evaluates to True if x is False and evaluates to False otherwise.

   c) Write an expression that evaluates to True if at least one of the variables is True and evaluates to False otherwise.

4. Given variables full and empty, write an expression that evaluates to True if at most one of the variables is True and evaluates to False otherwise.

5. You want an automatic wildlife camera to switch on if the light level is less than 0.01 or if the temperature is above freezing, but not if both conditions are true.

Your first attempt to write this is as follows:

```
if (light < 0.01) or (temperature > 0.0):
    if (light < 0.01) and (temperature > 0.0):
        pass
    else:
        camera.on()
```

A friend says that this is an exclusive or and that you could write it more simply as follows:

```
if (light < 0.01) != (temperature > 0.0):
    camera.on()
```

Is your friend right? If so, explain why. If not, give values for light and temperature that will produce different results for the two fragments of code.

6. In Section 2.7, *Built-in Functions*, on page 23, we saw the built-in function abs. Given a variable x, write an expression that evaluates to True if x and its absolute value are equal and evaluates to False otherwise. Associate the resulting value with a variable named result.

7. Write a function named different that has two parameters, a and b. The function should return True if a and b refer to different values and should return False otherwise.

8. You are given two float variables, population and land_area.

   a) Write an if statement that will print the population if it is less than 10,000,000.

   b) Write an if statement that will print the population if it is between 10,000,000 and 35,000,000.

   c) Write an if statement that will print "Densely populated" if the land density (number of people per unit of area) is greater than 100.

   d) Write an if statement that will print "Densely populated" if the land density (number of people per unit of area) is greater than 100 and that will print "Sparsely populated" otherwise.

9. Function to_celsius from Section 2.6, *Function Basics*, on page 20 converts from Fahrenheit to Celsius. Wikipedia, however, discusses eight temperature scales: Kelvin, Celsius, Fahrenheit, Rankine, Delisle, Newton, Rèaumur, and Rømer. Visit http://en.wikipedia.org/wiki/Comparison_of_temperature_scales to read about them.

a) Write a function convert_temperatures(t, source, target) that converts temperature t from source units to target units, where source and target are each one of "Kelvin", "Celsius", "Fahrenheit", "Rankine", "Delisle", "Newton", "Reaumur", and "Romer".

Hint: on the Wikipedia page there are eight tables, each with two columns and seven rows. That translates to an awful lot of if statements—at least 8 * 7, because each of the eight units can be converted to the seven other units. Possibly even worse, if you decided to add another temperature scale, you would need to add at least sixteen more if statements: eight to convert from your new scale to each of the current ones and eight to convert from the current ones to your new scale.

A better way is to choose one canonical scale, such as Celsius. Your conversion function could work in two steps: convert from the source scale to Celsius and then from Celsius to the target scale.

b) Now, if you added a new temperature scale, how many if statements would you need to add?

10. Assume we want to print a strong warning message if a pH value is below 3.0 and otherwise simply report on the acidity. We try this if statement:

cond/elif_wrongorder.cmd

```
>>> if ph < 7.0:
...     print "%s is acidic." % (ph)
... elif ph < 3.0:
...     print "%s is VERY acidic! Be careful." % (ph)
...
```

This prints the wrong message when a pH of 2.5 is entered. What is the problem, and how can you fix it?

11. The following code displays a message(s) about the acidity of a solution:

cond/acidity.cmd

```
ph = float(raw_input("Enter the ph level: "))
if ph < 7.0:
    print "It's acidic!"
elif ph < 4.0:
    print "It's a strong acid!"
```

a) What message(s) are displayed when the user enters 6.4?

b) What message(s) are displayed when the user enters 3.6?

c) Make a small change to one line of the code so that both messages are displayed when a value less than 4 is entered.

12. Why does the last example in Section 6.3, *Storing Conditionals*, on page 118 check to see whether someone is heavy (that is, that their weight exceeds the threshold) rather than light? If you wanted to write the second assignment statement as light = bmi < 22.0, what change(s) would you have to make to the lookup table?

Chapter 7

Repetition

This chapter revisits another fundamental kind of control flow: repetition. The for loops we saw in Section 5.4, *Processing List Items*, on page 81 are the simplest way to do this, but many situations require something a bit more powerful. Along with that "something," we will also encounter some of the tools that make experienced programmers more productive and learn how Python keeps track of what it's doing at any moment in time.

7.1 Counted Loops

Conditional statements let us decide whether to do something; loops let us do things many times. Section 5.4, *Processing List Items*, on page 81 introduced simple for loops, which can be used to do things with each element of a sequence in turn. To refresh your memory, these loops look like this:

```
for variable in <cf>list</cf>:
    block
```

and are used like this:

`loop/for_loop.cmd`

```
>>> for c in 'alpha':
...     print c
...
a
l
p
h
a
```

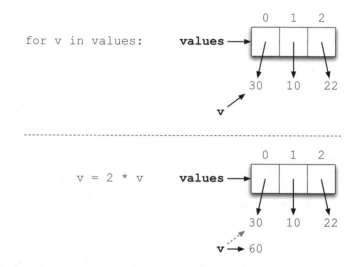

Figure 7.1: OVERWRITING A LOOP ITERATOR

But what if we want to change the elements of a list? For example, suppose we want to double all of the values in a list. We can't do this:

```
values[0] = 2 * values[0]
values[1] = 2 * values[1]
...
```

because we may not know the list's length (and because we'd have to rewrite our program every time the list's length changed). This doesn't work either:

```
for v in values:
    v = 2 * v
```

To see why, look at the memory model in Figure 7.1. Each loop iteration assigned an element of values to the variable v. Doubling that value inside the loop changes what v refers to but doesn't change what's in the original list.

Ranges of Numbers

In order to do what we want, we need to know the index of the list element we are working with. Getting that requires us to make a little detour to examine a built-in function called range, which generates a list of numbers.

Here are some examples:

loop/range_basic.cmd

```
>>> range(1, 5)
[1, 2, 3, 4]
>>> range(1, 10)
[1, 2, 3, 4, 5, 6, 7, 8, 9]
>>> range(5, 10)
[5, 6, 7, 8, 9]
>>> range(10)
[0, 1, 2, 3, 4, 5, 6, 7, 8, 9]
>>>
```

Notice that a call to range(start, stop) returns a list of integers from start to *the first integer before* stop. This is (deliberately) consistent with the way sequence indexing works: the expression seq[0:5] takes a slice of seq up to, but not including, the value at index 5.

To save typing, a call to range with a single argument is equivalent to a call to range(0, argument):

loop/range_single.cmd

```
>>> range(10)
[0, 1, 2, 3, 4, 5, 6, 7, 8, 9]
>>> range(1)
[0]
>>> range(0)
[]
```

The result of range is a list like any other. As an example, the following program calculates the sum of the integers from 1 to 100:

loop/for_rangebasic.cmd

```
>>> sum = 0
>>> for i in range(1, 101):
...     sum += i
...
>>> sum
5050
```

Again, notice that the upper bound passed to range is one more than the greatest integer we actually want.

By default, range generates numbers that increase by 1 successively— this is called its *step size*. We can specify a different step size for range with an optional third parameter.

Here, we produce a list of leap years in the first half of this century:

loop/for_rangestepping.cmd

```
>>> range(2000, 2050, 4)
[2000, 2004, 2008, 2012, 2016, 2020, 2024, 2028, 2032, 2036, 2040, 2044, 2048]
```

The step size can also be negative, but when it is, the starting index should be *larger* than the stopping index:

loop/for_rangestepping2.cmd

```
>>> range(2050, 2000, -4)
[2050, 2046, 2042, 2038, 2034, 2030, 2026, 2022, 2018, 2014, 2010, 2006, 2002]
```

Otherwise, range's result will be empty:

loop/for_rangestepping_empty.cmd

```
>>> range(2050, 2000, 4)
[]
>>> range(2000, 2050, -4)
[]
```

Let's return to our original goal of doubling the elements of a list. If the list is called values, then len(values) is the number of elements it contains, and the expression range(len(values)) produces a list containing exactly the indices for values:

loop/range_len.cmd

```
>>> values = ['a', 'b', 'c']
>>> len(values)
3
>>> range(3)
[0, 1, 2]
>>> range(len(values))
[0, 1, 2]
```

If we use that list of indices in a for loop, we will iterate over the indices for the list, rather than the values in the list itself:

loop/range_len_2.cmd

```
>>> values = ['a', 'b', 'c']
>>> for i in range(len(values)):
...     print i
...
0
1
2
```

We can use this to get values out of the list:

loop/range_len_3.cmd

```
>>> values = ['a', 'b', 'c']
>>> for i in range(len(values)):
...     print i, values[i]
...
0 a
1 b
2 c
```

and to overwrite list elements:

loop/range_len_4.cmd

```
>>> values = ['a', 'b', 'c']
>>> for i in range(len(values)):
...     values[i] = 'X'
...
>>> values
['X', 'X', 'X']
```

We now have everything we need to solve our original problem:

loop/range_len_5.cmd

```
>>> values = [1, 2, 3]
>>> for i in range(len(values)):
...     values[i] = 2 * values[i]
...
>>> values
[2, 4, 6]
```

We can tidy this up a bit using a combined operator:

loop/range_len_6.cmd

```
>>> values = [1, 2, 3]
>>> for i in range(len(values)):
...     values[i] *= 2
...
>>> values
[2, 4, 6]
```

The enumerate Function

Looping over a list using its indices is such a common operation that Python provides a built-in function called enumerate to help do it. Given a sequence—a list, a tuple, or a string—enumerate returns a list of pairs. The first element of each pair is an index, and the second is the sequence's value at that index.

For example:

loop/enumerate.cmd

```
>>> for x in enumerate('abc'):
...     print x
...
(0, 'a')
(1, 'b')
(2, 'c')
>>> for x in enumerate([10, 20, 30]):
...     print x
...
(0, 10)
(1, 20)
(2, 30)
```

Using this gives us another way to write our double-the-values loop:

loop/enumerate_2.cmd

```
>>> values = [1, 2, 3]
>>> for pair in enumerate(values):
...     i = pair[0]
...     v = pair[1]
...     values[i] = 2 * v
...
>>> values
[2, 4, 6]
```

This is easier to read when we write it like this:

loop/enumerate_3.cmd

```
>>> values = [1, 2, 3]
>>> for (i, v) in enumerate(values):
...     values[i] = 2 * v
...
>>> values
[2, 4, 6]
```

What's happening here is that Python actually allows *multivalued assignment*. If there are several variables on the left of an assignment statement and an equal number of values on the right, Python matches them up and does all the assignments at once:

loop/multi_assign.cmd

```
>>> x, y = 1, 2
>>> x
1
>>> y
2
```

This also works if the values on the right side are in a list, string, or other kind of sequences—Python "explodes" the sequence on the right and then assigns the elements to the variables on the left:

`loop/multi_assign_explode.cmd`

```
>>> first, second, third = [1, 2, 3]
>>> first
1
>>> second
2
>>> third
3
>>> first, second, third = 'abc'
>>> first
'a'
>>> second
'b'
>>> third
'c'
```

Knowing this, we can understand what happened in the for loop shown earlier:

```
for (i, v) in enumerate(values):
    values[i] = 2 * v
```

On the first iteration of the loop, enumerate(values) produced the tuple (0, values[0]). Python saw that the loop was using two variables as its indices, so it broke the tuple apart, assigning 0 to i and values[0] to v. The next iteration produced 1, values[1], and so on.

Nested Loops, Revisited

As you saw in Section 5.4, *Nested Loops*, on page 82, loops can be nested inside other loops. Here is an example where we use nested loops to color every other line of an image black; the result of running this code is shown in Figure 7.2, on the next page:

`loop/for_nested.py`

```
import media

lake = media.load_picture('lake.png')
width, height = media.get_width(lake), media.get_height(lake)

for y in range(0, height, 2): # Skip odd-numbered lines
    for x in range(0, width):
        p = media.get_pixel(lake, x, y)
        media.set_color(p, media.black)

media.show(lake)
```

Figure 7.2: LAKE_LINES.PNG

The nested loops result in a full set of iterations for the inner loop, for *every* iteration of the outer loop.

Looping Over Several Objects

It's possible to use the same loop to interact with different objects. In the following example, we'll superimpose a baseball over a lake. We do this by looping over the pixels in all the rows and columns of the baseball image and copying them one by one into the lake image. The top-left corner of both images is located at (0, 0). We can position the baseball away from the corner by adding offsets when we refer to indices in the lake image; the result is shown in Figure 7.3, on the facing page.

```
import media

baseball = media.load_picture('baseball.png')
lake = media.load_picture('lake.png')
width, height = media.get_width(baseball), media.get_height(baseball)

for y in range(0, height):
```

Figure 7.3: BASEBALL_LAKE.PNG

```
for x in range(0, width):
    # Position the top-left of the baseball at (50, 25)
    from_p = media.get_pixel(baseball, x, y)
    to_p = media.get_pixel(lake, 50 + x, 25 + y)
    media.set_color(to_p, media.get_color(from_p))

media.show(lake)
```

Ragged Lists

Nothing says that nested lists all have to be the same length:

`loop/different_lengths.cmd`

```
>>> info = [['Isaac Newton', 1643, 1727],
            ['Charles Darwin', 1809, 1882],
            ['Alan Turing', 1912, 1954, 'alan@bletchley.uk']]
>>> for item in info:
...     print len(item)
...
3
3
4
```

These sorts of lists are called *ragged lists*. Ragged lists can be tricky to process if the data is not uniform; for example, trying to assemble a list of email addresses for data where some addresses are missing requires a bit of careful thought.

Ragged data does arise normally. For example, if a record is made each day of the time at which a person who is trying to quit smokes a cigarette, each day will have a different number of entries. The code is fairly straightforward:

loop/nested_for.cmd

```
>>> times = [["9:02", "10:17", "13:52", "18:23", "21:31"],
...          ["8:45", "12:44", "14:52", "22:17"],
...          ["8:55", "11:11", "12:34", "13:46", "15:52", "17:08", "21:15"],
...          ["9:15", "11:44", "16:28"],
...          ["10:01", "13:33", "16:45", "19:00"],
...          ["9:34", "11:16", "15:52", "20:37"],
...          ["9:01", "12:24", "18:51", "23:13"]]
>>> for day in times:
...     for time in day:
...             print time,
...     print
...
9:02 10:17 13:52 18:23 21:31
8:45 12:44 14:52 22:17
8:55 11:11 12:34 13:46 15:52 17:08 21:15
9:15 11:44 16:28
10:01 13:33 16:45 19:00
9:34 11:16 15:52 20:37
9:01 12:24 18:51 23:13
```

7.2 while Loops

for loops are very useful if you know how many iterations of the loop you need. However, there are situations where it's impossible to know in advance how many times you will want the loop body executed. That's what a while loop is used for. while loops are sometimes called *conditional* loops, since they iterate only as long as some condition is true. Their general form is as follows:

```
while condition:
    block
```

The condition of a while loop is an expression, just like the condition of an if statement. When Python encounters a while loop, it evaluates the condition. If that condition is false, Python skips the loop body. If the condition is true, on the other hand, Python executes the loop

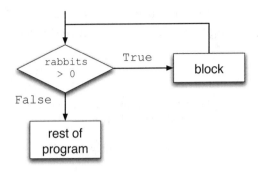

Figure 7.4: WHILE LOOPS

body once and then goes back to the top of the loop and reevaluates the condition. If it's still true, the loop body is executed again. This is repeated—condition, body, condition, body—until the condition is false, at which point Python stops executing the loop.

Here's a trivial example:

loop/simple_while.cmd

```
>>> rabbits = 3
>>> while rabbits > 0:
...     print rabbits
...     rabbits -= 1
...
3
2
1
```

Notice that this loop did *not* print 0. When the number of rabbits reaches zero, the loop expression is false, so the body is not executed (see Figure 7.4).

As a more useful example, we can calculate the growth of a bacterial colony using a simple exponential growth model, which is essentially a calculation of compound interest:

$$P(t + 1) = P(t) + rP(t)$$

In this formula, *P(t)* is the population size at time *t*, and *r* is the growth rate. Let's see how long it takes the bacteria to double their numbers:

loop/whileloop.py

```
time = 0
population = 1000   # 1000 bacteria to start with
growth_rate = 0.21 # 21% growth per minute
while population < 2000:
    population = population + growth_rate * population
    print population
    time = time + 1
print "It took %d minutes for the bacteria to double." % time
print "...and the final population was %6.2f bacteria." % population
```

Because the time variable was updated inside the loop, its value after the loop was the time of the last iteration, which is exactly what we want. Running this program gives us the answer we were looking for:

loop/whileloop_output.cmd

```
1210.0
1464.1
1771.561
2143.58881
It took 4 minutes for the bacteria to double.
...and the final population was 2143.59 bacteria.
```

Infinite Loops

The preceding example used population < 2000 as a loop condition so that the loop stopped when the population reached double its initial size *or more*. What would happen if we stopped only when the population was *exactly* double its initial size?

loop/while_infinite.py

```
# Use multi-valued assignment to set up controls.
time, population, growth_rate = 0, 1000, 0.21

# Don't stop until we're exactly double original size.
while population != 2000:
    population = population + growth_rate * population
    print population
    time = time + 1
print "It took %d minutes for the bacteria to double." % time
```

Here is this program's output:

```
loop/while_infinite_output.cmd
```

```
1210.0
1464.1
1771.561
2143.58881
2593.7424601
...3,680 lines or so later...
inf
inf
inf
...and so on forever...
```

Whoops—since the population is never exactly 2,000 bacteria, the loop never stops.[1] A loop like this one is called an *infinite loop*, because the computer will execute it forever (or until you kill your program, whichever comes first). In Wing 101, you kill your program by selecting Restart Shell from the Options menu, and from the command-line shell, you can kill it by pressing Ctrl-C. Infinite loops are a common kind of bug; the usual symptoms include printing the same value over and over again, or *hanging* (doing nothing at all).

Here's a more subtle example of an infinite loop. The following function counts the number of times a fragment occurs in a string of DNA. It starts searching at index 0. Subsequent searches start at the index of the last match:

```
loop/debug.py
```

```python
def count_fragments(fragment, dna):
    count = -1
    last_match = 0
    while last_match != -1:
        count += 1
        last_match = dna.find(fragment, last_match)
    return count
```

Let's try calling it with some bits of DNA:

```
loop/debug.cmd
```

```
>>> count_fragments('atc', 'gttacgtggatg')
0
>>> count_fragments('gtg', 'gttacgtggatg')
```

---

1. The first set of dots represents more than 3,000 values, each 21 percent larger than the one before. Eventually, these values are too large for the computer to represent, so it displays inf (or on some computers 1.#INF), which is its way of saying "effectively infinity."

Figure 7.5: THE WING 101 DEBUGGER

It works when the fragment doesn't occur in the DNA. However, when the fragment does appear, the function seems to run forever. Let's try to diagnose the problem using a *debugger*. Wing 101 has one (see Figure 7.5); so should you.

The easiest way to figure out what's going on is to set a *breakpoint* where the function is called. In Wing 101, you can do this by clicking in the margin directly to the left of the line, as illustrated in Figure 7.6, on the next page.

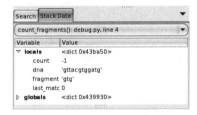

```
debug py

1   def count_fragments(fragment, dna):
2       count = -1
3       last_match = 0
4       while last_match != -1:
5           count += 1
6           last_match = dna.find(fragment, last_match)
7       return count
8
9   count_fragments('atc', 'gttacgtggatg')
10 ● count_fragments('gtg', 'gttacgtggatg')
11
```

Figure 7.6: SETTING A BREAKPOINT

```
Search  Stack Data                          ▼

count_fragments(): debug.py, line 4         ▼

Variable          Value
▽ locals          <dict 0x43ba50>
    count         -1
    dna           'gttacgtggatg'
    fragment      'gtg'
    last_matc     0
▷ globals         <dict 0x439930>
```

Figure 7.7: THE STACK DATA TAB

Start the debugging session by clicking the Debug button. You'll notice that the line with the breakpoint gets highlighted. Click the Step Into button to make the debugger look at the details of the function call.

Now that we're inside, we can *step over* individual statements. We don't want to step into any more functions at this level because we're concerned only about what's happening in our own function.

Keep stepping over the code until you reach the beginning of the while loop. While you're stepping, take a look at the Stack Data tab (see Figure 7.7). You can see the values of your local variables there.

Step over the statements in the loop a few times while watching how the values of the local variables change. Notice that count keeps increasing, but last_match doesn't change! It turns out that after we find the first match, we find it over and over again in subsequent searches.

Edit the value of last_match in the Stack Data tab by double-clicking it. Change it from 5 to 6, and continue stepping. That should let the function run to completion.

Now that we confirmed what our bug is, we need to go back and change our code. What we really want to do is search from last_match + 1:

loop/debug2.py

```
def count_fragments(fragment, dna):
    count = -1
    last_match = 0
    while last_match != -1:
        count += 1
        last_match = dna.find(fragment, last_match + 1)
    return count
```

Now let's try running it with different input:

loop/debug2.cmd

```
>>> count_fragments('gtg', 'gttacgtggatg')
1
>>> count_fragments('gtt', 'gttacgtggatg')
0
```

The first case works. The second case is obviously wrong because 'gtt' occurs right at the beginning of the string. It turns out that we inserted a bug along with our fix! Now that you know how to use the debugger, you can diagnose this problem on your own.

The Call Stack

Python keeps track of any running functions using a *runtime stack* (see Figure 7.8, on the next page). We can think of the stack as a series of records, called *frames* (see Figure 7.9, on the facing page), which pile up on top of each other as functions are called. Only the top frame is active; the rest are paused, waiting until functions above them are finished.

Code outside of any function is executed in a special frame that is at the bottom of the stack; this frame is called <module> because it is executing at the module level.

When a function is called, Python creates a new frame for it and adds the frame to the top of the stack. These frames store information about each function call and the order they were called in. The most recently called function's frame always sits at the top of the stack.

As we will see later in this chapter, each stack frame stores a function's *parameters* and *local variables*. It also contains a reference to the next statement Python will execute when the function finishes. This is known as the *return address*.

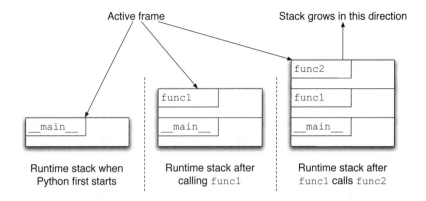

Figure 7.8: RUNTIME STACK

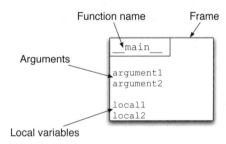

Figure 7.9: A STACK FRAME

Finally, the frame has space set aside for storing the function's *return value*, which we will see later in the chapter.

When a function finishes executing, Python then checks the stack to see what it should run next. This information is stored in the return address of the frame at the top of the stack. Once Python knows where to go, it removes the frame.

When your Python program is finished executing, there will be no more frames on the stack.

7.3 User Input Loops

We can use the raw_input function in a loop to make the chemical formula translation example from Section 6.2, *if Statements*, on page 111 interactive:

loop/userinputloop_infinite.py

```
while True:
    formula = raw_input("Please enter a chemical formula: ")
    if formula == "H2O":
        print "Water"
    elif formula == "NH3":
        print "Ammonia"
    elif formula == "CH3":
        print "Methane"
    else:
        print "Unknown compound"
```

In this case, we'd like the loop to continually process user input, so the loop condition is just True. Running the program looks like this:

loop/userinputloop_infinite_output.cmd

```
Please enter a chemical formula: NH3
Ammonia
Please enter a chemical formula: H2O
Water
Please enter a chemical formula: NaCl
Unknown compound
...
```

where ... shows that the cycle repeats until the user kills the program or turns off her computer. Since that isn't a particularly friendly user interface, let's modify the loop condition to give users a way to stop the program cleanly:

loop/userinputloop.py

```
text = ""
while text != "quit":
    text = raw_input("Please enter a chemical formula (or 'quit' to exit): ")
    if text == "quit":
        print "...exiting program"
    elif text == "H2O":
        print "Water"
    elif text == "NH3":
        print "Ammonia"
    elif text == "CH3":
        print "Methane"
    else:
        print "Unknown compound"
```

Since the loop condition checks the value of text, we have to assign it a value before the loop begins. Now we can run the program as usual but exit whenever we want:

loop/userinputloop_output.cmd

```
Please enter a chemical formula (or 'quit' to exit): CH3
Methane
Please enter a chemical formula (or 'quit' to exit): H2O
Water
Please enter a chemical formula (or 'quit' to exit): quit
...exiting program
```

7.4 Controlling Loops

As a rule, for and while loops execute all the statements in their body on each iteration. However, it is sometimes handy to be able to break that rule. Python provides two ways of controlling the iteration of a loop: break, which exits the loop body immediately, and continue, which skips ahead to the next iteration.

The break Statement

Sometimes a loop's task is finished before its final iteration. Using what we have seen so far, though, we still have to finish iterating. For example, to find which line in a file contains the string "Earth," we would have to write something like this:

loop/filesearch_nobreak.py

```
current_line = 1
earth_line = 0
file = open("data.txt", "r")
for line in file:
    line = line.strip()
    if line == "Earth":
        earth_line = current_line
    current_line = current_line + 1
print "Earth is at line %d" % earth_line
```

Here we require two variables: one for the current line number and another to remember the desired line number until after the loop. This is a little bit clumsy and also inefficient: if "Earth" is the first line of the file, this program is still going to read everything that comes after it.

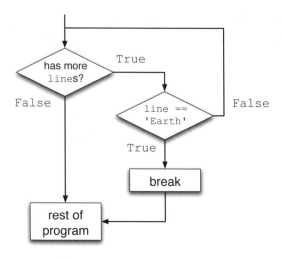

Figure 7.10: THE BREAK STATEMENT

To fix this, we can exit the loop early using a break statement, which jumps out of the loop body immediately:

loop/filesearch_break.py

```python
earth_line = 1
file = open("data.txt", "r")
for line in file:
    line = line.strip()
    if line == "Earth":
        break
    earth_line = earth_line + 1
print "Earth is at line %d" % earth_line
```

We can see this in Figure 7.10. Notice that because the loop exits early, the counter variable earth_line retains the value it had when the break was executed, so we need only one variable. However, if the file contains more than one occurrence of "Earth," this program will produce a different answer than the previous one. This program will display the index of the first line found, while the previous program would remember and display the index of the *last* matching line.

One more thing about break: it exits only the *innermost* loop that it's contained in. This means that in a nested loop, a break statement inside the inner loop will exit only the inner loop, not both loops.

The continue Statement

Another way to bend the rules for iteration is to use the continue statement, which causes Python to skip immediately ahead to the next iteration of a loop. For example, let's assume that the file data.txt could
include comment lines starting with a # character:

loop/fileinput_continue_data.cmd

```
# Pluto is only 0.002 times the mass of Earth.
Pluto
Mercury
# Mars is half Earth's diameter, but only
#   0.11 times Earth's mass.
Mars
Venus
Earth
Uranus
```

If we used the previous version of this program, it would count the
commented lines as well, giving us an incorrect answer. Instead, we
can use continue to skip comments in the file:

loop/filesearch_continue.cmd

```
entry_number = 1
file = open("data.txt", "r")
for line in file :
    line = line.strip()
    if line.startswith("#"):
        continue
    if line == "Earth":
        break
    entry_number = entry_number + 1
print "Earth is the %dth-lightest planet." % (entry_number)
```

When continue is executed, it *immediately* begins the next iteration of
the loop and skips any statements in the loop body that appear after it.
This allows us to skip the statement where entry_number is incremented.

Using continue is one way to skip comment lines, but this can also
be accomplished by using the conditional statements that were introduced earlier in this chapter. In the previous code, continue prevents
the comment line from being processed; in other words, if the line is
not a comment, it should be processed.

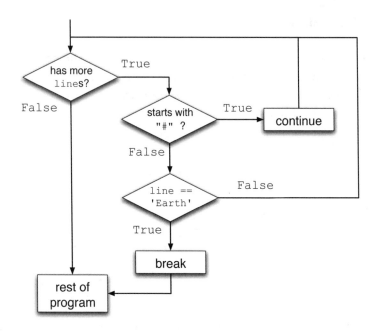

Figure 7.11: THE CONTINUE STATEMENT

The form of the previous sentence matches that of an if statement, and the updated code is as follows:

`loop/filesearch_if.py`

```python
entry_number = 1
file = open("data.txt", "r")
for line in file :
    line = line.strip()
    if not line.startswith("#"):
        if line == "Earth":
            break
        entry_number = entry_number + 1
print "Earth is the %dth-lightest planet." % (entry_number)
```

Whether you favor if or continue is largely a matter of personal taste.[2] As always, the most important thing is to be consistent: switching back and forth between the two is more likely to confuse your readers than consistently using either one.

---

2. That is our way of saying that the authors and reviewers of this book split almost evenly as to which they thought was better.

7.5   Style Notes

Conditional statements give us control over of the flow of execution of our programs. When there are multiple paths of execution, we have choices to make about the structure of our conditional statements. For example, consider the following:

loop/complex_cond.py

```python
def f(a, b, c):
  if a:
    if b:
      print 'hi'
    elif c:
      print 'bonjour'
    else:
      print 'hola'
  else:
    print 'Select a language.'
```

Under what conditions will "hi" be printed? "hola"? The word "hi" is printed when both a and b are True, and "hola" is printed when a is True, but b and c are not. To make this clearer, we can rewrite our conditional statement without the nesting:

loop/complex_cond_2.py

```python
def f(a, b, c):
  if a and b:
    print 'hi'
  elif a and c:
    print 'bonjour'
  elif a:
    print 'hola'
  else:
    print 'Select a language'
```

With multiple ways to write equivalent conditional statements, care must be taken to structure our code so that it is easy to understand. Reducing the amount of nesting is one way to improve the readability of the code, particularly if there are several nested conditionals.

break and continue have their place but should be used sparingly since they can make programs harder to understand. When people see while and for loops in programs, their first assumption is that the whole body will execute every time, in other words, that the body can be treated as a single "super statement" when trying to understand the program. If the loop contains break or continue, though, that assumption is false.

Sometimes, only part of the statement body will execute, which means the reader has to keep two scenarios in mind.

There are always alternatives: well-chosen loop conditions (as in Section 7.3, *User Input Loops*, on page 142) can replace break, and if statements can be used to skip statements instead of continue. It is up to the programmer to decide which option makes the program clearer and which makes it more complicated. As we said in Section 5.11, *Comments*, on page 95, programs are written for human beings; taking a few moments to make your code as clear as possible, or to make clarity a habit, will pay dividends for the lifetime of the program.

7.6 Summary

In this chapter, we learned the following:

- Program statements in Python can be grouped into blocks using indentation.
- Choosing whether to execute a block is one of the fundamental ways to control a program's behavior. In Python, such choices are expressed using if, elif, and else. The first two base their decision on the value of a Boolean expression, while else is executed only if all other tests fail.
- Repeating a block is another fundamental way to control a program's behavior. Using a for loop to iterate over the elements of a structure is one example, but for can also be used to create counted loops that iterate over a range of integers.
- The most general kind of repetition is the while loop, which continues executing as long as some arbitrary Boolean condition is true. However, the condition is tested only at the top of the loop. If that condition is never false, the loop will execute forever. The break and continue statements can be used to change the way loops execute.
- Control structures like loops and conditionals can be nested inside one another to any desired depth.
- Python and other languages keep track of nested function calls using a call stack. Each time a function is called, a new frame containing that functions parameters and local variables is put on the top of the stack. When the function returns, the frame is discarded.
- Programs can use raw_input to get input from users interactively.

7.7 Exercises

Here are some exercises for you to try on your own:

1. Your lab partner claims to have written a function that replaces each value in a list with twice the preceding value (and the first value with 0). For example, if the list [1, 2, 3] is passed as an argument, the function is supposed to turn it into [0, 2, 4]. Here's the code:

loop/buggy_scan.py

```python
def double_preceding(values):
    if values == []:
        pass # do nothing to the empty list
    else:
        temp = values[0]
        values[0] = 0
        for i in range(1, len(values)):
            values[i] = 2 * temp
            temp = values[i]
```

Explain what the bug in this function is, and fix it.

2. You are given two lists, rat_1 and rat_2, that contain the daily weights of two rats over a period of ten days. Write statements to do the following:

   a) If the weight of Rat 1 is greater than that of Rat 2 on day 1, print "Rat 1 weighed more than Rat 2 on Day 1."; otherwise, print "Rat 1 weighed less than Rat 2 on Day 1."

   b) If Rat 1 weighed more than Rat 2 on day 1 and if Rat 1 weighs more than Rat 2 on the last day, print "Rat 1 remained heavier than Rat 2."; otherwise, print "Rat 2 became heavier than Rat 1."

   c) If your solution to the previous question used nested if statements, then do it without nesting, or vice versa.

3. Print the numbers in the range 33 to 49 (inclusive).

4. Print the numbers from 1 to 10 in descending order, all on one line.

5. Calculate the average of numbers in the range 2 to 22 using a loop to find the total, and then calculate the average.

6. Consider the following function:

`loop/shrinking_list.py`

```python
def remove_neg(num_list):
    '''Remove the negative numbers from the list num_list.'''
    for item in num_list:
        if item < 0:
            num_list.remove(item)
```

When remove_negs([1, 2, 3, -3, 6, -1, -3, 1]) is executed, the result is [1, 2, 3, 6, -3, 1]. The for loop traverses the elements of the list, and when a negative value (like -3 at position 3) is reached, it is removed, shifting the subsequent values one position earlier in the list (so 6 moves into position 3). The loop then continues on to process the next item, skipping over the value that moved into the removed item's position. If there are two negative numbers in a row (like -1 and -3), then the second one will not be removed. Rewrite the code to avoid this problem.

7. Using nested for loops, print a right triangle of the character *T* on the screen where the triangle is one character wide at its narrowest point and seven characters wide at its widest point:

```
T
TT
TTT
TTTT
TTTTT
TTTTTT
TTTTTTT
```

8. Using nested for loops, print the triangle described in the previous question with its hypotenuse on the left side:

```
      T
     TT
    TTT
   TTTT
  TTTTT
 TTTTTT
TTTTTTT
```

9. Redo the previous two questions using while loops instead of for loops.

10. The variables rat_1_weight and rat_2_weight store the weights of two rats at the beginning of an experiment. The variables rat_1_rate and rat_2_rate are the rate that the rats' weights are expected to increase each week (for example, 4 percent per week).

a) Using a while loop, calculate how many weeks it would take for the weight of the first rat to become 25 percent heavier than it was originally.

b) Assume that the two rats have the same initial weight, but rat 1 is expected to gain weight at a faster rate than rat 2. Using a while loop, calculate how many weeks it would take for rat 1 to be 10 percent heavier than rat 2.

11. Transformations are some of the most common operations in image-processing software. Arbitrary rotations require some trigonometry but 90 degree rotations can be done using for loops. Design a function that uses nested for loops to rotate an image 90 degrees clockwise.

12. Reflections are another type of image transformation. Reflected images appear flipped over when compared to the original.

a) When you look into a typical mirror, the image you see is a horizontal reflection of reality. Use nested for loops to transform an image in the same way by flipping it along the y-axis.

b) Use nested for loops to flip an image along the x-axis.

13. Scaling is another common image transformation. Downscaling makes an image smaller, while upscaling makes it larger. Create a function that uses nested for loops to downscale an image so that each of its new dimensions are half of the original. For example, your function should transform a 100 x 50 pixel image into a 50 x 25. The new image should look like it is 1/4th the size of the original.

14. The mosaic filter is a common artistic effect in image processing programs. The simple version of this filter divides an image into a grid of equal-sized squares. The color of each square is determined by the pixels that make up the square.

To keep things simple, assume each square is 10 pixels wide. The color of the square is the average of the colors of the 100 pixels inside. The average of two colors can be computed like this: red = (red_1 + red_2)/2, green = (green_1 + green_2)/2, blue = (blue_1 + blue_2)/2. Assuming the original image dimensions are divisible by 10, design a function that implements the mosaic filter described here.

15. When the red, green, and blue components of a pixel are equal, the observed color is black, white, or a shade of gray. You can transform a color image into a grayscale image by converting each pixel to a shade of gray that approximates the brightness of the original color. The easiest way to do this is to replace each color component for a pixel with the average of all the color components.

   a) Design a function that uses nested for loops that transforms a color image into grayscale using the technique described earlier.

   b) The method of producing grayscale images in the previous exercise assumes the human eye is equally sensitive to each of the three color components. In reality, this is not the case. The human eye is much more sensitive to greens than the other colors. How would you modify your solution so that greens influence the brightness of the image more than the reds and blues?

Chapter 8

File Processing

We now have the tools we need—functions, modules, lists, loops, and conditionals—to solve problems that scientists face every day. Scientific data is often stored in plain-text files, which can be organized in several different ways. The most straightforward format is one piece of data per line; for example, the rainfall in Oregon for each separate day in a study period might be stored on a line of its own. Alternatively, each line might store the values for an entire week or month, with a *delimiter* such as a space, tab, or comma used to separate values to make the data easier for humans to read.

Often, data is more complex. For example, a study might keep track of the heights, weights, and ages of the participants. Each *record* can appear on a line by itself with the pieces of data in each record separated by delimiters. Some records might even span multiple lines, in which case the format will usually have some kind of a separator (such as a blank line) between records or use special symbols to mark the start or end of each record.

Modules to read (or *parse*) many common formats are part of the standard Python library or will have been written by whoever created the format you are working with. However, it is still common to encounter specialized formats for which readers don't exist. This chapter will show you how to handle a variety of file formats from fairly simple single-line records to more complex multiline records, as well as several variations of each.

8.1 One Record per Line

The following data, taken from the Time Series Data Library (TSDL) [Hynnd], describes the number of colored fox fur pelts produced in Hopedale, Labrador, in the years 1834–1842. (The full data set has values for the years 1834–1925.)

```
fileproc/hopedale.txt
```

```
Coloured fox fur production, HOPEDALE, Labrador, 1834-1842
#Source: C. Elton (1942) "Voles, Mice and Lemmings", Oxford Univ. Press
#Table 17, p.265--266
      22
      29
       2
      16
      12
      35
       8
      83
     166
```

The first line contains a description of the data. The next two lines contain comments about the data, each of which begins with a # character. Each piece of actual data appears on a single line.

Reading a File

For now, we will treat all lines the same (data, headers, and comments) and read all lines of the file. As we saw in Section 5.10, *Files as Lists*, on page 92, this loop reads and prints a file line by line:

```
fileproc/read_file_1.py
```

```python
input_file = open("hopedale.txt", "r")
for line in input_file:
    line = line.strip()
    print line
input_file.close()
```

Files Over the Internet

These days, of course, the file containing the data we want could well be on a machine half a world away. Provided it is accessible over the Internet, though, it is just as easy to work with. The module urllib contains a function called urlopen that opens a web page for reading and returns a file-like object that you can use exactly as if you were reading a local file.

For example, the Hopedale data not only exists on our machine, but it's also on a web page.[1] We can print this web page line by line using a module called urllib and commands that are very similar to those we've use with files:

```
fileproc/read_url.py
```

```python
import urllib

url = "http://www-personal.buseco.monash.edu.au/~hyndman/TSDL/ecology1/hopedale.dat"

web_page = urllib.urlopen(url)
for line in web_page:
    line = line.strip()
    print line
web_page.close()
```

Note that this example will work only if your machine is actually connected to the Internet. Let's return to our example of reading and printing a file line by line:

```
fileproc/read_file_1.py
```

```python
input_file = open("hopedale.txt", "r")
for line in input_file:
    line = line.strip()
    print line
input_file.close()
```

We can improve this in several ways. One big issue is that the filename is *hard-coded*; in other words, the name of a particular file is stored in the program, which means the program can't be used to process any other files. To fix this, we use what we learned in Section 5.10, *Command-Line Arguments*, on page 95; we place the code that does the work in a function that takes the name of the file as a parameter and call that function with sys.argv[1] as an argument:

```
fileproc/read_file_2.py
```

```python
import sys

def process_file(filename):
    '''Open, read, and print a file.'''

    input_file = open(filename, "r")
    for line in input_file:
        line = line.strip()
        print line
    input_file.close()
```

---

1. At the time of writing, the URL for the file is http://www-personal.buseco.monash.edu.au/ ~hyndman/TSDL/ecology1/hopedale.dat (you can look at it online!).

```
if __name__ == "__main__":
    process_file(sys.argv[1])
```

This is more flexible, because we can now pass the program the name of a file when we run it. To do this in Wing 101, right-click the editing pane, select Properties, select the Debug tab, and enter the run arguments. However, it will work only with files, not with other input streams such as standard input or a URL using module urllib. We fix this by opening the file (or URL or input stream) *outside* of the function and passing in the file object instead:

`fileproc/read_file_3.py`

```
import sys

def process_file(reader):
    '''Read and print the contents of reader.'''

    for line in reader:
        line = line.strip()
        print line

if __name__ == "__main__":
    input_file = open(sys.argv[1], "r")
    process_file(input_file)
    input_file.close()
```

This change allows us to call the same function with an open web page instead of a local file:

`fileproc/read_file_4.py`

```
import sys
import urllib

def process_file(reader):
    '''Read and print the contents of reader.'''

    for line in reader:
        line = line.strip()
        print line

if __name__ == "__main__":
    webpage = urllib.urlopen(sys.argv[1])
    process_file(webpage)
    webpage.close()
```

Skipping the Header

Of course, we usually don't just want to print data—if we did, we could open the file in an editor and read it. Instead, we typically want to find the smallest value, sum the values, or process it in some other way.

Before we can do that, though, we need to figure out how to skip the file's header. To do this, we need to read the description line and all the comment lines following it. Of course, not all files start with a description line like this one does, so we won't always want to discard the first line. We can stop when we read the first real piece of data, which will be the first line after the description that doesn't start with a #:

In English, we might try this algorithm to process such a file:

```
Skip the first line in the file.
Skip over the comment lines in the file.
For each of the remaining lines in the file:
    Process the data on that line.
```

The problem with this approach is that we can't tell whether a line is a comment line until we've read it, but we can read a line from a file only once—there's no simple way to "back up" in the file. An alternative approach is to read the line, skip it if it's a comment, and process it if it's not. Once we've processed the first line of data, we process the remaining lines:

```
Skip the first line in the file.
Find and process the first line of data in the file.
For each of the remaining lines:
    Process the data on that line.
```

The thing to notice about this algorithm is that it processes lines in two places: once when it finds the first "interesting" line in the file and once when it handles all of the following lines:

`fileproc/tsdl.py`

```python
import sys

def skip_header(r):
    '''Skip the header in reader r, and return the first
    real piece of data.'''

    # Read the description line and then the comment lines.
    line = r.readline()
    line = r.readline()
    while line.startswith('#'):
        line = r.readline()

    # Now line contains the first real piece of data.
    return line

def process_file(r):
    '''Read and print open reader r.'''
```

```
        # Find the first piece of data.
        line = skip_header(r).strip()
        print line

        # Read the rest of the data.
        for line in r:
            line = line.strip()
            print line

if __name__ == "__main__":
    input_file = open(sys.argv[1], 'r')
    process_file(input_file)
    input_file.close()
```

In skip_header, we return the first line of read data, because once we've found it, we can't read it again (we can go forward but not backward). We will want to use skip_header in all of the file-processing functions in this section. Rather than copying the code each time we want to use it, we can put the function in a file called tsdl.py for Time Series Data Library and get it in other programs using import tsdl, as shown in the next example. This allows us to reuse the skip_header code, and if it needs to be modified, then there is only one copy of the function to edit.

We can finally process the Hopedale data set to find the smallest number of fox pelts produced in any year. As we progress through the file, we keep the smallest value seen so far in a variable called smallest. That variable is initially set to the value on the first line, since it's the smallest (and only) value seen so far:

`fileproc/read_smallest.py`

```
import sys
import tsdl

def smallest_value(r):
    '''Read and process reader r to find the smallest
    value after the TSDL header.'''

    line = tsdl.skip_header(r).strip()
    print line

    # Now line contains the first data value; this is also the
    # smallest value found so far, because it is the only one we have seen.
    smallest = int(line)

    for line in r:
        line = line.strip()
        value = int(line)
```

```
        # If we find a smaller value, remember it.
        if value < smallest:
            smallest = value

    return smallest

if __name__ == "__main__":
    input_file = open(sys.argv[1], "r")
    print smallest_value(input_file)
    input_file.close()
```

We could also use this:

```
smallest = min(smallest, value)
```

to keep track of the smallest value in the loop in smallest_value.

Data with Missing Values: Fox Pelts

We also have data for colored fox production in Hebron, Labrador:

fileproc/hebron.txt

```
Coloured fox fur production, Hebron, Labrador, 1834-1839
#Source: C. Elton (1942) "Voles, Mice and Lemmings", Oxford Univ. Press
#Table 17, p.265--266
#remark: missing value for 1836
    55
    262
    -
    102
    178
    227
```

The hyphen indicates that data for the year 1836 is missing. Unfortunately, calling read_smallest on the Hebron data produces this error:

fileproc/read_smallest_hebron.cmd

```
>>> import read_smallest
>>> read_smallest.process_file(open('hebron.txt', 'r'))
Traceback (most recent call last):
  File "<stdin>", line 1, in <module>
  File "read_smallest.py", line 15, in process_file
    value = int(line)
ValueError: invalid literal for int() with base 10: '-'
```

The problem is that '-' isn't an integer, so calling int('-') fails. This isn't an isolated problem. In general, we will often need to skip blank lines, comments, or lines containing other "nonvalues" in our data. Real data sets often contain omissions or contradictions; dealing with them is just a fact of scientific life.

To fix our code, we must add a check inside the loop that processes a line only if it contains a real value. In the TSDL data sets, missing entries are always marked with hyphens, so we just need to check for that before trying to convert the string we have read to an integer:

`fileproc/read_smallest_skip.py`

```python
import sys
from tsdl import skip_header

def smallest_value_skip(r):
    '''Read and process reader r to find the smallest value after
    the TSDL header.  Skip missing values, which are indicated
    with a hyphen.'''

    line = skip_header(r).strip()

    # Now line contains the first data value; this is also the
    # smallest value found so far.
    smallest = int(line)

    for line in r:
        line = line.strip()

        # Only process line if it has a valid value.
        if line != '-':
            value = int(line)

            # Process value; if we find a smaller value, remember it.
            if value < smallest:
                smallest = value

    return smallest

if __name__ == "__main__":
    input_file = open(sys.argv[1], "r")
    print smallest_value_skip(input_file)
    input_file.close()
```

Notice that the comparison of value with smallest is nested inside the check for hyphens. If it were not, then if the line contained a hyphen, comparing value with smallest would result in an error.

Individual Whitespace-Delimited Data

The file [Hynnd] contains information about lynx pelts in the years 1821–1934. All data values are integers, each line contains many values, the values are separated by whitespace, and for reasons best known to the file's author, each value ends with a period.

```
fileproc/lynx.txt
```

```
Annual Number of Lynx Trapped, MacKenzie River, 1821-1934
#Original Source: Elton, C. and Nicholson, M. (1942)
#"The ten year cycle in numbers of Canadian lynx",
#J. Animal Ecology, Vol. 11, 215--244.
#This is the famous data set which has been listed before in
#various publications:
#Cambell, M.J. and Walker, A.M. (1977) "A survey of statistical work on
#the MacKenzie River series of annual Canadian lynx trappings for the years
#1821-1934 with a new analysis", J.Roy.Statistical Soc. A 140, 432--436.
  269.  321.  585.  871. 1475. 2821. 3928. 5943. 4950. 2577.  523.   98.
  184.  279.  409. 2285. 2685. 3409. 1824.  409.  151.   45.   68.  213.
  546. 1033. 2129. 2536.  957.  361.  377.  225.  360.  731. 1638. 2725.
 2871. 2119.  684.  299.  236.  245.  552. 1623. 3311. 6721. 4245.  687.
  255.  473.  358.  784. 1594. 1676. 2251. 1426.  756.  299.  201.  229.
  469.  736. 2042. 2811. 4431. 2511.  389.   73.   39.   49.   59.  188.
  377. 1292. 4031. 3495.  587.  105.  153.  387.  758. 1307. 3465. 6991.
 6313. 3794. 1836.  345.  382.  808. 1388. 2713. 3800. 3091. 2985. 3790.
  674.   81.   80.  108.  229.  399. 1132. 2432. 3574. 2935. 1537.  529.
  485.  662. 1000. 1590. 2657. 3396.
```

To process this, we must break each line into pieces and strip off the periods. Our algorithm is the same as it was for the fox pelt data: find and process the first "real" line in the file, and then process each of the subsequent lines. However, the notion of "processing a line" needs to be examined further, because there are many values per line. Our refined algorithm, shown next, uses nested loops to handle the notion of "for each line and for each value on that line":

```
Find the first line containing real data after the header.
For each piece of data in the current line:
    Process that piece.

For each other line of data:
    For each piece of data in the current line:
        Process that piece.
```

Once again, we are processing lines in two different places. That is a strong hint that we should write a helper function to avoid duplicate code. Rewriting our algorithm, and making it specific to the problem of finding the largest value, makes this clearer:

```
Find the first line of real data after the header.
Find the largest value in that line.

For each other line of data:
    Find the largest value in that line.
    If that value is larger than the previous largest, remember it.
```

The *helper function* required is one that finds the largest value in a line, and it must split the line up. The string method split will split around the whitespace, but we still have to remove the periods at the ends of values.

We can also simplify our code by initializing largest to -1, because that value is guaranteed to be smaller than any of the (positive) values in the file. That way, no matter what the first real value is, it will be larger than the "previous" value (our -1) and replace it.

fileproc/read_lynx_1.py

```python
import sys

def find_largest(line):
    '''Return the largest value in line, which is a
    whitespace-delimited string of integers.'''

    # The largest value seen so far.
    largest = -1

    for value in line.split():

        # Remove the trailing period.
        v = int(value[:-1])

        # If we find a larger value, remember it.
        if v > largest:
            largest = v

    return largest
```

We now face the same choice as with skip_header: we can put find_largest in a module (possibly tsdl), or we can include it in the same file as the rest of the code. We choose the latter this time, because the code is specific to this particular data set and problem:

fileproc/read_lynx.py

```python
import sys
from tsdl import skip_header

def find_largest(line):
    '''Return the largest value in line, which is a
    whitespace-delimited string of integers.'''

    # The largest value seen so far.
    largest = -1

    for value in line.split():
```

```
        # Remove the trailing period.
        v = int(value[:-1])

        # If we find a larger value, remember it.
        if v > largest:
            largest = v

    return largest

def process_file(r):
    '''Read and process reader r.'''

    line = skip_header(r).strip()

    # The largest value so far.
    largest = find_largest(line)

    # Check the rest of the lines for larger values.
    for line in r:
        large = find_largest(line)
        if large > largest:
            largest = large

    return largest

if __name__ == "__main__":
    input_file = open(sys.argv[1], "r")
    print process_file(input_file)
    input_file.close()
```

Notice how simple the code in process_file looks! This happened only because we decided to write helper functions. To show you how much clearer this is, here is the same code without using find_largest as a helper method:

fileproc/read_lynx_expanded.py

```
import sys
from tsdl import skip_header

def process_file(r):
    '''Read and process reader r.'''

    line = skip_header(r).strip()

    # The largest value seen so far.
    largest = -1

    for value in line.split():
```

```
        # Remove the trailing period.
        v = int(value[:-1])

        # If we find a larger value, remember it.
        if v > largest:
            largest = v

    # Check the rest of the lines for larger values.
    for line in r:
        # The largest value seen so far.
        large = -1

        for value in line.split():

            # Remove the trailing period.
            v = int(value[:-1])

            # If we find a larger value, remember it.
            if v > large:
                large = v

        if large > largest:
            largest = large

    return largest

if __name__ == "__main__":
    input_file = open(sys.argv[1], "r")
    print process_file(input_file)
    input_file.close()
```

8.2 Records with Multiple Fields

Here is some United States housing data for 1983 and 1984, also taken from [Hynnd]. The first column is the monthly housing starts (thousands of units), the second is the total construction contracts (millions of dollars), and the third is the average interest rate for a new home mortgage (percent):

fileproc/housing.dat

```
91.3    11.358   13
96.3    11.355   12.62
134.6   16.100   12.97
135.8   16.315   12.02
174.9   19.205   12.21
173.2   20.263   11.9
161.6   16.885   12.02
```

```
176.8   19.441   12.01
154.9   17.379   12.08
159.3   16.028   11.8
136     15.401   11.82
108.3   13.518   11.94
109.1   14.023   11.8
130     14.442   11.78
137.5   17.916   11.56
172.7   17.655   11.55
180.7   21.990   11.68
184     20.036   11.61
162.1   19.224   11.91
147.4   19.367   11.89
148.5   16.923   12.03
152.3   18.413   12.27
126.2   16.616   12.27
98.9    14.220   12.05
```

This data differs from the previous example, because although there are multiple values per line, in this case each value represents something different. We want to compare total housing starts and construction contracts from 1983 to 1984; for the moment, we don't care about interest rates.

What if we decide to ask more questions about this data in the future? Instead of rereading the data from the file, we can store the data for future use. But how will we store it? We can create twelve lists, one for each month, or two lists, one for housing starts and one for total construction contracts, and store the data by column. Another option is to create a list of lists to keep all the data together. Twelve variables feels like too many, so let's store the data by column using two lists. (A lot of program design is based on what "feels" right. There are no universal hard-and-fast rules for good design; there are only trade-offs and consequences.) Using the two lists to store the data, we compare housing starts and construction contracts from 1983 to 1984:

fileproc/housing.py

```python
import sys

def housing(r):
    '''Return the difference between the housing starts and
    construction contracts in 1983 and in 1984 from reader r.'''

    # The monthly housing starts, in thousands of units.
    starts = []

    # The construction contracts, in millions of dollars.
    contracts = []
```

```
    # Read the file, populating the lists.
    for line in r:
        start, contract, rate = line.split()
        starts.append(float(start))
        contracts.append(float(contract))

    return (sum(starts[12:24]) - sum(starts[0:12]),
            sum(contracts[12:24]) - sum(contracts[0:12]))

if __name__ == "__main__":
    input_file = open(sys.argv[1], "r")
    print housing(input_file)
    input_file.close()
```

The result is the tuple (46.400000000000091, 17.577000000000027), showing that both housing starts and construction contracts rose from 1983 to 1984.

This program answered our question, but it could still be improved. Its first shortcoming is that it throws away the interest rate data; although we don't need this right now, someone might in future, so we should create a third list and store it. The second improvement is to separate the parsing and processing of the data, that is, to have one function that reads the data and another that does calculations on it. That way, we can reuse the parsing code every time we have new questions.

`fileproc/housing_2.py`

```
import sys

def read_housing_data(r):
    '''Read housing data from reader r, returning lists of starts,
    contracts, and rates.'''

    starts = []
    contracts = []
    rates = []

    for line in r:
        start, contract, rate = line.split()
        starts.append(float(start))
        contracts.append(float(contract))
        rates.append(rate)

    return (starts, contracts, rates)

def process_housing_data(starts, contracts):
    '''Return the difference between the housing starts and
    construction contracts in 1983 and in 1984.'''
```

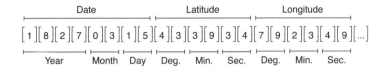

Figure 8.1: A FIXED-WIDTH FILE FORMAT

```
    return (sum(starts[12:24]) - sum(starts[0:12]),
            sum(contracts[12:24]) - sum(contracts[0:12])))

if __name__ == "__main__":
    input_file = open(sys.argv[1], "r")
    starts, contracts, rates = read_housing_data(input_file)
    print process_housing_data(starts, contracts)
    input_file.close()
```

Many programs go one step further and separate parsing, processing, and reporting (the printing of results). That way, both the input and output can be used in other programs without having to be rewritten, and programs can process data from other sources [Wil05].

8.3 Positional Data

Some file formats don't use delimiters to separate fields. Instead, each field is in a fixed location on the line. For example, characters 1–8 might store the date (with four digits for the year, two for the month, and two for the day), characters 9–14 and 15–20 the latitude and longitude (as degrees, minutes, and seconds), and the 24 characters after that the temperature, humidity, and pressure as decimal numbers, each eight characters long (see Figure 8.1).

Processing files like this is relatively straightforward, because slicing strings is easy in Python. Here's a function that reads a file in the format just described. Its result is a list of tuples; each tuple is a single record, and the fields in each tuple are that record's values.

fileproc/fixed_width_1.py

```
def read_weather_data(r):
    '''Read weather data from reader r in fixed-width format.
    The fields are:
        1   8   YYYYMMDD (date)
        9   14  DDMMSS   (latitude)
```

```
15  20    DDMMSS    (longitude)
21  26    FF.FFF    (temp, deg. C)
27  32    FF.FFF    (humidity, %)
33  38    FF.FFF    (pressure, kPa)
The result is a list of tuples:
((Yr, Mo, Day), (Deg, Min, Sec), (Deg, Min, Sec), (Temp, Hum, Press))
'''

result = []
for line in r:
    year = int(line[0:4])
    month = int(line[4:6])
    day = int(line[6:8])
    lat_deg = int(line[8:10])
    lat_min = int(line[10:12])
    lat_sec = int(line[12:14])
    long_deg = int(line[14:16])
    long_min = int(line[16:18])
    long_sec = int(line[18:20])
    temp = float(line[20:26])
    hum = float(line[26:32])
    press = float(line[32:38])
    result.append(((year, month, day),
                  (lat_deg, lat_min, lat_sec),
                  (long_deg, long_min, long_sec),
                  (temp, hum, press)))
return result
```

This function does indeed do what we need, but an experienced programmer would find fault with it. The biggest criticism would be that it would be very easy to mistype some of those twenty-four slice indices and wind up taking too much or too little data, like this:

```
long_min = int(line[16:18]) # missing 18!
long_sec = int(line[19:20])
temp = float(line[20:26])
```

Also, if the data format ever changes—for example, if this function needs to read files that used decimal degrees for latitude and longitude—then all the indices after the point of change would need to be updated.

Here's a more elegant solution:[2]

`fileproc/fixed_width_2.py`

```python
def read_weather_data(r):
    '''Read weather data from reader r in fixed-width format.
    The field widths are:
        4,2,2    YYYYMMDD (date)
        2,2,2    DDMMSS    (latitude)
        2,2,2    DDMMSS    (longitude)
        6,6,6    FF.FFF    (temp, deg. C; humidity, %; pressure, kPa)
    The result is a list of values (not tuples):
    (YY, MM, DD, DD, MM, SS, DD, MM, SS, Temp, Hum, Press)'''

    fields = ((4, int), (2, int), (2, int),       # date
              (2, int), (2, int), (2, int),       # latitude
              (2, int), (2, int), (2, int),       # longitude
              (6, float), (6, float), (6, float)) # data
    result = []
    # For each record
    for line in r:
        start = 0
        record = []
        # for each field in the record
        for (width, target_type) in fields:
            # convert the text
            text = line[start:start+width]
            field = target_type(text)
            # add it to the record
            record.append(field)
            # move on
            start += width
        # add the completed record to the result
        result.append(record)
    return result
```

The basic idea is that each field is a fixed width, so after processing a field of width *W*, we just move *W* characters forward in the string to find the next field. And since the users of this function don't want text back, but integers and floating-point numbers, we store a reference to the appropriate conversion function right beside each field's width. An interesting feature of this example is that the functions are stored in tuples just like other data.

---

2. Astute readers will notice that it returns a single tuple per record, rather than a tuple of tuples. This will be fixed in the exercises.

8.4 Multiline Records

Not every data record will fit onto a single line. Here is a file in simplified Protein Data Bank (PDB) format that describes the arrangements of atoms in ammonia:

`fileproc/ammonia.pdb`

```
COMPND        AMMONIA
ATOM       1  N   0.257  -0.363   0.000
ATOM       2  H   0.257   0.727   0.000
ATOM       3  H   0.771  -0.727   0.890
ATOM       4  H   0.771  -0.727  -0.890
END
```

The first line is the name of the molecule. All subsequent lines down to the one containing END specify the ID, type, and XYZ coordinates of one of the atoms in the molecule.

Reading this file is straightforward using the tools we have built up in this chapter. But what if the file contained two or more molecules, like this:

`fileproc/multimol.pdb`

```
COMPND        AMMONIA
ATOM       1  N   0.257  -0.363   0.000
ATOM       2  H   0.257   0.727   0.000
ATOM       3  H   0.771  -0.727   0.890
ATOM       4  H   0.771  -0.727  -0.890
END
COMPND        METHANOL
ATOM       1  C  -0.748  -0.015   0.024
ATOM       2  O   0.558   0.420  -0.278
ATOM       3  H  -1.293  -0.202  -0.901
ATOM       4  H  -1.263   0.754   0.600
ATOM       5  H  -0.699  -0.934   0.609
ATOM       6  H   0.716   1.404   0.137
END
```

As always, we tackle this problem by dividing into smaller ones and solving each of those in turn. Our first algorithm is as follows:

```
while there are more molecules in the file:
    read a molecule from the file
    append it to the list of molecules read so far
```

Simple, except the only way to tell whether there is another molecule left in the file is to try to read it. Our modified algorithm is as follows:

```
reading = True
while reading:
    try to read a molecule from the file
```

```
    if there is one:
        append it to the list of molecules read so far
    else:  # nothing left
        reading = False
```

In Python, this is as follows:

`fileproc/multimol.py`

```python
def read_all_molecules(r):
    '''Read zero or more molecules from reader r,
    returning a list of the molecules read.'''

    result = []
    reading = True
    while reading:
        molecule = read_molecule(r)
        if molecule:
            result.append(molecule)
        else:
            reading = False
    return result
```

The work of actually reading a single molecule has been put in a function of its own that must return some false value (such as None) if it can't find another molecule in the file. This function checks the first line it tries to read to see whether there is actually any data left in the file. If not, it returns immediately to tell read_all_molecules that the end of the file has been reached. Otherwise, it pulls the name of the molecule out of the first line and then reads the molecule's atoms one at a time down to the END line:

`fileproc/multimol_2.py`

```python
def read_molecule(r):
    '''Read a single molecule from reader r and return it,
    or return None to signal end of file.'''

    # If there isn't another line, we're at the end of the file.
    line = r.readline()
    if not line:
        return None

    # Name of the molecule: "COMPND    name"
    key, name = line.split()

    # Other lines are either "END" or "ATOM num type x y z"
    molecule = [name]
    reading = True
```

```
while reading:
    line = r.readline()
    if line.startswith('END'):
        reading = False
    else:
        key, num, type, x, y, z = line.split()
        molecule.append((type, x, y, z))

return molecule
```

Notice that this function uses exactly the same trick to spot the END marking the end of a single molecule as the first function used to spot the end of file.

8.5 Looking Ahead

Let's add one final complication. Suppose that molecules didn't have END markers but instead just a COMPND line followed by one or more ATOM lines. How would we read multiple molecules from a single file in that case?

At first glance, it doesn't seem much different from the problem we just solved: read_molecule could extract the molecule's name from the COMPND line and then read ATOM lines until it got either an empty string signaling the end of the file or another COMPND line signaling the start of the next molecule. But once it has read that COMPND line, the line isn't available for the next call to read_molecule, so how can we get the name of the second molecule (and all the ones following it)?

To solve this problem, our functions must always "look ahead" one line. Let's start with the function that reads multiple molecules:

`fileproc/lookahead.py`

```
def read_all_molecules(r):
    '''Read zero or more molecules from reader r,
    returning a list of the molecules read.'''

    result = []
    line = r.readline()
    while line:
        molecule, line = read_molecule(r, line)
        result.append(molecule)
    return result
```

This function begins by reading the first line of the file. Provided that line is not the empty string (that is, the file being read is not empty),

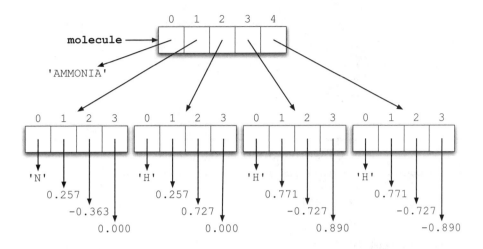

Figure 8.2: A PDB FILE

it passes both the stream to read from and the line into read_molecule, which is supposed to return two things: the next molecule in the file and the first line immediately after the end of that molecule (or an empty string if the end of file has been reached).

This simple description is enough to get us started writing the read_molecule function. The first thing it has to do is check that line is actually the start of a molecule. It then reads lines from stream one at a time, looking for one of three situations:

- The end of file, which signals the end of both the current molecule and the file

- Another COMPND line, which signals the end of this molecule and the start of the next one

- An ATOM, which is to be added to the current molecule

The most important thing is that when this function returns, it returns both the molecule *and* the next line so that its caller can keep processing. The result is probably the most complicated function we have seen so far, but understanding the idea behind it will help you understand how it works.

Figure 8.3: LOOKING AHEAD

fileproc/lookahead_2.py

```python
def read_molecule(r, line):
    '''Read a molecule from reader r.  The variable 'line'
    is the first line of the molecule to be read; the result is
    the molecule, and the first line after it (or the empty string
    if the end of file has been reached).'''

    fields = line.split()
    molecule = [fields[1]]

    line = r.readline()
    while line and not line.startswith('COMPND'):
        fields = line.split()
        key, num, type, x, y, z = fields
        molecule.append((type, x, y, z))
        line = r.readline()

    return molecule, line
```

8.6 Writing to Files

In addition to extracting data from files, there are times when we'd like
to modify or create files using Python. For example, when processing
data from a file, we may want to create a new file containing the results.
We may also want to take two data files and merge them into a single
file or split a single file into different files.

To open a file, we provide the filename and one of three modes 'r', 'w', or
'a', which stand for read, write, and append, respectively. If the mode
isn't provided (that is, we call open with only one argument), then the
default mode is 'r'.

To create a new file or to replace the contents of an existing file, we use
the write mode. If the filename does not exist already, then a new file

is created; otherwise, the file contents are replaced. For example, let's put "Computer Science" in the file test.txt:

```
output_file = open("test.txt", "w")
output_file.write("Computer Science")
output_file.close()
```

Rather than replacing the file contents, we can also add to a file using the append mode. When we write to a file that is opened in append mode, the data we write is added to the end of the file, and the current file contents are not overwritten. For example, to add to our previous file test.txt, we can append the line "Software Engineering":

```
output_file = open("test.txt", "a")
ouput_file.write("Software Engineering")
output_file.close()
```

In each of the previous examples, we called write only once, but we would typically call it multiple times.

The next example is more complex, and it involves both reading from and writing to a file. Our input file contains two numbers per line separated by a space. The output file will contain three numbers: the two from the input file and their sum (all separated by spaces):

```
def sum(input_file, output_filename):
    '''Reads the data from open file descriptor input_file, which contains
    two floats per line separated by a space.  For each line from
    input_file, a line is written to the file named output_filename
    containing the two floats from the corresponding line of input_file
    plus a space and the sum of the two floats.'''

    output_file = open(output_filename, 'w')

    for line in input_file:
        operands = line.split()
        print 'operands', operands
        sum = float(operands[0]) + float(operands[1])
        new_line = line.rstrip() + ' ' + str(sum) + '\n'
        output_file.write(new_line)

    output_file.close()
```

8.7 Summary

In this chapter, we learned the following:

- Data stored in files is usually formatted in one of a small number of ways, from value per line to multiline records with explicit end-of-record markers. Each format can be processed in a stereotypical way.
- Data processing programs should be broken into input, processing, and output stages so that each can be reused independently.
- Programs that take filenames as command-line arguments are more flexible, and therefore more useful, than ones in which these names are hard-coded.
- Files can be read (content retrieved), written to (content replaced), and added to (new content appended). When a file is opened in writing mode and it does not exist, a new file is created.
- Data files come in many different formats, so custom code is often required, but we can reuse as much as possible by writing helper functions.
- To make the functions usable by different types of readers, the reader (file, web page or input stream) is opened outside the function, passed as an argument to the function, and then closed outside the function.

8.8 Exercises

Here are some exercises for you to try on your own:

1. All of the file-reading functions we have seen in this chapter read forward through the file from the first character or line to the last. How would you write a function that would read backward through a file?

2. The file reader we developed in Section 8.3, *Positional Data*, on page 167 returns a single tuple for each entire record. Modify it so that if the field format is specified like this:

```
fields = (
  ((4, int), (2, int), (2, int)),       # date
  ((2, int), (2, int), (2, int)),       # latitude
  ((2, int), (2, int), (2, int)),       # longitude
  ((6, float), (6, float), (6, float))  # data
)
```

then each record will be converted into a tuple of tuples, like this:

```
(
    (2007, 5, 3),              # date
    (24, 17, 37),              # latitude
    (38, 56,  5),              # longitude
    (100.0, 121.3, 16.37)      # data
)
```

Explain why a tuple of tuples would make life easier for the programs that are using this function.

3. The format descriptor used by the fixed-width file reader of Section 8.3, *Positional Data*, on page 167, specifies the width of each field. However, formats are sometimes specified in terms of starting positions. For example, look at Figure 8.1, on page 167; the fixed-width file format could be specified as this:

```
fields = (
    (0, int), (4, int), (6, int),              # date
    (8, int), (10, int), (12, int),            # latitude
    (14, int), (16, int), (18, int),           # longitude
    (20, float), (26, float), (32, float)      # data
)
```

Write a function that takes a format specified this way, converts it into a width-based format, and then reads data from the specified file. (Functions like this are called *wrapper functions*, since they are "wrapped around" existing code so that it can be used in different ways.)

4. Modify the file reader in read_smallest_skip.py of Section 8.1, *Skipping the Header*, on page 156 so that can handle files with no data.

5. Modify the file reader in read_smallest_skip.py of Section 8.1, *Skipping the Header*, on page 156 so that it uses a continue inside the loop instead of an if. Which form do you find easier to read?

6. Modify the PDB file reader of Section 8.4, *Multiline Records*, on page 170 so that it ignores blank lines and comment lines in PDB files. A blank line is one that contains only space and tab characters (that is, one that looks empty when viewed). A comment is any line beginning with the keyword CMNT.

7. Modify the PDB file reader to check that the serial numbers on atoms start at 1 and increase by 1. What should the modified function do if it finds a file that doesn't obey this rule?

## Chapter 9

Sets and Dictionaries

So far, the only way we have seen to store multiple values is to put them in a sequence, such as a list or a tuple. In this chapter, we will investigate two other kinds of collections called *sets* and *dictionaries*. These allow us to create programs that are simpler and more efficient than those we could write using sequences alone.

9.1 Sets

A set is an unordered collection of distinct items. *Unordered* means that items are not stored in any particular order. Something is either in the set or not, but there's no notion of it being the first, second, or last item. *Distinct* means that any item appears in a set at most once; in other words, there are no duplicates.

Sets are fundamental to mathematics and are built in to modern versions of Python. To create a new empty set, simply type set(). To create a set with values already in it, type set((2, 3, 5)). It is important to notice that the initial values are specified in a single argument, which is a tuple. We could instead use a list, like set([2, 3, 5]), but cannot pass the values one by one, like set(2, 3, 5).

It's equally important to understand that the order of the values doesn't matter, nor does the number of times each value is entered. The expressions set((3, 5, 2)) and set((2, 3, 5, 5, 2, 3)) create exactly the same result: a set containing just three values (see Figure 9.1, on the following page).

Set Operations

In mathematics, set operations include union, intersection, add, and remove. In Python, these are implemented as methods (for a complete

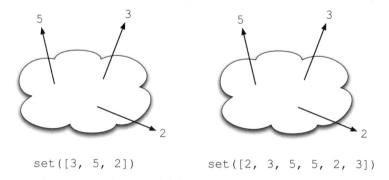

set([3, 5, 2])　　　　　set([2, 3, 5, 5, 2, 3])

Figure 9.1: CREATING A SET

list, see Figure 9.2, on the next page). Note that most operations create a new set: only add, remove, and clear modify the current set. The following program shows these methods in action:

`setdict/setexamples.cmd`

```
>>> ten = set(range(10))
>>> lows = set([0, 1, 2, 3, 4])
>>> odds = set([1, 3, 5, 7, 9])
>>> lows.add(9)
>>> lows
set([0, 1, 2, 3, 4, 9])
>>> lows.difference(odds)
set([0, 2, 4])
>>> lows.intersection(odds)
set([1, 3, 9])
>>> lows.issubset(ten)
True
>>> lows.issuperset(odds)
False
>>> lows.remove(0)
>>> lows
set([1, 2, 3, 4, 9])
>>> lows.symmetric_difference(odds)
set([2, 4, 5, 7])
>>> lows.union(odds)
set([1, 2, 3, 4, 5, 7, 9])
>>> lows.clear()
>>> lows
set([])
```

Method	Purpose	Example	Result
add	Adds an element to a set	lows.add(9)	None
clear	Removes all elements from a set	lows.clear()	None
difference	Creates a set with elements from one set, but not the other	lows.difference(odds)	set((0, 2, 4)))
intersection	Creates a set with elements that are in both sets	lows.intersection(odds)	set((1, 3)))
issubset	Asks are all of one set's elements contained in another?	lows.issubset(ten)	True
issuperset	Asks does one set contain all of another's elements?	lows.issuperset(odds)	False
remove	Removes an element from a set	lows.remove(0)	None
symmetric_difference	Creates a set with elements that are in exactly one set	lows.symmetric_difference(odds)	set((0, 2, 4, 5, 7, 9)))
union	Creates a set with elements that are in either set	lows.union(odds)	set((0, 1, 2, 3, 4, 5, 7, 9)))

Figure 9.2: SET OPERATIONS, WHERE TEN = SET(RANGE(10)), LOWS = SET([0, 1, 2, 3, 4]), AND ODDS = SET([1, 3, 5, 7, 9])

Many set methods can also be written using operators. If acids and bases are two sets, for example, then acids | bases creates a new set containing their union (that is, all the elements from both acids and bases), while acids <= bases tests whether all the values in acids are also in bases. All the operators that sets support are listed in Figure 9.3, on the following page.

Arctic Birds

To see how sets are used, suppose we have several files recording observations of birds in the Canadian Arctic and we want to know which species we have seen. Each file is formatted like this:

setdict/birdwatching.txt

```
canada goose
canada goose
long-tailed jaeger
canada goose
snow goose
canada goose
canada goose
northern fulmar
```

Method Call	Operator
set1.difference(set2)	set1 - set2
set1.intersection(set2)	set1 & set2
set1.issubset(set2)	set1 <= set2
set1.issuperset(set2)	set1 >= set2
set1.union(set2)	set1 | set2
set1.symmetric_difference(set2)	set1^set2

Figure 9.3: SET OPERATIONS

Here's our program:

`setdict/birdwatching.py`

```python
import sys

# Find the different bird types observed.
birds = set()
for filename in sys.argv[1:]:
    infile = open(filename, 'r')
    for line in infile:
        name = line.strip()
        birds.add(name)
    infile.close()

# Print the birds.
for b in birds:
    print b
```

The first statement after the import creates a new empty set and assigns it to the variable birds. The loop then reads the names of birds from each of the input files specified on the command line. Any whitespace before or after the bird's name is stripped away by line.strip(); the program then uses birds.add(name) to make sure the new name is in the set. If the name is not already there, set.add puts it in the set; otherwise, the set isn't changed.

Once all the names have been read, the program loops over the values in the set to print them. This works exactly like a loop over the values in a list, except that the order in which values are encountered is arbitrary: there is no guarantee that they will come out in the order in which they were added, in alphabetical order, in order by length, or anything else.

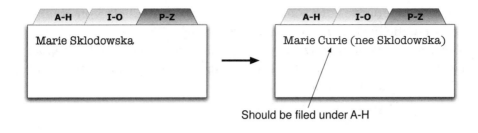

Should be filed under A-H

Figure 9.4: MOVING ITEMS IN A FILING CABINET

Set Storage

Sets are stored in a data structure called a *hash table*. Each time an item is added to a set, Python calculates a *hash code* for the item, which is an integer that is guaranteed to be the same for items with equal values:

`setdict/hashcode.cmd`

```
>>> help(hash)
Help on built-in function hash in module __builtin__:

hash(...)
    hash(object) -> integer

    Return a hash value for the object.  Two objects with the same
    value have the same hash value.  The reverse is not necessarily
    true, but likely.

>>> hash(123)
123
>>> hash('123') # a string
1911471187
```

To see whether a value is in a set, Python simply recalculates the hash code for that value and checks the corresponding location in the hash table. This is a lot faster than searching the whole set every time a value needs to be looked up. However, this scheme works only if an item's hash code cannot change after it has been added to the hash table. To see why, consider what would happen if you filed patient records in alphabetical order but then went back and changed someone's name (see Figure 9.4). Their record would now be out of place, so if someone else tried to look it up, they wouldn't find it.

Because hash codes are computed from values, if a list's contents are changed, the hash code for that list will change. For this reason, Python allows sets to contain only immutable values (see Section 5.2, *Modifying Lists*, on page 77). Again, Booleans, numbers, strings, and tuples are allowed, but lists are not:

`setdict/hashcode_seq.cmd`

```
>>> hash((1, 2, 3))
-378539185
>>> hash([1, 2, 3])
Traceback (most recent call last):
  File "<stdin>", line 1, in <module>
TypeError: list objects are unhashable
```

This is actually one of the reasons tuples were invented: they allow multipart values like ('Albert', 'Einstein') to be added to sets.

But this means that we can't store a set of sets. Sets themselves can't be immutable, since we need to add and remove values, so a set can't contain another one. To solve this problem, Python has another data type called a *frozen set*. As the name implies, frozen sets are sets whose contents can't be changed, just as tuples are lists whose values can't be modified. An empty frozen set (which isn't particularly useful) is created using frozenset(); to create a frozen set that contains some values, use frozenset(values), where values is a list, tuple, set, or other collection.

9.2 Dictionaries

Back to bird watching. Suppose we want to know how often each kind of bird was seen. Our first attempt uses a list of pairs, each a list storing the name of a bird and the number of times it has been seen so far:

`setdict/listfordict.py`

```
import sys

# Find all the birds.
birds = []
for filename in sys.argv[1:]:
    infile = open(filename, 'r')

    # For each bird, find its entry and increment the count.
    for line in infile:
        name = line.strip()
        found = False
        for entry in birds:
            if entry[0] == name:
```

```
            entry[1] += 1
            found = True
    if not found:
        birds.append([name, 1])

    infile.close()

# Print.
for (name, count) in birds:
    print name, count
```

This gives the right answer, but there are two things wrong with it. The first is that it is complex. The more nested loops our programs contain, the harder they are to understand, fix, and extend. The second is that it is inefficient. Suppose we were interested in beetles instead of birds and that we had millions of observations of tens of thousands of species. Scanning the list of names each time we want to add one new observation would take a long, long time, even on a fast computer (a topic we will return to in Chapter 11, *Searching and Sorting*, on page 209).

Can we use a set to solve both problems at once? Sets can look up values in a single step; why not combine each bird's name and the number of times it has been seen into a two-valued tuple and put those tuples in a set?

The problem with this idea is that we can look for values only if we know what those values are. In this case, we won't. We will know only the name of the species, not how many times it has already been seen.

The right answer is to use another data structure called a *dictionary*. Also known as a *map*, a dictionary is an unordered mutable collection of key/value pairs (see Figure 9.5, on the following page). In plain English, dictionaries are like phone books. They associate a value (such as a phone number) with a key (like a name). The keys form a set. Any particular key can appear at most once in a dictionary, and like the elements in sets, keys must be immutable (though the values associated with them do not have to be).

Dictionaries are created by putting key/value pairs inside braces. To get the value associated with a key, we put the key in square brackets:

setdict/simpledict.cmd

```
>>> birds = {'canada goose' : 3, 'northern fulmar' : 1}
>>> birds
{'canada goose' : 3, 'northern fulmar' : 1}
>>> birds['northern fulmar']
1
```

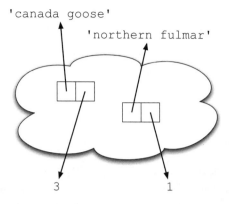

'canada goose'

'northern fulmar'

3   1

Figure 9.5: STRUCTURE OF A DICTIONARY

As you'd expect, the empty dictionary is written {}. Indexing a dictionary with a key it doesn't contain produces an error, just like an out-of-range index for a list:

setdict/badkey.cmd

```
>>> birds = {'canada goose' : 3, 'northern fulmar' : 1}
>>> birds['canada goose']
3
>>> birds['long-tailed jaeger']
Traceback (most recent call last):
  File "<stdin>", line 1, in ?
KeyError: 'long-tailed jaeger'
```

To test whether a key is in a dictionary, use k in d:

setdict/dictin.cmd

```
>>> birds = {'eagle' : 999, 'snow goose' : 33}
>>> if 'eagle' in birds:
...    print 'eagles have been seen'
...
eagles have been seen
>>> del birds['eagle']
>>> if 'eagle' in birds:
...    print 'oops: why are eagles still there?'
...
```

Updating and Membership

Updating dictionaries is easy. Just assign a value to a key. If the key is already in the dictionary, this changes the value associated with it.

If the key was not present, it is added, along with the value:

`setdict/dictupdate.cmd`

```
>>> birds = {}
>>> birds['snow goose'] = 33
>>> birds['eagle'] = 999 # oops
>>> birds
{'eagle' : 999, 'snow goose' : 33}
>>> birds['eagle'] = 9
>>> birds
{'eagle' : 9, 'snow goose' : 33}
```

To remove an entry from a dictionary, use del d[k], where d is the dictionary and k is the key being removed. Only entries that are present can be removed; trying to remove one that isn't there causes an error:

`setdict/dictdel.cmd`

```
>>> birds = {'snow goose' : 33, 'eagle' : 9}
>>> del birds['snow goose']
>>> birds
{'eagle' : 9}
>>> del birds['gannet']
Traceback (most recent call last):
  File "<stdin>", line 1, in <module>
KeyError: 'gannet'
```

Loops

Since dictionaries are collections, we're going to want to loop over their contents. We do this with for key in somedict, which assigns each of the keys in the dictionary to the loop variable in turn:

`setdict/loop.cmd`

```
>>> birds = {'canada goose' : 183, 'long-tailed jaeger' : 71,
             'snow goose' : 63, 'northern fulmar', 1}
>>> for x in birds:
...     print x, birds[x]
...
'northern fulmar' 1
'long-tailed jaeger' 71
'canada goose' 183
'snow goose' 63
```

As with set elements, Python loops over the entries in the dictionary in an arbitrary order. There is no guarantee that they will be seen alphabetically or in the order they were added to the dictionary.

Notice, by the way, that looping over dictionaries is slightly different from looping over lists. When Python loops over a list, the values in the list are assigned to the loop variable. When it loops over a dictionary, on the other hand, it assigns the keys. Python's designers chose to do this because

- looping over the indices of a list isn't very interesting, since the program would always get the sequence 0, 1, 2, ...; and

- it's a lot easier to go from a dictionary key to the associated value than it is to take the value and find the associated key.

Dictionary Methods

Like lists, tuples, and sets, dictionaries are objects. Their methods are described in Figure 9.6, on the next page, while the following program shows how they are used:

`setdict/dictmeth.py`

```
scientists = {'Newton' : 1642, 'Darwin' : 1809, 'Turing' : 1912}

print 'keys:', scientists.keys()
print 'values:', scientists.values()
print 'items:', scientists.items()
print 'get:', scientists.get('Curie', 1867)

temp = {'Curie' : 1867, 'Hopper' : 1906, 'Franklin' : 1920}
scientists.update(temp)
print 'after update:', scientists

scientists.clear()
print 'after clear:', scientists
```

As you can see from its output (shown next), the keys and values methods return the dictionary's keys and values, respectively, while items returns a list of (key, value) pairs. get returns the value associated with a key or returns some user-specified value if the key isn't in the dictionary; we'll see a use for this shortly. Finally, update copies keys and values from one dictionary into another, and clear erases the dictionary's contents.

`setdict/dictmeth.out`

```
keys: ['Turing', 'Newton', 'Darwin']
values: [1912, 1642, 1809]
items: [('Turing', 1912), ('Newton', 1642), ('Darwin', 1809)]
get: 1867
after update: {'Curie': 1867, 'Darwin': 1809, 'Franklin': 1920,
               'Turing': 1912, 'Newton': 1642, 'Hopper': 1906}
after clear: {}
```

Method	Purpose	Example	Result
clear	Empties the dictionary.	d.clear()	Returns None, but d is now empty.
get	Returns the value associated with a key, or a default value if the key is not present.	d.get('x', 99)	Returns d['x'] if "x" is in d, or 99 if it is not.
keys	Returns the dictionary's keys as a list. Entries are guaranteed to be unique.	birthday.keys()	['Turing', 'Newton', 'Darwin']
items	Returns a list of (key, value) pairs.	birthday.items()	[('Turing', 1912), ('Newton', 1642), ('Darwin', 1809)]
values	Returns the dictionary's values as a list. Entries may or may not be unique.	birthday.values()	[1912, 1642, 1809]
update	Updates the dictionary with the contents of another.	See the example on the facing page.	

Figure 9.6: DICTIONARY METHODS

One common use of items is to loop over the keys and values in a dictionary together:

```
for (key, value) in dictionary.items():
    ...do something with the key and value...
```

This is inefficient for large dictionaries, since items actually constructs a list of (key, value) pairs. A similar method called iteritems hands these pairs back one by one on demand:

```
for (key, value) in dictionary.iteritems():
    ...do something with the key and value...
```

Dictionary Example

Back to birdwatching once again. We want to count the number of times each species has been seen. To do this, we create a dictionary that is initially empty. Each time we read an observation from a file, we check to see whether we have seen that bird before, that is, whether the bird's name is already a key in our dictionary. If it is, we add one to its count. If it isn't, we add the name to the dictionary with the value 1. Here is the program that does this:

setdict/countbirds1.py

```
import sys

# Count all the birds.
count = {}
for filename in sys.argv[1:]:
    infile = open(filename, 'r')
    for line in infile:
        name = line.strip()
        if name in count:
            count[name] = count[name] + 1
        else:
            count[name] = 1

    infile.close()

# Print.
for b in count:
    print b, count[b]
```

We can shorten this program a bit using the method dict.get. This returns either the value associated with a key or some default value that we provide. In this case, we get either the number of times we've already seen a species or zero, add one to whichever value the method returns, and store that back in the dictionary:

setdict/countbirds2.py

```
import sys

# Count all the birds.
count = {}
for filename in sys.argv[1:]:
    infile = open(filename, 'r')
    for line in infile:
        name = line.strip()
        count[name] = count.get(name, 0) + 1
    infile.close()
```

```
# Print.
keys = count.keys()
keys.sort()
for b in keys:
    print b, count[b]
```

Using dict.get saves three lines, but some programmers find it harder to understand at a glance.

This program contains another innovation as well. Instead of printing the birds' names in whatever order the dictionary chose to use, we get the dictionary's keys as a list, sort that list alphabetically, and then loop over that. This way, the entries appear in a sensible order. We can make this more readable by using Python's built-in sorted function:

setdict/countbirds3.py

```
import sys

# Count all the birds.
count = {}
for filename in sys.argv[1:]:
    infile = open(filename, 'r')
    for line in infile:
        name = line.strip()
        count[name] = count.get(name, 0) + 1
    infile.close()

# Invert the dictionary.
freq = {}
for (name, times) in count.items():
    if times in freq:
        freq[times].append(name)
    else:
        freq[times] = [name]

# Print.
for key in sorted(freq):
    print key
    for name in freq[key]:
        print ' ', name
```

9.3 Inverting a Dictionary

We might want to print the birds in another order—in order of frequency, for example. To do this, we need to *invert* the dictionary; that is, use the values as keys and the keys as values. This is a little trickier than it first appears. There's no guarantee that the values are unique, so we have to handle *collisions*. For example, if we invert the dictionary {'a':1, 'b':1, 'c':1}, the key will be 1, but it's not clear what the value would be.

The solution is to use some sort of collection, such as a list, to store the inverted dictionary's values. If we go this route, the inverse of the dictionary shown earlier would be {1:['a','b','c']}. Here's a program to do what we want:

setdict/countbirds4.py

```python
import sys

# Count all the birds.
count = {}
for filename in sys.argv[1:]:
    infile = open(filename, 'r')
    for line in infile:
        name = line.strip()
        count[name] = count.get(name, 0) + 1
    infile.close()

# Invert the dictionary.
freq = {}
for (name, times) in count.items():
    if times in freq:
        freq[times].append(name)
    else:
        freq[times] = [name]

# Print.
for key in sorted(freq):
    print key
    for name in freq[key]:
        print ' ', name
```

The exercises will ask you to break this into functions to make it more readable.

9.4 Summary

In this chapter, we learned the following:

- Sets are used in Python to store unordered collections of unique values. They support the same operations as sets in mathematics.

- Sets are stored in hash tables to make lookup efficient. For this to work, each item must have a hash code that does not change during its lifetime. This means that mutable values like lists and sets cannot themselves be stored in sets. Instead, programs must use tuples and frozen sets.

- Dictionaries are used to store unordered collections of key/value pairs. They are also stored using hash tables for efficiency's sake and also require keys to be immutable.

- Looking things up in sets and dictionaries is much faster than searching through lists. If you have a program that is doing the latter, consider changing your choice of data structures.

9.5 Exercises

Here are some exercises for you to try on your own:

1. Write a function called find_dups that takes a list of integers as its input argument and returns a set of those integers that occur two or more times in the list.

2. Python's set objects have a method called pop that removes and returns an arbitrary element from the set. If a set gerbils contains five cuddly little animals, for example, calling gerbils.pop() five times will return those animals one by one, leaving the set empty at the end. Use this to write a function called mating_pairs that takes two equal-sized sets called males and females as input and returns a set of pairs; each pair must be a tuple containing one male and one female. (The elements of males and females may be strings containing gerbil names or gerbil ID numbers—your function must work with both.)

3. The PDB file format is often used to store information about molecules. A PDB file may contain zero or more lines that begin with the word AUTHOR (which may be in uppercase, lowercase, or mixed case), followed by spaces or tabs, followed by the name of the person who created the file. Write a function that takes a list of filenames as an input argument and returns the set of all author names found in those files.

4. Draw a memory model of the data structure produced by the following statement:

```
vowels = set(frozenset('aeiou'))
```

5. The keys in a dictionary are guaranteed to be unique, but the values are not. Write a function called count_values that takes a single dictionary as an argument and returns the number of distinct values it contains. Given the input {'red':1, 'green':1, 'blue':2}, for example, it would return 2.

6. After doing a series of experiments, you have compiled a dictionary showing the probability of detecting certain kinds of subatomic particles. The particles' names are the dictionary's keys, and the probabilities are the values: {'neutron':0.55, 'proton':0.21, 'meson':0.03, 'muon':0.07, 'neutrino':0.14}. Write a function that takes a single dictionary of this kind as input and returns the particle that is least likely to be observed. Given the dictionary shown earlier, for example, the function would return 'meson'.

7. Write a function called count_duplicates that takes a dictionary as an argument and returns the number of values that appear two or more times.

8. Write a function called fetch_and_set that takes a dictionary and two arbitrary values, key and new_value, as arguments. If key is already in the dictionary, this function returns the value associated with it while replacing that value with new_value. If the key is not present, the function raises a KeyError exception with the error message 'Unable to replace value for nonexistent key'.

9. A *balanced color* is one whose red, green, and blue values add up to 1.0. Write a function called is_balanced that takes a dictionary whose keys are 'R', 'G', and 'B' as its input and returns True if they represent a balanced color.

10. Write a function called dict_intersect that takes two dictionaries as arguments and returns a dictionary that contains only the key/value pairs found in both of the original dictionaries.

11. Programmers sometimes use a dictionary of dictionaries as a simple database. For example, to keep track of information about famous scientists, they might use something like this:

setdict/dict_of_dicts.py

```
{
  'jgoodall'  : {'surname'  : 'Goodall',
                 'forename' : 'Jane',
                 'born'     : 1934,
                 'died'     : None,
```

```
                        'notes'    : 'primate researcher'
                        'author'   : ['In the Shadow of Man', 'The Chimpanzees of Gombe']},
       'rfranklin' : {'surname'   : 'Franklin',
                        'forename' : 'Rosalind',
                        'born'     : 1920,
                        'died'     : 1957,
                        'notes'    : 'contributed to discovery of DNA'},
        'rcarson'   : {'surname'   : 'Carson',
                        'forename' : 'Rachel',
                        'born'     : 1907,
                        'died'     : 1964,
                        'notes'    : 'raised awareness of effects of DDT',
                        'author'   : ['Silent Spring']}
    }
```

Write a function called db_headings that returns the set of keys used in *any* of the inner dictionaries. In this example, the function should return set('author', 'forename', 'surname', 'notes', 'born', 'died').

12. Write another function called db_consistent that takes a dictionary of dictionaries in the format described in the previous question and returns True if and only if every one of the inner dictionaries has exactly the same keys. (This function would return False for the previous example, since Rosalind Franklin's entry does not contain the 'author' key.)

13. Make the final bird-counting program in Section 9.3, *Inverting a Dictionary*, on page 191, more readable by breaking it into several functions.

14. A *sparse vector* is a vector whose entries are almost all zero, like [1, 0, 0, 0, 0, 0, 3, 0, 0, 0]. Storing all those zeroes in a list wastes memory, so programmers often use dictionaries instead to keep track of just the nonzero entries. For example, the vector shown earlier would be represented as {0:1, 6:3}, since the vector it is meant to represent has the value 1 at index 0 and the value 3 at index 6.

   a) Write a function called sparse_add that takes two sparse vectors stored as dictionaries and returns a new dictionary representing their sum.[1]

---

1. The sum of two vectors is just the element-wise sum of their elements. For example, the sum of [1, 2, 3] and [4, 5, 6] is [5, 7, 9].

b) Write another function called sparse_dot that calculates the dot product of two sparse vectors.[2]

c) Your boss has asked you to write a function called sparse_len that will return the length of a sparse vector (just as Python's len returns the length of a list). What do you need to ask her before you can start writing it?

---

2. The dot product of two vectors is the sum of the products of corresponding elements. For example, the dot product of $[1, 2, 3]$ and $[4, 5, 6]$ is 4+10+18, or 32.

Chapter 10

Algorithms

For the past few chapters, you have used built-in functions such as max and sort on lists. This chapter will examine how they work and thus introduce a systematic way of solving problems when there is no function or method that does exactly what you want.

An *algorithm* is a set of steps that accomplishes a task, such as synthesizing caffeine. Although programs require algorithms to be written in programming languages like Python, it is easier to discuss and plan an algorithm using a mixture of a human language like English and a little mathematics.

Our algorithm-writing technique is called *top-down design*. You start by describing your solution in English and then mark the phrases that correspond directly to Python statements. Those that do not correspond should be rewritten in more detail in English, until everything in your description can be written in Python.

Top-down design sounds easy, but doing it requires a little practice. As we work through the examples in the rest of this chapter, we will see why our initial attempts at translation will have implementations that *look* reasonable but often have bugs. This is common in many fields. In mathematics, for example, the first versions of "proofs" often handle common cases well but fail for odd cases [Lak76]. Mathematicians deal with this by looking for counter examples, and programmers (good programmers, at least) deal with it by testing their code as they write it.

Most important, this chapter focuses *only* on top-down design; we have skipped the discussion of testing to make sure our code works. In fact, the first versions we wrote had minor bugs in them, and we found them only by doing thorough testing. We will talk more about this in Chapter 12, *Construction*, on page 233.

10.1 Searching

To start, suppose we have data showing the number of humpback whales sighted off the coast of British Columbia over the past ten years:

809   834   477   478   307   122   96   102   324   476

We want to know how changes in fishing practices have impacted the whales' numbers. Our first question is, which year had the lowest number of sightings during those years? This code tells us just that:

`alg/search1.cmd`

```
>>> counts = [809, 834, 477, 478, 307, 122, 96, 102, 324, 476]
>>> min(counts)
96
```

If we want to know in which year the population bottomed out, we can use index to find the position of the minimum:

`alg/search2.cmd`

```
>>> counts = [809, 834, 477, 478, 307, 122, 96, 102, 324, 476]
>>> low = min(counts)
>>> min_index = counts.index(low)
>>> print min_index
6
```

or more succinctly:

`alg/search3.cmd`

```
>>> counts = [809, 834, 477, 478, 307, 122, 96, 102, 324, 476]
>>> counts.index(min(counts))
6
```

Although this does the job, it seems a little inefficient to search through the data to find the minimum value and then search again to find that value's index. Intuitively speaking, there ought to be a way to find both in just one pass.

Now what if we want to find the indices of the *two* smallest values? Lists don't have a method to do this directly, so we will have to write a function ourselves.

There are at least three ways we could do this, each of which will be subjected to top-down design:

- *Find, remove, find.* Find the index of the minimum, remove that element from the list, and find the index of the new minimum element in the list.

- *Sort, identify minimums, get indices.* Sort the list, get the two smallest numbers, and then find their indices in the original list.

- *Walk through the list.* Examine each value in the list in order, keep track of the two smallest values found so far, and update these values when a new smaller value is found.

At the end of all three, we'll return a tuple of the two smallest indices.

Find, Remove, Find

Here is the algorithm again, rewritten with one instruction per line:

alg/find_remove_find1.py

```
def find_two_smallest(L):
    '''Return a tuple of the indices of the two smallest values in list L.'''

    find the index of the minimum element in L
    remove that element from the list
    find the index of the new minimum element in the list
    return the two indices
```

To refine "find the index of the minimum element in L," we skim the help for list and find that there are no methods that do exactly that. We'll refine it:

alg/find_remove_find2.py

```
def find_two_smallest(L):
    '''Return a tuple of the indices of the two smallest values in list L.'''

    get the minimum element in L
    find the index of that minimum element
    remove that element from the list
    find the index of the new minimum element in the list
    return the two indices
```

Those first two statements match Python functions and methods: min does the first, and list.index does the second.

We see that list.remove does the third, and the refinement of "find the index of the new minimum element in the list" is also straightforward:

`alg/find_remove_find3.py`

```python
def find_two_smallest(L):
    '''Return a tuple of the indices of the two smallest values in list L.'''

    smallest = min(L)
    min1 = L.index(smallest)
    L.remove(smallest)
    next_smallest = min(L)
    min2 = L.index(next_smallest)

    return the two indices
```

Since we removed the smallest element, we need to put it back. Also, when we remove a value, the indices of the following values shift down by one. So, when smallest was removed, in order to get the indices of the two lowest values in the *original* list, we need to add 1 to min2:

`alg/find_remove_find4.py`

```python
def find_two_smallest(L):
    '''Return a tuple of the indices of the two smallest values in list L.'''

    smallest = min(L)
    min1 = L.index(smallest)
    L.remove(smallest)
    next_smallest = min(L)
    min2 = L.index(next_smallest)

    put smallest back into L
    if min1 comes before min2, add 1 to min2
    return the two indices
```

That's enough refinement (finally!) to do it all in Python:

`alg/find_remove_find5.py`

```python
def find_two_smallest(L):
    '''Return a tuple of the indices of the two smallest values in list L.'''

    smallest = min(L)
    min1 = L.index(smallest)
    L.remove(smallest)
    next_smallest = min(L)
    min2 = L.index(next_smallest)

    L.insert(min1, smallest)
    if min1 <= min2:
        min2 += 1

    return (min1, min2)
```

That seems like a lot of work, and it is. Even if you go right to code, you'll be thinking through all those steps.

Sort, Identify Minimums, Get Indices

We again restate the algorithm, rewritten with one instruction per line:

`alg/sort_then_find1.py`

```
def find_two_smallest(L):
    '''Return a tuple of the indices of the two smallest values in list L.'''

    sort a copy of L
    get the two smallest numbers
    find their indices in the original list L
    return the two indices
```

That looks straightforward; we can use list.sort, and then the smallest items will be at the front. Being careful, we notice that we should work on a copy of L—never change the contents of parameters unless the docstrings says to!

`alg/sort_then_find2.py`

```
def find_two_smallest(L):
    '''Return a tuple of the indices of the two smallest values in list L.'''

    temp_list = L[:]
    temp_list.sort()
    smallest = temp_list[0]
    next_smallest = temp_list[1]
    find their indices in the original list
    return the two indices
```

Now we can find the indices and return them the same way we did in find-remove-find:

`alg/sort_then_find3.py`

```
def find_two_smallest(L):
    '''Return a tuple of the indices of the two smallest values in list L.'''

    temp_list = L[:]
    temp_list.sort()
    smallest = temp_list[0]
    next_smallest = temp_list[1]
    min1 = L.index(smallest)
    min2 = L.index(next_smallest)
    return (min1, min2)
```

Walk Through the List

We'll start the same way as for the first two:

alg/walk_through1.py

```python
def find_two_smallest(L):
    '''Return a tuple of the indices of the two smallest values in list L.'''

    examine each value in the list in order
    keep track of the indices of the two smallest values found so far
    update these values when a new smaller value is found
    return the two indices
```

We'll also move the second line before the first one because it describes the whole process; it isn't a single step. Also, when we see phrases like *each value*, we think of iteration; the third line is part of that iteration, so we'll indent it:

alg/walk_through2.py

```python
def find_two_smallest(L):
    '''Return a tuple of the indices of the two smallest values in list L.'''

    keep track of the indices of the two smallest values found so far
    examine each value in the list in order
        update these values when a new smaller value is found
    return the two indices
```

Every loop has three parts: an initialization section to set up the variables we'll need, a loop condition, and a loop body. Here, the initialization will set up min1 and min2, which will be the indices of the smallest two items; a natural choice is to set them to the first two elements of the list:

alg/walk_through3.py

```python
def find_two_smallest(L):
    '''Return a tuple of the indices of the two smallest values in list L.'''

    set min1 and min2 to the indices of the smallest and next-smallest
    values at the beginning of L

    examine each value in the list in order
        update these values when a new smaller value is found
    return the two indices
```

We can turn that first line into a couple lines of code; we've left our English version in as a comment:

alg/walk_through4.py

```python
def find_two_smallest(L):
    '''Return a tuple of the indices of the two smallest values in list L.'''
```

```
# set min1 and min2 to the indices of the smallest and next-smallest
# values at the beginning of L
if L[0] < L[1]:
    smallest, next_smallest = 0, 1
else:
    smallest, next_smallest = 1, 0

examine each value in the list in order
    update these values when a new smaller value is found
return the two indices
```

We have a couple choices now. We can iterate with a for loop over the values, a for loop over the indices, or a while loop over the indices. Since we're trying to find indices and we want to look at all of the elements in the list, we'll use a for loop over the indices—and we'll start at index 2 because we've examined the first two values already. At the same time, we'll refine the statement in the body of the loop to mention min1 and min2.

`alg/walk_through5.py`

```
def find_two_smallest(L):
    '''Return a tuple of the indices of the two smallest values in list L.'''

    # set min1 and min2 to the indices of the smallest and next-smallest
    # values at the beginning of L
    if L[0] < L[1]:
        min1, min2 = 0, 1
    else:
        min2, min1 = 0, 1

    # examine each value in the list in order
    for i in range(2, len(values)):
        update min1 and/or min2 when a new smaller value is found
    return the two indices
```

Now for the body of the loop. We'll pick apart "update min1 and/or min2 when a new smaller value is found."

If L[i] is smaller than both, then we have a new smallest item, so min1 currently holds the second smallest and min2 currently holds the third smallest. We need to update both of them.

If L[i] is larger than min1 and smaller than min2, we have a new second smallest.

If L[i] is larger than both, we skip it.

alg/walk_through6.py

```python
def find_two_smallest(L):
    '''Return a tuple of the indices of the two smallest values in list L.'''

    # set min1 and min2 to the indices of the smallest and next-smallest
    # values at the beginning of L
    if L[0] < L[1]:
        min1, min2 = 0, 1
    else:
        min2, min1 = 1, 0

    # examine each value in the list in order
    for i in range(2, len(L)):

        L[i] is larger than both min1 and min2, smaller than both, or
        in between.
        if L[i] is larger than both min1 and min2, skip it
        if L[i] is smaller than min1 and min2, update them both
        if L[i] is in between, update min2

    return (min1, min2)
```

All of those are easily translated to Python; in fact, we don't even need code for the "larger than both" case:

alg/walk_through7.py

```python
def find_two_smallest(L):
    '''Return a tuple of the indices of the two smallest values in list L.'''

    # set min1 and min2 to the indices of the smallest and next-smallest
    # values at the beginning of L
    if L[0] < L[1]:
        min1, min2 = 0, 1
    else:
        min2, min1 = 1, 0

    # examine each value in the list in order
    for i in range(2, len(L)):

        # L[i] is larger than both min1 and min2, smaller than both, or
        # in between.

        # New smallest?
        if L[i] < L[min1]:
            min2 = min1
            min1 = i

        # New second smallest?
        elif L[i] < L[min2]:
            min2 = i

    return (min1, min2)
```

10.2 Timing

Profiling a program means measuring how long it takes to run and how much memory it uses. These two measures—space and time—are fundamental to the theoretical study of algorithms. They are also pretty important from a pragmatic point of view. Fast programs are more useful than slow ones, and programs that need more memory than what your computer has aren't particularly useful at all.

We ran the three functions we developed to find the two lowest values in a list on 1,400 monthly readings of air pressure in Darwin, Australia, from 1882 to 1998.[1] The execution times were as follows:

Algorithm	Running Time (ms)
Find, remove, find	1.117
Sort, identify, index	2.128
Walk through the list	1.472

Notice how small these times are. No human being can notice the difference between one and two milliseconds; if this code never has to process lists with more than 1,400 values, we would be justified in choosing an implementation based on simplicity or clarity, rather than speed.

But what if we wanted to process millions of values? Find-remove-find outperforms the other two algorithms on 1,400 values, but how much does that tell us about how they will perform on data sets 1,000 times larger? That will be the subject of Chapter 11, *Searching and Sorting*, on page 209.

10.3 Summary

In this chapter, we learned the following:

- The most effective way to design algorithms is to use top-down design, in which goals are broken down into subgoals until the steps are small enough to be translated directly into a programming language.

- The performance of a program can be characterized by how much time and memory it uses. This can be determined experimentally by profiling its execution.

---

1. See http://www.stat.duke.edu/~mw/ts_data_sets.html.

- Almost all problems have more than one correct solution. Choosing between them often involves a trade-off between simplicity and performance.

- Code that has side effects is harder to understand and debug than code that does not, so in general functions should return values rather than modifying their arguments or external data structures.

10.4 Exercises

Here are some exercises for you to try on your own:

1. A DNA sequence is a string made up of the letters A, T, G, and C. To find the complement of a DNA sequence, As are replaced by Ts, Ts by As, Gs by Cs, and Cs by Gs. For example, the complement of AATTGCCGT is TTAACGGCA.

    a) Write an outline in English of the algorithm you would use to find the complement.

    b) Reexamine your algorithm. Will any characters be changed to their complement and then changed back to their original value? If so, rewrite your outline. Hint: convert one character at a time, rather than all of the As, Ts, Gs, or Cs at once.

    c) Write the complement(sequence) function.

2. a) Write a loop (including initialization) that uses a loop to find both the minimum value in a list and that value's index in one pass through the list.

    b) Write the min_index(sequence) function that returns the minimum value and that value's index in a tuple.

    c) You might also want to find the maximum value and its index. Write a new function min_or_max_index(sequence, bool) where if find_min is true, it returns the minimum and its index, and where if find_min is false, it returns the maximum and its index.

3. Write a set of nose tests for the find-two-smallest functions. Think about what kinds of data are interesting, long lists or short lists, and what order the items are in. Here is one list to test with: [1, 2]. What other interesting ones are there?

4. What happens if the functions to find the two smallest values in a list are passed a list of length 1? What should happen, and why? How about length 0? Modify one of the docstrings to describe what happens.

Chapter 11

Searching and Sorting

A huge part of computer science involves studying how to organize, store, and retrieve data. Searching and sorting are fundamental parts of programming, and they are also a good way to explain how computer scientists compare the efficiency of different algorithms and to explain what they mean by *efficiency*. In this chapter, we will develop several algorithms for searching and sorting lists and then use them to explore what it means for one algorithm to be faster than another.

11.1 Linear Search

As you have already seen, Python lists have a method called index that searches for a particular item:

searchsort/index_help.txt

```
index(...)
    L.index(value, [start, [stop]]) -> integer -- return first index of value
```

Method index starts at the front of the list and examines each item in turn. For reasons that will soon become clear, this technique is called *linear search*. We'll examine three different but related versions.

Basic Linear Search

Here's the first version of linear search; this is a common version:

searchsort/linear_search_1.py

```python
def linear_search(v, L):
    '''Return the index of the first occurrence of v in list L, or return len(L)
    if v is not in L.'''

    i = 0
```

```
# Keep going until we reach the end of L or until we find v.
while i != len(L) and L[i] != v:
    i = i + 1

return i
```

This version uses variable i as the current index and marches through the values in L. The first check in the loop condition, i != len(L), makes sure we look at only valid indices; if we were to omit that check, then if v is not in L, we would end up trying to access L[len(L)]. This, of course, would not be valid.

The second check, L[i] != v, causes the loop to exit when we find v. The loop body increments i; we enter the loop when we haven't reach the end of L and when L[i] isn't the value we are looking for.

At the end, we return i's value, which is either the index of v (if the second loop check was false) or is len(L) if v was not in L.

for loop Version of Linear Search

The first version requires two checks each time through the loop. The first check (i != len(L)) is almost unnecessary; it evaluates to true almost every time through the loop, so the only effect it has is to make sure we don't attempt to index past the end of the list.

Here's the second version, where we try to get around this problem using Python's for loop:

searchsort/linear_search_2.py

```
def linear_search(v, L):
    '''Return the index of the first occurrence of v in list L, or return len(L)
    if v is not in L.'''

    i = 0
    for value in L:
        if value == v:
            return i

        i += 1

    return len(L)
```

With this version, we no longer need the first check because the for loop controls the number of iterations. This for loop version is significantly faster than basic linear search; we'll see in a bit how much faster.

Sentinel Search

The last linear search we will study is called *sentinel search*.[1] Remember that a problem with basic linear search is that we check i != len(L) every time through the loop even though it can never be false except when v is not in L. So, we'll play a trick: we'll add v to the end of L before searching so that we're guaranteed to find it! And we need to remove it before the function exits so that the list looks unchanged at the end:

searchsort/linear_search_3.py

```
def linear_search(v, L):
    '''Return the index of the first occurrence of v in list L, or return len(L)
    if v is not in L.'''

    # Add the sentinel.
    L.append(v)

    i = 0

    # Keep going until we find v.
    while L[i] != v:
        i = i + 1

    # Remove the sentinel.
    L.pop()

    return i
```

Timing the Searches

Here is a program that we used to time the three searches on a list with 1 million values:

searchsort/linear_time_1.py

```
import time
import linear_search_1
import linear_search_2
import linear_search_3

def time_it(search, v, L):
    '''Time how long it takes to run function search to find value v in list L.'''

    t1 = time.time()
    search(v, L)
    t2 = time.time()

    return (t2 - t1) * 1000.
```

---

1. A sentinel is a guard whose job it is to stand watch.

```
def print_times(v, L):
    '''Print the number of milliseconds it takes for linear_search(v, L)
    to run for list.index, basic linear search, the for loop linear search,
    and sentinel search.'''

    # Get list.index's running time.
    t1 = time.time()
    L.index(v)
    t2 = time.time()
    index_time = (t2 - t1) * 1000.

    # Get the other three running times.
    basic_time = time_it(linear_search_1.linear_search, v, L)
    for_time = time_it(linear_search_2.linear_search, v, L)
    sentinel_time = time_it(linear_search_3.linear_search, v, L)

    print "%d\t%.02f\t%.02f\t%.02f\t%.02f" % \
        (v, basic_time, for_time, sentinel_time, index_time)

L = range(1000001)
linear_search_1.linear_search(10, L)
print_times(10, L)
print_times(500000, L)
print_times(1000000, L)
```

Function time_it runs whatever search function it is given on v and L and returns how long the search takes. Function print_times calls time_it with the various linear search functions we have been exploring and prints the search times.

Linear Search Running Time

The running times of the three linear searches with that of Python's list.index are compared in Figure 11.1, on the facing page. This comparison used a list of 1,000,001 items and three test cases: an item near the front, an item roughly in the middle, and the last item. Except for the first case, where the speeds differ by only a few percent points, our basic linear search takes about seven times as long as the one built into Python, and the for loop search and sentinel search take about four times as long.

What is more interesting is the way the *running times* of these functions increase with the number of items they have to examine. Roughly speaking, when they have to look through twice as much data, every one of them takes twice as long. This is reasonable, because indexing

Case	basic	for	sentinel	list.index
First	0.01	0.01	0.03	0.01
Middle	138	69	62	17
Last	273	139	124	35

Figure 11.1: RUNNING TIMES FOR LINEAR SEARCH, MILLISECONDS

a list, adding 1 to an integer, and evaluating the loop control expression require the computer to do a fixed amount of work. Doubling the number of times the loop has to be executed therefore doubles the total number of operations, which in turn should double the total running time. This is why this kind of search is called *linear*: the time to do it grows linearly with the amount of data being processed.

11.2 Binary Search

Is there a faster way to find values than linear search? The answer is yes—we can do much better, provided the list is sorted.

To understand how, think about finding a name in a phone book. You open the book in the middle, glance at a name on the page, and immediately know which half to look in next. After checking only two names, you have eliminated $\frac{3}{4}$ of the numbers in the phone book. Even in a large city like Toronto, whose phone book has hundreds of thousands of entries, finding the name you want takes only a few steps.

This technique is called *binary search*, because each step divides the remaining data into two equal parts: values that come before the one being looked for and values that come after it. To figure out how fast it is, think about how big a list can be searched in a fixed number of steps. One step divides two values; two steps divide four; three steps divide 2^3 = 8, four divide 2^4 = 16, and so on. Turning this around, N values can be searched in roughly $log_2 N$ steps.[2] As shown in Figure 11.2, on the next page, this increases much less quickly than the time needed for linear search.

---

2. More exactly, N values can be searched in $\lceil log_2 N \rceil$ steps, where $\lceil \rceil$ is the ceiling function that rounds a value up to the nearest integer.

N	Steps Required
100	7
1000	10
1,0000	14
10,0000	17
100,000	24
1,000,000	27

Figure 11.2: LOGARITHMIC GROWTH

The key to binary search is to keep track of three parts of the list: the left part, which contains values that come before the value we are searching for; the right part, which contains values that come after the value we are searching for; and the middle part, which contains values that we haven't yet examined—the unknown section. We'll use two variables to keep track of the boundaries: i will mark the index of the first unknown value, and j will mark the index of the last unknown value.

At the beginning of the algorithm, the unknown section makes up the entire list, so we will set i to 0 and j to the length of the list minus one. We are done when that unknown section is empty—when we've examined every item in the list. This happens when i == j + 1—when the values *cross*. (When i == j, there is still one item left in the unknown section.)

To make progress, we will set either i or j to near the middle of the range between them, which is at (i + j) / 2.

Think for a moment about the value at (i + j) / 2. If it is less than v, we need to move i up, while if it is greater than j, we should move j down. But where exactly do we move them? When we move i up, we don't want to set it to the midpoint exactly, because L[i] is not included in the range; instead, we set it to one past the middle, in other words, to (i + j) / 2 + 1. Similarly, when we move j down, we move it to (i + j) / 2 - 1.

The completed function is as follows:

searchsort/binary_search.py

```
def binary_search(v, L):
    """Return the index of the leftmost occurrence of v in list L, or -1 if
    v is not in L."""
```

```
# Mark the left and right indices of the unknown section.
i = 0
j = len(L) - 1

while i != j + 1:
    m = (i + j) / 2
    if L[m] < v:
        i = m + 1
    else:
        j = m - 1

if 0 <= i < len(L) and L[i] == v:
    return i
else:
    return -1
```

Of course, no code is really complete until it has been tested. We tested the various linear searches but did not show the tests; they are similar to these:

`searchsort/binary_test.py`

```
'''Test binary search.'''

import nose
from binary_search import binary_search

# The list to search with.
VALUES = [1, 3, 4, 4, 5, 7, 9, 10]

def test_first():
    '''Test a value at the beginning of the list.'''
    assert binary_search(1, VALUES) == 0

def test_duplicate():
    '''Test a duplicate value.'''
    assert binary_search(4, VALUES) == 2

def test_middle():
    '''Test searching for the middle value.'''
    assert binary_search(5, VALUES) == 4

def test_last():
    '''Test searching for the last value.'''
    assert binary_search(10, VALUES) == 7

def test_missing_start():
    '''Test searching for a missing value at the start.'''
    assert binary_search(-3, VALUES) == -1
```

Case	list.index	binary_search	Ratio
First	0.03	0.05	0.66
Middle	107	0.04	2643
Last	15.73	0.04 (Wow!)	4304

Figure 11.3: RUNNING TIMES FOR BINARY SEARCH

```python
def test_missing_middle():
    '''Test searching for a missing value in the middle.'''
    assert binary_search(2, VALUES) == -1

def test_missing_end():
    '''Test searching for a missing value at the end.'''
    assert binary_search(11, VALUES) == -1

if __name__ == '__main__':
    nose.runmodule()
```

Binary Search Running Time

Binary search is more complicated to write and understand than linear search. Is it fast enough to make the extra effort worthwhile? To find out, we can compare it to list.index. As before, we search for the first, middle, and last items in a list with 100,001 elements.

The results are impressive (see Figure 11.3). Binary search is up to several thousand times faster than its linear counterpart when searching 1 million items. Most important, if we double the number of items, binary search takes only one more iteration, while the time for list.index nearly doubles. Note also that although the time taken for linear search grows in step with the index of the item found, there is no such pattern for binary search. No matter where the item is, it takes the same number of steps.

Built-in Binary Search

The Python standard library's bisect module includes binary search functions that are slightly faster than our binary search. bisect_left returns the index where an item should be inserted in a list to keep it in sorted order, assuming it is sorted to begin with. insort_left actually does the insertion. The word *left* in their name signals that they find the leftmost (lowest index) position where they can do their jobs; the complementary functions bisect_right and insort_right find the rightmost.

563	7590	1708	2142	3323	6197	1985	1316	1824	472
1346	6029	2670	2094	2464	1009	1475	856	3027	4271
3126	1115	2691	4253	1838	828	2403	742	1017	613
3185	2599	2227	896	975	1358	264	1375	2016	452
3292	538	1471	9313	864	470	2993	521	1144	2212
2212	2331	2616	2445	1927	808	1963	898	2764	2073
500	1740	8592	10856	2818	2284	1419	1328	1329	1479

Figure 11.4: ACRES LOST TO FOREST FIRES IN CANADA (IN 000s), 1918–87

11.3 Sorting

Now let's look at a slightly harder problem. Figure 11.4, taken from [Hynnd], shows the number of acres burned in forest fires in Canada from 1918 to 1987. One way to find out how much forest was destroyed in the *N* worst years is to sort the list and then take the last *N* values (Section 10.1, *Sort, Identify Minimums, Get Indices*, on page 201):

`searchsort/sort1.py`

```python
def find_largest(N, L):
    """Return the N largest values in L in order from smallest to largest."""

    copy = L[:]
    copy.sort()
    return copy[:N]
```

This algorithm is short, clean, and easy to understand, but it relies on a bit of black magic. How *does* list.sort work, anyway? And how efficient is it?

It turns out that many sorting algorithms have been developed over the years, each with its own strengths and weaknesses. Broadly speaking, they can be divided into two categories: those that are simple but inefficient and those that are efficient but harder to understand and implement. We'll examine two of the former kind; the rest rely on techniques typically taught in a second course.

Selection Sort

Selection sort works by partitioning the list in two. The section at the front contains values that are now in sorted order; the one at the back contains values that have yet to be sorted. As you can probably guess

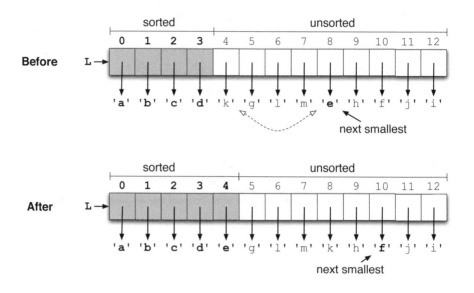

Figure 11.5: SELECTION SORT

from this description, selection sort works by repeatedly finding the next smallest item in the unsorted section and placing it at the end of the sorted section (see Figure 11.5). This works because we are selecting the items in order. We first select the smallest item and move it to the front; then we select the second-smallest item and move it to the second spot, and so on.

Here's the selection sort algorithm, partially in English:

`searchsort/sort2.py`

```python
def selection_sort(L):
    """Reorder the items in L from smallest to largest."""

    i = 0
    while i != len(L):
        # Find the index of the smallest item in L[i:].
        # Swap that smallest item with L[i].
        i = i + 1
```

In this algorithm, i acts as a marker for the beginning of the unsorted section.

We can replace the second comment with a single line of code:[3]

`searchsort/sort3.py`

```python
def selection_sort(L):
    """Reorder the values in L from smallest to largest."""

    i = 0
    while i != len(L):
        # Find the index of the smallest item in L[i:].
        L[i], L[smallest] = L[smallest], L[i]
        i = i + 1
```

Now all that's left is finding the index of the smallest item in L[i:]. This is complex enough that it's worth putting it in a function of its own:

`searchsort/sort4.py`

```python
def selection_sort(L):
    """Reorder the values in L from smallest to largest."""

    i = 0
    while i != len(L):
        smallest = find_min(L, i)
        L[i], L[smallest] = L[smallest], L[i]
        i = i + 1

def find_min(L, b):
    """Return the index of the smallest value in L[b:]."""

    smallest = b # The index of the smallest so far.
    i = b + 1
    while i != len(L):
        if L[i] < L[smallest]:
            # We found a smaller item at L[i].
            smallest = i

        i = i + 1

    return smallest
```

Function find_min runs along L[b:], keeping track of the index of the minimum item so far in variable smallest. When it finds a smaller item, it updates smallest.

---

3. Most Python programmers would probably write the loop header as for i in range(len(L)), rather than incrementing i explicitly in the body of the loop. We're doing the latter here to make it clearer when the loop ends and to show why.

As always, our function isn't done until it has been tested:

searchsort/sort4test.py

```python
from sort4 import selection_sort
import nose

def run_test(original, expected):
    '''Sort list original and compare it to list expected.'''
    selection_sort(original)
    assert original == expected

def test_empty():
    '''Test sorting empty list.'''
    run_test([], [])

def test_one():
    '''Test sorting a list of one value.'''
    run_test([1], [1])

def test_two_ordered():
    '''Test sorting an already-sorted list of two values.'''
    run_test([1, 2], [1, 2])

def test_two_reversed():
    '''Test sorting a reverse-ordered list of two values.'''
    run_test([2, 1], [1, 2])

def test_three_identical():
    '''Test sorting a list of three equal values.'''
    run_test([3, 3, 3], [3, 3, 3])

def test_three_split():
    '''Test sorting a list with an odd value out.'''
    run_test([3, 0, 3], [0, 3, 3])

if __name__ == '__main__':
    nose.runmodule()
```

Insertion Sort

Like selection sort, *insertion sort* keeps a sorted section at the beginning of the list. Rather than scan all of the unsorted section for the next smallest item, though, it takes the next item from the unsorted section and inserts it where it belongs in the sorted section.

In outline, this is as follows:

searchsort/sort5.py

```python
def insertion_sort(L):
    """Reorder the values in L from smallest to largest."""
```

```
i = 0
while i != len(L):
    # Insert L[i] where it belongs in L[0:i+1].
    i = i + 1
```

This is exactly the same code as for selection sort; the difference is in the comment in the loop.

How does insert work? It works by finding out where L[b] belongs and then moving it. Where does it belong? It belongs after every value less than or equal to it and before every value that is greater than it.[4] We need the check i != 0 in case L[b] is smaller than every value in L[0:b]:

searchsort/sort7.py

```
def insertion_sort(L):
    """Reorder the values in L from smallest to largest."""

    i = 0
    while i != len(L):
        insert(L, i)
        i = i + 1

def insert(L, b):
    """Insert L[b] where it belongs in L[0:b + 1];
       L[0:b - 1] must already be sorted."""

    # Find where to insert L[b] by searching backwards from L[b] for a smaller item.
    i = b
    while i != 0 and L[i - 1] >= L[b]:
        i = i - 1

    # Move L[b] to index i, shifting the following values to the right.
    value = L[b]
    del L[b]
    L.insert(i, value)
```

This passes all the tests we wrote earlier for selection sort.

Performance

We have two algorithms of roughly equal complexity. Which should we use?

---

4. We could equally well say "After every value less than it and before every value that is greater than or equal to it." This would produce a slightly different function, but the end result would still be a sorted list.

It's easy enough to write a program to compare their running times, along with that for list.sort:

`searchsort/sort_time.py`

```python
import time
from sort4 import selection_sort
from sort7 import insertion_sort
from ms import mergesort

def built_in(L):
    '''Call list.sort --- we need our own function to do this
    so that we can treat it as we treat our own sorts.'''
    L.sort()

def print_times(L):
    '''Print the number of milliseconds it takes for selection sort
    and insertion sort to run.'''

    print len(L),
    for func in (selection_sort, insertion_sort, mergesort, built_in):
        if func in (selection_sort, insertion_sort) and len(L) > 4000:
            continue

        L_copy = L[:]
        t1 = time.time()
        func(L_copy)
        t2 = time.time()
        print "\t%.1f" % ((t2 - t1) * 1000.),
    print

for list_size in [10, 1000, 2000, 3000, 4000, 5000, 10000, 20000, 40000, 80000]:
    L = range(list_size)
    L.reverse()
    print_times(L)
```

The results are shown in Figure 11.6, on the facing page. Something is very clearly wrong, because our sorting functions are tens of thousands of times slower than the built-in function. What's more, the time required by our routines is growing faster than the size of the data. On 1,000 items, for example, selection sort takes about 0.5 milliseconds per item, but on 10,000 items, it needs about 4 milliseconds per item—an eightfold increase! What is going on?

To answer this, we examine what happens in the inner loops of our two algorithms. On the first iteration of selection sort, the inner loop examines *every* element to find the smallest. On the second iteration, it looks at all but one; on the third, it looks at all but two, and so on.

List Length	Selection Sort	Insertion Sort	list.sort
10	0.1	0.1	0.0
1000	481	300	0.1
2000	1640	1223	0.2
3000	3612	2772	0.4
4000	6536	4957	0.6
5000	10112	7736	0.6
10000	40763	32382	1.3

Figure 11.6: RUNNING TIMES FOR SELECTION AND INSERTION SORT, MILLISECONDS

If there are N items in the list, then the number of iterations of the inner loop, in total, is roughly $N + (N\text{-}1) + (N\text{-}2) + ... + 1$, or $\frac{N(N+1)}{2}$. Putting it another way, the number of steps required to sort N items is roughly proportional to N^2+N. For large values of N, we can ignore the second term and say that the time needed by selection sort grows as the square of the number of values being sorted. And indeed, examining the timing data further shows that doubling the size of the list increases the running time by four.

The same analysis can be used for insertion sort, since it also examines one element on the first iteration, two on the second, and so on. (It's just examining the already-sorted values, rather than the unsorted values.)

So, why is insertion sort slightly faster? The reason is that, on average, only half of the values need to be scanned in order to find the location in which to insert the new value, while with selection sort, *every* value in the unsorted section needs to be examined in order to select the smallest one. *But, wow, list.sort is so much faster!*

11.4 More Efficient Sorting Algorithms

The analysis of selection and insertion sort begs the question: how can list.sort be so much more efficient? The answer is the same as it was for binary search: by taking advantage of the fact that some values are already sorted.

N	N^2	$Nlog_2N$
10	100	3.32
100	10,000	6.64
1000	1,000,000	9.96

Figure 11.7: SORTING TIMES

A First Attempt

Consider the following function:

searchsort/binsort.py

```python
import bisect

def bin_sort(values):
    '''Sort values, creating a new list.'''
    result = []
    for v in values:
        bisect.insort_left(result, v)
    return result
```

This code uses bisect.insort_left to figure out where to put each value from the original list into a new list that is kept in sorted order. As we have already seen, doing this takes time proportional to log_2N, where N is the length of the list. Since N values have to be inserted, the overall running time ought to be $Nlog_2N$. As shown in Figure 11.7, this grows much more slowly with the length of the list than N^2.

Unfortunately, there's a flaw in this analysis. It's correct to say that bisect.insort_left needs only log_2N time to figure out where to insert a value, but actually inserting it takes time as well. To create an empty slot in the list, we have to move all the values above that slot up one place. On average, this means copying half of the list's values, so the cost of insertion is proportional to N. Since there are N values to insert, our total time is $N(N + log_2N)$. For large values of N, this is once again roughly proportional to N^2.

11.5 Mergesort: An $Nlog_2N$ Algorithm

There are several well-known fast sorting algorithms; mergesort, quicksort, and heapsort are the ones you are most likely to encounter in a future CS course. Most of them involve techniques that we haven't yet taught you, but mergesort can be written to be more accessible. Mergesort is built around the idea that taking two sorted lists and merging them is proportional to the number of items in both lists. We'll start with very small lists and keep merging them until we have a single sorted list.

Merging Two Sorted Lists

Given two lists L1 and L2, we can produce a new sorted list by running along L1 and L2 and comparing pairs of elements.

Here is the code for merge:

`searchsort/merge.py`

```python
def merge(L1, L2):
    """Merge sorted lists L1 and L2 and return the result."""

    newL = []
    i1 = 0
    i2 = 0

    # For each pair of items L1[1], L2[i2], copy the smaller into newL.
    while i1 != len(L1) and i2 != len(L2):
        if L1[i1] <= L2[i2]:
            newL.append(L1[i1])
            i1 += 1
        else:
            newL.append(L2[i2])
            i2 += 1

    # Gather any leftover items from the two sections.
    # Note that one of them will be empty because of the loop condition.
    newL.extend(L1[i1:])
    newL.extend(L2[i2:])

    return newL
```

i1 and i2 are the indices into L1 and L2, respectively; in each iteration, we compare L1[i1] to L2[i2] and copy the smaller item to the resulting list. At the end of the loop, we have run out of items in one of the two lists, and the two extend calls will append the rest of the items to the result.

Mergesort

Here is the header for mergesort:

`searchsort/mergesort_header.py`

```python
def mergesort(L):
    """Sort L in increasing order."""
```

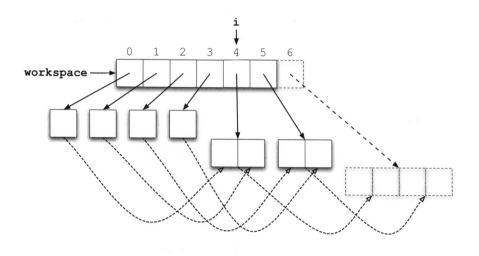

Figure 11.8: LIST OF LISTS IN MERGESORT

Mergesort uses function merge to do the bulk of the work. Here is the algorithm, which creates and keeps track of a list of lists:

- Take list L, and make a list of one-item lists from it.

- As long as there are two lists left to merge, merge them, and append the new list to the list of lists.

The first step is straightforward:

```
searchsort/mergesort_make_list.py
```

```python
# Make a list of 1-item lists so that we can start merging.
workspace = []
for i in range(len(L)):
    workspace.append([L[i]])
```

The second step is trickier. If we remove the two lists, then we'll run into the same problem that we ran into in binsort: all the following lists will need to shift over, which takes time proportional to the number of lists.

Instead, we'll keep track of the index of the next two lists to merge. Initially, they will be at indices 0 and 1, and then 2 and 3, and so on (Figure 11.9, on page 228). Here's our refined algorithm:

- Take list L, and make a list of one-item lists from it.

- Start index i off at 0.

- As long as there are two lists, at indices i and i + 1, merge them, append the new list to the list of lists, and increment i by 2.

With that, we can go straight to code:

searchsort/mergesort_function.py

```
def mergesort(L):
    """Sort L."""

    # Make a list of 1-item lists so that we can start merging.
    workspace = []
    for i in range(len(L)):
        workspace.append([L[i]])

    # The next two lists to merge are workspace[i] and workspace[i + 1].
    i = 0

    # As long as there are at least two more lists to merge, merge them.
    while i < len(workspace) - 1:
        L1 = workspace[i]
        L2 = workspace[i + 1]
        newL = merge(L1, L2)
        workspace.append(newL)
        i += 2

    # Copy the result back into L.
    if len(workspace) != 0:
        L[:] = workspace[-1][:]
```

Notice that, since we're always making new lists, we need to copy the last of the merged lists back into parameter L.

Mergesort Analysis

Mergesort, it turns out, is $Nlog_2N$, where N is the number of items in L. It may help to refer to Figure 11.9, on the next page.

The first part of the function, creating the list of one-item lists, takes N iterations, one for each item.

The second loop, in which we continually merge lists, will take some care to analyze. We'll start with the very last iteration, in which we are merging two lists with about $\frac{N}{2}$ items. As we've seen, function merge copies each element into its result exactly once, so with these two lists, this merge step takes roughly N steps.

On the previous iteration, there are two lists of size $\frac{N}{4}$ to merge into one of the two lists of size $\frac{N}{2}$, and on the iteration before that there are another two lists of size $\frac{N}{2}$ to merge into the second list of size $\frac{N}{2}$. Each

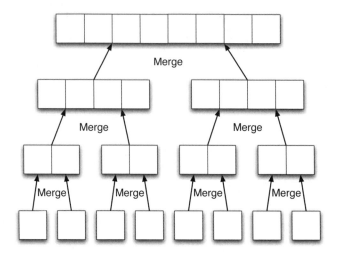

Figure 11.9: STEPS IN MERGESORT

of these two merges takes roughly $\frac{N}{2}$ steps, so the two together take roughly N steps in total.

On the iteration before that, there are a total of eight lists of size $\frac{N}{8}$ to merge into the four lists of size $\frac{N}{4}$. Four merges of this size together also take roughly N steps.

We can subdivide a list with N items a total of log_2N times, using an analysis much like we used for binary search. Since at each "level" there are a total of N items to be merged, each of these log_2N levels takes roughly N steps. Hence, mergesort take time proportional to $Nlog_2N$.

11.6 Summary

In this chapter, we learned the following:

- Linear search is the simplest way to find a value in a list, but on average, the time required is directly proportional to the length of the list.

- Binary search is much faster—the average time is proportional to the logarithm of the list's length—but it works only if the list is in sorted order.

Big-Oh and All That

Our method of analyzing the performance of searching and sorting algorithms might seem like hand-waving, but there is actually a well-developed mathematical theory behind it. If f and g are functions, then the expression $f(x) = O(g(x))$ is read "f is big-oh of g" and means that for sufficiently large values of x, $f(x)$ is bounded above by some constant multiple of $g(x)$, or equivalently that the function g gives us an upper bound on the values of the function f. Computer scientists use this to group algorithms into families, such as those sorting functions that execute in N^2 time and those that execute in $Nlog_2 N$ time.

These distinctions have important practical applications. In particular, one of the biggest puzzles in theoretical computer science today is whether two families of algorithms (called P and NP for reasons that we won't go into here) are the same or not. Almost everyone thinks they are not, but no one has been able to prove it (despite the offer of a million-dollar prize for the first correct proof). If it turns out that they *are* the same, then many of the algorithms used to encrypt data in banking and military applications (as well as on the Web) will be much more vulnerable to attack than expected.

- Similarly, the average running time of simple sorting algorithms like selection sort is proportional to the square of the input size N, while the running time of more complex sorting algorithms grows as $Nlog_2 N$.

- Looking at how the running time of an algorithm grows as a function of the size of its inputs is the standard way to analyze and compare algorithms' efficiency.

11.7 Exercises

Here are some exercises for you to try on your own:

1. Binary search is significantly faster than the built-in search but requires that the list is sorted. As you know, the running time for the best sorting algorithm is on the order of $Nlog_2 N$, where N is the length of the list. If we search a lot of times on the same list of data, it makes sense to sort it once before doing the searching; roughly

how many times do we need to search in order to make sorting and then searching faster, instead of using the built-in search?

2. Given the unsorted list [6, 5, 4, 3, 7, 1, 2], show what the contents of the list would be after each iteration of the loop as it is sorted using the following:

   a) Selection sort

   b) Insertion sort

3. Another sorting algorithm is *bubble sort*. Bubble sort involves keeping a sorted section at the end of the list. The list is traversed, pairs of elements are compared, and larger elements are swapped into the higher position. This is repeated until all element are sorted.

   a) Using the English description of bubble sort, write an outline of the bubble sort algorithm in English.

   b) Continue using top-down design until you have a Python algorithm.

   c) Turn it into a function bubble_sort(L).

   d) Write Nose test cases for bubble_sort.

4. In the description of bubble sort in the previous question, the sorted section of the list was at the end of the list. In this question, bubble sort will maintain the sorted section of the beginning of the list. Make sure that you are still implementing bubble sort!

   a) Rewrite the English description of bubble sort from the previous question with the necessary changes so that the sorted elements are at the beginning of the list instead of the end.

   b) Using your English description of bubble sort, write an outline of the bubble sort algorithm in English.

   c) Write the bubble_sort_2(L) function.

   d) Write Nose test cases for bubble_sort_2.

5. Modify the timing program to compare bubble sort with insertion and selection sort. Explain the results.

6. Modify the timing program to compare Python's built-in list.sort method with insertion and selection sort. Clearly, the built-in sort does not use insertion, selection, or bubble sort; instead, some

advanced tricks are being used in order to get a huge speedup. You will learn these tricks in your next computer science course.

7. The analysis of bin_sort said, "Since N values have to be inserted, the overall running time is $Nlog_2N$." Point out a flaw in this reasoning, and explain whether it affects the overall conclusion.

8. There are at least two ways to come up with loop conditions. One of them is to answer the question "When is the work done?" and then negate it. In function merge in Section 11.5, *Merging Two Sorted Lists*, on page 225, the answer is "when we run out of items in one of the two lists," which is described by this expression: i1 == len(L1) or i2 == len(L2). Negating this leads to our condition i1 != len(L1) and i2 != len(L2).

   Another way to come up with a loop condition is to ask "What are the valid values of the loop index?" In function merge, the answer to this is 0 <= i1 < len(L1) and 0 <= i2 < len(L2); since i1 and i2 start a zero, we can drop the comparisons with zero, giving us i1 < len(L1) and i2 < len(L2).

   Is there another way to do it? Have you tried both approaches? Which do you prefer?

9. In function mergesort in Section 11.5, *Mergesort*, on page 225, there are two calls to extend. They are there because, when the preceding loop ends, one of the two lists still has items in it that have not been processed. Rewrite that loop so that these extend calls are not needed.

Chapter 12

Construction

A good scientist can do a lot with a handheld magnifying glass and a pair of tweezers. However, she can do a lot more with a fully equipped lab. The same is true for programming. In theory, you can write any program at all using nothing but arithmetic and conditionals, but useful software is a lot easier to build if you have more tools at your disposal.

This chapter will introduce a few of those tools. Some are part of the Python language and will allow you to code something using a couple of statements that might otherwise take up an entire page. Others are mental tools, such as testing and debugging techniques, ways to handle errors, and patterns worth naming because they come up so frequently. Together, they help you become more fluent as a programmer.

12.1 More on Functions

Good programmers break their code down into functions that can be reused. Therefore, it's not surprising that Python (as well as other languages) provides a number of tools for making functions more flexible.

Default Parameter Values

Default parameter values are the first of these tools. Here's an example:

`construct/default_define.py`

```python
def total(values, start=0, end=None):
    '''Add up the values in a list. If none are given, the total is zero. If
    'start' is not specified, start at the beginning. If 'end' is specified,
    go up to but not including that index; otherwise, go to the end of the
    list.'''
```

```
    if not values:
        return 0

    if end is None:
        end = len(values)

    result = 0
    for i in range(start, end):
        result += values[i]
    return result
```

This function has three parameters: a list of values and two indices that specify which part of the list to sum up. What makes it different is that start and end are "assigned" default values in the definition. If the caller doesn't override them, Python uses those defaults when the function is called. This means that the function can be called with one, two, or three parameters, as shown here:

construct/default_call.cmd

```
>>> numbers = [10, 20, 30]
>>> print "total(numbers, 0, 3):", total(numbers, 0, 3)
total(numbers, 0, 3): 60
>>> print "total(numbers, 2):", total(numbers, 2)
total(numbers, 2): 30
>>> print "total(numbers):", total(numbers)
total(numbers): 60
```

Specifying default parameter values often makes functions easier to use. If we didn't let callers specify start and end indices for total, they would have to slice their lists whenever they wanted to add up only a subset of values:

```
most = total(values[1:-1]) # add up all but the first and last
```

This is no extra typing but is less efficient, since slicing copies the values in the list. On the other hand, if total always required callers to specify start and end indices, then the most common case—summing up the whole list—would require more typing:

```
all = total(values, 0, len(values)) # more typing and harder to read
```

When you give a function's parameters default values, parameters without default values must come before those that that do. This is because when a function is called, values are matched with parameters from left to right; defaults are used only for those that are "left over" at the end of the parameter list. If Python were to let you define a function like this:

```
# Illegal!
def total(start=0, values, end=None):
    ...body as shown before...
```

then the call total(x) could be interpreted as either of these:

1. Assign the value of x to start, and then report an error because nothing has been assigned to values.

2. Assign 0 to start and the value of x to values.

The second is probably what the caller wanted, but the computer can't know that. Worse, with more parameters, there is a greater chance of confusing one parameter (or one kind of parameter) for another. Thus, the left-to-right rule described earlier lets everyone involved—the function's creator and its user—keep track of which values will be assigned to which parameters.

One note before we leave this example: if you look closely at total's definition, you'll see that start's default value is 0 (which is a legal index), but end's is None (which is not). Why not assign end a more useful default, such as len(values)? The answer is that we can't, because Python evaluates the default value when the function is defined, and at that point, we don't know what list is going to be passed in for values. We will discuss the implications of this in more detail in the exercises.

Variable Parameter Lists

Default parameter values are useful, but they still aren't enough to let us write functions like max, which can take any number of arguments at all. We *could* do this by requiring callers to pass a list of values, but Python can actually do this for us. Take a close look at the parameter in this function:

`construct/our_max.cmd`

```
>>> def our_max(*values):
...         '''Find the maximum of any number of values.'''
...
...     if not values:
...             return None
...     m = values[0]
...     for v in values[1:]:
...             if v > m:
...                 m = v
...     return m
...
>>> our_max(1)
1
>>> our_max(1, 2)
2
>>> our_max(3, 1, 2, 5, 4, -17)
5
```

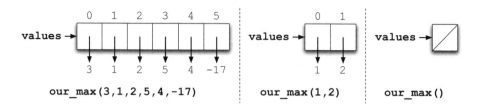

Figure 12.1: HOW VARIABLE ARGUMENTS WORK

The key here is the * in front of values. This tells Python to take all the arguments passed into the call, put them in a tuple, and assign that tuple to values. For example, if we call our_max(1, 2), values is assigned (1, 2); when our_max is called with six values, values is assigned a six-element tuple, while if no arguments are provided, values is assigned an empty tuple (see Figure 12.1).

A starred parameter does not always have to appear on its own. Functions are free to define any number of regular parameters before it. These are matched up with the actual arguments as usual, and anything left over is then placed in the tuple assigned to the starred parameter:

construct/append_all.cmd

```
>>> def append_all(old, *new):
...     for n in new:
...         old.append(n)
...     return old
...
>>> values = []
>>> append_all(values, 1, 2, 3)
[1, 2, 3]
>>> append_all(values) # not actually appending anything
[1, 2, 3]
```

One thing Python *doesn't* allow is two or more starred arguments in a single function, because matching values to them would be ambiguous. For example, if a function is defined as follows:

```
# Illegal!
def f(*front, *back):
    ...body of function...
```

and then called with f(1, 2, 3), there are four possible assignments of the actual arguments to the parameters:

- a=(1, 2, 3), b=()

- a=(1, 2), b=(3,)

- a=(1,), b=(2, 3)

- a=(), b=(1, 2, 3)

Python also doesn't allow "regular" parameters to be defined after a starred parameter:

```
# Illegal!
def f(*front, y, z):
    ...body of function...
```

There's no technical reason to disallow this, because Python could match actual arguments to parameters right-to-left instead of left-to-right and then put the remainder in the starred parameter. On the other hand, there's no particular reason to allow it, either. Everything that can be done this way can be done by defining the starred parameter at the end of the parameter list.

Named Parameter

Python provides yet another way to call functions. Instead of passing arguments in a particular order, they can be paired with parameters by name, like this:

construct/named_params.cmd

```
>>> def describe_creature(name, species, age, weight):
...     return '%s (%s): %d years, %d kg' % (name, species, age, weight)
...
>>> print describe_creature(name='Charles Darwin', species='Homo sapiens',
                            age=28, weight=70)
Charles Darwin (Homo sapiens): 28 years, 70 kg
```

Why would we do this? Because if we specify arguments by name, we can put them in any order we want and get the same result:

construct/named_params_2.cmd

```
>>> print describe_creature(weight=70, species='Homo sapiens',
                            age=28, name='Charles Darwin')
Charles Darwin (Homo sapiens): 28 years, 70 kg
```

Being able to do this is particularly useful when working with functions that have a very large number of parameters. As we will see in Chapter 14, *Graphical User Interfaces*, on page 291, for example, a function that displays text in a GUI can take a dozen or more parameters to specify font, weight, colors, borders, and so on. In these cases, it is easier (and more readable) to specify the parameter names explicitly than to remember whether the border thickness comes before the border color, or vice versa.

12.2 Exceptions

Our next tool is a standard way of dealing with errors in programs. As you have no doubt discovered by now, Python doesn't like it when you try to use an out-of-bounds index into a list, use a key not in a dictionary, or use a string where you need an integer.

In each of these cases, Python reports the error by creating an *exception* that contains information about what went wrong. The program can deal with the exception right where it occurs or handle it somewhere else; it can also handle exceptions occurring in many different places in one location. As we'll see, this allows programmers to separate "normal" code from error-handling code, which makes both easier to read.

try and except

Consider this short program:

`construct/simpletry.cmd`

```
>>> try:
...     x = 1/0.3
...     print 'reciprocal of 0.3 is', x
...     x = 1/0.0
...     print 'reciprocal of 0.0 is', x
... except:
...     print 'error: no reciprocal'
reciprocal of 0.3 is 3.33333333333
error: no reciprocal
```

The keywords try and except are used for error handling, just like if and else are used for conditionals. If nothing goes wrong, Python executes the code in the try block and then skips over the except block entirely (see Figure 12.2, on the facing page). If any exceptions are *raised* in the try block, Python immediately jumps to the start of the except block and executes the code inside it. When this happens, we say that the exception has been *caught* and refer to the code that deals with it as an *exception handler*. Statements in the try block after the statement that raised the exception are *not* executed.

```
try:                                    try:
 ❶ x = 1/0.3                             ❶ x = 1/0.3
 ❷ print 'reciprocal of 0.3 is', x       ❷ print 'reciprocal of 0.3 is', x
except:                                  ❸ x = 1/0.0
    print 'error: no reciprocal'            print 'reciprocal of 0.0 is', x
                                         except:
 ❸ (rest of program)                      ❹ print 'error: no reciprocal'

                                          ❺ (rest of program)

         No Error                                Division By Zero
```

Figure 12.2: A SIMPLE TRY/EXCEPT

We can also tell Python what to do when an exception *isn't* raised by adding an else block to the try/except:

```
construct/exceptelse.cmd
```
```
>>> def invert(x):
...     try:
...         i = 1.0 / x
...     except:
...         print 'caught exception for', x
...     else:
...         print 'reciprocal of', x, 'is', i
...
>>> invert(1)
reciprocal of 1 is 1.0
>>> invert(0)
caught exception for 0
```

Here, the statements in the else block are executed only if everything inside the try block was executed without error. If we were sure we knew all the places that exceptions could be thrown, we could put these statements inside the try block. Even then, it is often clearer to put them in an else block so that people reading the code can see that these statements are to be executed only if the try block completed normally.

Exception Objects

When Python raises an exception, it creates an object to hold information about what went wrong. Typically, this object will contain an error message, along with a filename and line number to help the programmer pinpoint the problem.

Different kinds of errors raise exceptions of different types, which allows a program to choose which kinds of errors to handle by specifying an exception type in the except. For example:

`construct/excepttype.cmd`

```
>>> values = [-1, 0, 1]
>>> for i in range(4):    # one more than len(values)
...     try:
...         r = 1.0 / values[i]
...         print 'reciprocal of', values[i], 'at', i, 'is', r
...     except IndexError:
...         print 'index', i, 'out of range'
...     except ArithmeticError:
...         print 'unable to calculate reciprocal of', values[i]
reciprocal of -1 at 0 is -1.0
unable to calculate reciprocal of 0
reciprocal of 1 at 2 is 1.0
index 3 out of range
```

Here, the first except block handles only indexing errors; arithmetic errors (such as dividing by zero) are handled by the second block. If we want to know exactly what went wrong, we must modify the except statement so that Python knows which variable to assign the exception object to:

`construct/exceptobj.cmd`

```
>>> values = [-1, 0, 1]
>>> for i in range(4):    # one more than len(values)
...     try:
...         r = 1.0 / values[i]
...         print 'reciprocal of', values[i], 'at', i, 'is', r
...     except IndexError, e:
...         print 'error:', e
...     except ArithmeticError, e:
...         print 'error:', e
reciprocal of -1 at 0 is -1.0
error: float division
reciprocal of 1 at 2 is 1.0
error: list index out of range
```

Python tests except blocks in order. Whichever matches first gets to handle the exception. The order matters because exceptions are arranged in a hierarchy, as shown in Figure 12.3, on the next page. This allows a program to handle ZeroDivisionErrors one way and all other ArithmeticErrors another, but only if the handler for the first comes before the handler for the second. An except that doesn't specify an exception class catches everything, so if there is one, it must appear last, like the else in an if-elif-else chain.

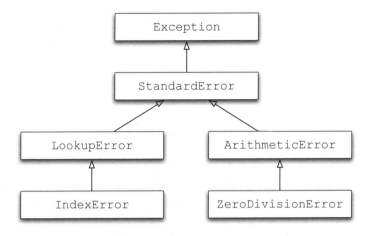

Figure 12.3: EXCEPTION HIERARCHY

Functions and Exceptions

What if Python can't find a matching exception handler in a particular try/except block? For example, what happens when Python tries to divide by zero in the following code?

```
construct/uncaught.py
values = [-1, 0, 1]
for i in range(4):    # one more than len(values)
    try:
        r = 1.0 / values[i]
        print 'reciprocal of', values[i], 'at', i, 'is', r
    except IndexError, e:
        print 'error:', e
```

The answer is that Python keeps a stack of exception handlers, just like its stack of function calls (see Figure 12.4, on the following page). When an exception is raised, Python takes handlers off the exception handler stack one by one until it finds a handler that matches and then executes it. This means that the code to handle an exception can be a long way away from the place where the exception occurred. It also means that one exception handler can take care of exceptions from many pieces of code.

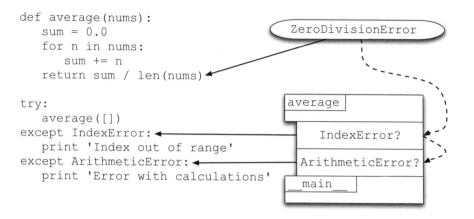

```
def average(nums):
    sum = 0.0
    for n in nums:
        sum += n
    return sum / len(nums)

try:
    average([])
except IndexError:
    print 'Index out of range'
except ArithmeticError:
    print 'Error with calculations'
```

Figure 12.4: THE EXCEPTION HANDLER STACK

For example, suppose we are using several functions that calculate statistics on numbers stored in lists. Some of those functions might raise exceptions because of division by zero. We don't particularly care which function call is at fault, so we can deal with them all at once like this:

`construct/exceptfunc.cmd`

```
def average(nums):
    sum = 0.0
    for n in nums:
        sum += n
    return sum / len(nums)

...other function definitions skipped...

values = read_values_from_file()
try:
    print 'average:', average(values)
    print 'median:', median(values)
    print 'standard deviation:', std_dev(values)
except ArithmeticError:
    print 'Error in calculations'
```

As you can see, the code that handles the error is outside the functions that are doing the work. This means that the functions can focus on doing their jobs and let whoever is calling them worry about how to handle mistakes.

Raising Exceptions

You don't have to wait for Python to notice that something has gone wrong—you can raise an exception yourself using the raise keyword, followed by the type of exception that you want to raise. When you do this, it's good style to include an error message to explain what went wrong:

`construct/raise.cmd`

```
>>> def divide(top, bottom):
...     if bottom == 0:
...         raise ValueError('divisor is zero')
...     else:
...         return top / bottom
...
>>> for i in range(-1, 2):
...     try:
...         print divide(1, i)
...     except ValueError, e:
...         print 'caught exception for', i
...
-1
caught exception for 0
1
```

You will still sometimes see the raise statement written like this:

```
raise ValueError, 'divisor is zero'
```

However, that style is now *deprecated*; that is, Python's creator has said that it will be removed from the language one day, so new programs shouldn't use it (and old ones should be fixed).

Exceptional Style

When working with exceptions, you should always follow two rules. First, always indicate errors in functions by raising exceptions, rather than returning None, -1, False, or some other "special" value.[1] This adds clarity by separating error-handling code from "normal" code; in addition, experience shows that, sooner or later, you are going to want some of your functions to return those special values, at which point you will have no way of distinguishing success from failure. Alternatively, you

---

1. Note that Python's own str.find breaks this rule by returning -1 if something can't be found instead of throwing an exception. In this case, practicality beats purity. Returning -1 is only slightly more efficient than raising an exception, but substring searches are so common that Python's designers decided it was worth it.

will need to completely rewrite the code so that it both raises exceptions and returns the appropriate values.

The second rule is often phrased as, "Throw low, catch high." This means that you should throw lots of very specific exceptions in the lower levels of your program but catch them only at a higher level in the exception hierarchy where you can take corrective action. For example, instead of writing code like this:

```
def first():
    try:
        ...body of first function...
    except Exception, e:
        print 'error occurred', e

def second():
    try:
        ...body of second function...
    except Exception, e:
        print 'error occurred', e

if __name__ == '__main__':
    first()
    second()
```

a programmer should write this:

```
def first():
    ...body of first function...

def second():
    ....body of second function...

if __name__ == '__main__':
    try:
        first()
        second()
    except Exception, e:
        print 'error occurred', e
```

Handling errors in a small number of places like this makes it easy to change the way they are handled. If, for example, you decide to write application errors to a log file as well as print them to the screen, you have to change only one piece of code in the second example. Similarly, if this program were made part of a larger application with a graphical interface that required errors to be displayed in dialogs rather than on the command line, there would be exactly one place to make the change.

12.3 Testing

Now that we have looked at how to deal with errors, we can discuss
how to test programs so that they don't happen. The first thing to point
out is that testing on its own is not enough to produce high-quality
software. As Steve McConnell said in [McC04], "Trying to improve the
quality of software by doing more testing is like trying to lose weight by
weighing yourself more often." Every time you sit down to test a piece
of software, you should therefore start by asking yourself a few simple
questions: What kind of problem am I looking for? What's the most
efficient way to find out if the problem exists?

Terminology

Let's start by defining some terms. A *functional test* looks at the behavior of the system as a whole, just as its eventual users will. A *unit test*
exercises just one isolated component of a program. For example, here's
a simple-minded unit test of a function that compares two strings and
returns -1, 0, or 1 if the first comes before, is the same as, or comes
after the second alphabetically:

construct/compare_strings.py

```python
if my_compare('abc', 'def') == -1:
    print 'success'
else:
    print 'failure'
```

In Nose, this would be as follows:

construct/compare_strings_nose.py

```python
import nose

def test_compare():
    '''Test comparison of unequal strings.'''

    assert my_compare('abc', 'def') == -1

if __name__ == '__main__':
    nose.runmodule()
```

Two more frequently used terms are *black-box testing* and *glass-box
testing*. As the name suggests, black-box testing considers only the
inputs and outputs of the code being tested, not its implementation.
(The term is borrowed from electrical engineering, where a black box is
often the thing being tested.) In glass-box testing, on the other hand,
the tester is able to look inside the program and see how it works.

Glass-box testing may sound more effective, since the tester is able to see which parts of the code to stress. In practice, though, knowing how something is implemented often leads to psychological bias. Thus, it is therefore often better to treat the code the same way its eventual users will and test it by comparing its actual behavior to its specification.

Regression testing is another term that comes up fairly often. It is the practice of rerunning tests to make sure that recent changes haven't broken anything. Regression testing is practical only if the tests are automated and if changes to program behavior are relatively infrequent. If the first condition doesn't hold, then human beings must retest manually every time the program changes. This is boring, expensive, and error-prone, so in practice, most projects don't do it.

The second condition is a corollary of the first. If the program's behavior is changing on a daily basis, then the project's automated tests have to be rewritten every day as well, which cancels out the advantages of automation. This is one of the main reasons why it's important to spend time up front on design before writing code.

Unit Testing

For now we will focus on unit testing, since that's what programmers do while they're programming. If you would like to know more, [AW06, Whi03, WT04] are practical guides on what to look for in desktop and web applications and how to find security holes.

As discussed in Section 4.5, *Testing*, on page 61, a unit test can have one of three outcomes: pass, fail, or error. To classify a result, though, you must know how the code being tested is supposed to behave; that is, you must have some kind of *specification*. The more precise that specification is, the easier it will be to determine whether the code is doing what it's supposed to do.

Independence

For unit testing to be useful, every test must be *independent*; in other words, the outcome of one test must not depend on the outcome of other tests. There are two reasons for this. First, if this rule is violated, then every time we change a test that runs early, we have to check all subsequent tests to see whether they have been affected. The second, and more important, reason is that failures in early tests can hide bugs that later tests are supposed to find.

For example, try running this code:

construct/test_side_effects.py

```python
import nose

numbers = [1, 3, -1, 5]

def test_max():
    assert max(numbers) == 5

def test_min():
    assert min(numbers) == -1

def test_append():
    old_len = len(numbers)
    numbers.append(99)
    assert len(numbers) == old_len + 1

if __name__ == '__main__':
    nose.runmodule()
```

If Nose decides to run the tests in the order they're given, everything will be OK. But if Nose runs the tests in a different order or if someone decides to put the tests in alphabetical order, test_max will suddenly start to fail, because test_append is changing the values it is being run on.[2] As a rule, therefore, the data structures manipulated in the test, called its *fixture*, should be used only once.

Limitations

Now for the bad news. In practice, it's practically impossible to completely test any nontrivial piece of software. Suppose that you have a function that compares two seven-digit phone numbers and returns True if the first is greater than the second. There are (10^{7^2}) possible inputs; if you can compare 100 million pairs of numbers per second, it will take 15.5 days to check all combinations. If the inputs are seven-character alphabetic strings, rather than numbers, it will take a little more than twenty-five years, and that's just the first function—your program probably contains dozens, or thousands, many of which will be much more complex.

---

2. Of course, part of the problem is the use of the global variable numbers. If each test function used a local variable, it would be safe for test_append to its list.

Luckily, testing isn't as futile as this analysis makes it sound. In practice, it's usually enough to test the following:

- *Boundary cases*, such as sorting an empty list or list containing a single value
- The *Simplest interesting cases*, such as sorting lists containing two values (one where the items are in order and one where they are not)
- The *General cases*, such as sorting a longer list

If your code works for these cases, there's a good chance it will work for all other cases as well.

Of course, you should also test cases that are expected to fail, since error handling is part of a function's specification too. Test with invalid input or too little input or too much, and make sure it fails the way the specification says it should. Finally, do a few sanity checks. If information appears in two or more places, for example, check that all occurrences are still consistent after the action. For example, if a program stores both a list of numbers and their sum, make sure that the sum is still correct after any operation that manipulates the list.

Above all, remember that human beings are creatures of habit; we tend to make the same kinds of errors over and over again. So, good testers will test for common errors first, but great ones build catalogs of errors to refer back to whenever they test a new piece of code. Here are some tests that often turn up problems in code:

- For numbers: Zero; the largest and smallest allowed numbers; one less and one more than the largest and smallest values.
- For data structures: Empty structures; structures containing exactly one element; structures containing the maximum allowed number of elements; structures containing duplicates (for example, a letter appears three times in a string); structures containing aliased values (for example, a sublist appears three times in an outer list).
- For searching: No match found; one match found; multiple matches found; everything matches.

Over time, you'll commit fewer and fewer errors as you catalog them and, subsequently, become more conscious of them. And that's really the whole point of focusing on quality. The more you do it, the less likely it is for problems to arise.

Test-Driven Development

Since the late 1990s, a style of programming called *test-driven development* (TDD) has become increasingly popular. The idea behind it is that tests are actually specifications. Each test says, "Given these inputs, this code should produce this result." Therefore, programmers who practice TDD write their test cases *first* and then write the code to be tested.

This sounds backward, but studies have shown that it can actually make programmers more productive, for several reasons:

- Tests provide a more precise specification than sentences.
- TDD gives programmers a finish line to aim for: a function is finished when its unit tests all pass.
- TDD ensures that tests actually get written, since even the best programmers are often too tired or too rushed to write a good set of tests after the code appears to be working.
- Writing tests first gives programmers a chance to "test-drive" the code they're about to write before actually writing it. For example, if a programmers finds that it's awkward to create tests for the matrix functions she's about to write, she can change the interface before it is set in stone.

As an example of TDD, suppose we need to write a function that calculates a running sum of the values in a list. For example, if the list is $[1, 2, 3]$, the result should be $[1, 1{+}2, 1{+}2{+}3]$, which is $[1, 3, 6]$. This seems simple enough, but look at what's missing: it's not clear if a new list should be created or the old one should be overwritten, and there's no mention of how to handle errors.

Now look at this:

`construct/running_sum_tdd.py`

```python
import nose

def test_empty_list():
    assert running_sum([]) == []

def test_single_value():
    assert running_sum([1]) == [1]

def test_two_values():
    assert running_sum([1, 3]) == [1, 4]

def test_three_values():
    assert running_sum([1, 3, 7]) == [1, 4, 11]
```

```python
def test_negative_values():
    assert running_run([-1, 1]) == [-1, 0]

def test_mixed_types():
    assert running_sum([1, 3.0]) == [1, 4.0]

def test_string():
    try:
        running_sum('string')
        assert False
    except ValueError:
        pass
    except:
        assert False

def test_non_numeric():
    try:
        running_sum(['string'])
        assert False
    except ValueError:
        pass
    except:
        assert False
```

Even without docstrings, these tests tell us that the function

- has to be able to handle a mix of integer and floating-point values,

- doesn't have to add things that aren't numbers, and

- should produce a ValueError exception when given invalid input.

That's a pretty good specification.

12.4 Debugging

As most programmers have discovered, debugging[3] is what you get to do when you didn't do enough testing. Tracking down and eliminating bugs in your programs is part of every programmer's life, so this chapter introduces some techniques that can make debugging more efficient and give you more time to do the things you'd rather be doing.

Debugging a program is like diagnosing a medical condition. To find the cause, you start by working backward from the symptoms (or, in a

---

3. In 1945, Admiral Grace Hopper's team "debugged" Harvard University's Mark II Aiken Relay Calculator by removing a moth trapped in one of the relays. However, the term dates back to at least Thomas Edison's time.

program, its incorrect behavior), then come up with a solution, and test it to make sure it actually fixes the problem.

At least, that's the right way to do it. Many beginners make the mistake of skipping the diagnosis stage and trying to cure the program by changing things at random. Renaming a variable or swapping the order in which two functions are defined might actually fix the program, but millions of such changes are possible. Trying them one after another in no particular order can be an inefficient waste of many, many hours.

Here are some rules for tracking down the cause of a problem:

1. *Make sure you know what the program is supposed to do.* Sometimes this means doing the calculation by hand to see what the correct answer is. Other times, it means reading the documentation (or the assignment) carefully or writing a test.

2. *Repeat the failure.* You can debug things only when they go wrong, so find a test case that makes the program fail reliably. Once you have one, try to find a simpler one; doing this often provides enough clues to allow you to fix the underlying problem.

3. *Divide and conquer.* Once you have a test that makes the program fail, try to find the first moment where something goes wrong. Examine the inputs to the function or block of code where the problem first becomes visible. If they are wrong, look at how they were created, and so on.

4. *Change one thing at a time, for a reason.* Replacing random bits of code on the off-chance they might be responsible for your problem is unlikely to do much good. (After all, you got it wrong the first time....) Each time you make a change, rerun your test cases immediately.

5. *Keep records.* After working on a problem for an hour, you won't be able to remember the results of the tests you've run. Like any other scientist, you should keep records. Some programmers use a lab notebook; others keep a file open in an editor. Whatever works for you, make sure that when the time comes to seek help, you can tell your colleagues exactly what you've learned.

12.5 Patterns

It's hard to figure out what a program is supposed to do if it is cluttered or disorganized. Good design is therefore the most important programming tool of all.

One of the keys to organizing programs is to recognize that variables are usually used in stereotypical ways. Learning to recognize these *variable roles* helps us read code more quickly; it also helps us figure out when something is going wrong. The following sections, taken from [KS04], describe some typical roles.

Fixed Values

As the name suggests, a *fixed value* is a variable whose value doesn't change once it is assigned. Fixed values are often used to give human-readable names to "magic numbers" like 9.81 (Earth-normal gravity in meters per second squared) or 3.14159 (a rough approximation to pi). By convention, they are placed at the top of the program, as in the following example:

`construct/fixedvalue.cmd`

```
>>> SECONDS_PER_DAY = 24 * 60 * 60
>>> instant = 10**3
>>> while instant <= 10**7:
...     print "%10d seconds is %8.2f days" % \
...             (instant, (1.0 * instant / SECONDS_PER_DAY))
...     instant *= 10
     1000 seconds is      0.01 days
    10000 seconds is      0.12 days
   100000 seconds is      1.16 days
  1000000 seconds is     11.57 days
 10000000 seconds is    115.74 days
```

As this example shows, they are also often given uppercase names to make them stand out from "normal" values.

Stepper and Counter

A *stepper* is a variable that "steps through" a sequence of values in some predictable way. The index variables in for loops are almost always steppers; so is the time variable in the previous example. A stepper is very much like a *counter*, but the latter term normally refers to an integer that keeps track of how many things have been seen so far.

Most-Wanted Holder

Normally, we search for a value in a collection by checking each value in turn and keeping a reference to the best one seen so far. That reference is called a *most-wanted holder*, since it holds the value we want most. For example, here's a function that searches for the largest value in a list that is less than some threshold:

`construct/largethresh.py`

```python
def largest_below_threshold(values, threshold):
    '''Find the largest value below a specified threshold. If no value is
    found, returns None.'''

    result = None
    for v in values:
        if v < threshold:
            result = v
            break

    if result is None:
        return None

    for v in values:
        if result < v < threshold:
            result = v
    return result
```

Most-Recent Holder

A *most-recent holder* holds the value most recently seen from some sequence of values. In a sense, a stepper is just a special case of a most-recent holder. The only distinction is that the stepper is stepping through regular values (like the elements of a list), while a most-recent holder is assigned values that can come from anywhere. Here's an example:

`construct/mostrecent.py`

```python
# A really simple number-guessing game
while True:
    input = raw_input('Enter a number: ')
    try:
        val = int(input)
    except ValueError:
        print 'I said, a *number*...'
    if val == 7:
        print 'You guessed it!'
        break
    else:
        print 'Try again'
```

Since users can type in anything they want, this program *validates* the input (in other words, checks that it's at least plausible) before doing anything else with it.

Container

A *container* is a value that holds other values. Lists are clearly containers, but what about strings? They can be containers too, if we find ourselves adding or removing characters:

construct/container.cmd

```
>>> whole = 'selenium'
>>> for i in range(len(whole)/2):
...     print whole
...     whole = whole[1:-1]
selenium
eleniu
leni
ni
```

This example shows that patterns like "stepper" and "container" are a matter of interpretation, rather than part of the program itself. In the previous example, the string "selenium" isn't being modified in place— that's not allowed in Python. However, when we're writing the program, it's helpful to *think* of it that way. So, is whole a container of characters or a most-recent holder?

Gatherer

A *gatherer* (sometimes called an *accumulator*) collects individual values. For example, the variable result in the following code is a gatherer; it collects values by adding them:

construct/gatherer.py

```
def add_up(values):
    '''Return the sum of the values in a list, or 0 if the list is empty.'''

    result = 0
    for sum in values:
        result += sum
    return result
```

Temporary

A *temporary* is a variable that exists only for a short time. Temporaries are typically used to store partial results in order to make code easier to read. For example, here's a function that returns the two roots of a quadratic equation:

`construct/roots.py`

```
from math import sqrt

def roots(a, b, c):
    '''Return real roots of a quadratic, or None.'''

    temp = b**2 - 4*a*c
    if temp < 0:
        return None

    temp = sqrt(temp)
    left = (-b + temp) / (2 * a)
    right = (-b - temp) / (2 * a)
    return left, right
```

Compare this with a version that uses fewer lines but doesn't use a temporary:

`construct/roots_full.py`

```
from math import sqrt

def roots(a, b, c):
    '''Return real roots of a quadratic, or None.'''

    if sqrt(b**2 - 4*a*c) < 0:
        return None

    left = (-b + sqrt(b*2 - 4*a*c)) / (2 * a)
    right = (-b - sqrt(b**2 - 4*a*c)) / (2 * a)
    return left, right
```

Did you spot the bug in the second version? Code that seems to be repeated is never read as carefully as code that isn't; using temporaries to store intermediate results therefore reduces the chances of a lurking bug.

One-Way Flag

A *one-way flag* is a variable whose value changes just once to show that something has occurred.

For example, this function finds the lines in a data file that were added after a particular date:

`construct/afterdate.py`

```python
def after_date(input_file, date):
    '''Return the lines that were added to a file after a certain date.'''

    keep_it = False
    result = []
    for line in input_file:
        if keep_it:
            result.append(line)
        elif get_date(line) >= date:
            keep_it = True
    return result
```

The keep_it variable is initially set to False to signal that we haven't yet seen a line in the file added after the desired date. As soon as we do see that line, the flag becomes True.

12.6 Summary

In this chapter, we learned the following:

- Specifying default values for parameters can make functions easier to use; letting them take variable-length parameter lists can make them more flexible.

- When an error occurs in a program, the program should raise an exception with a meaningful type and an informative error message. Programs should catch exceptions only in a small number of places where they can do something to report or correct the error.

- Functional testing looks at the program as a whole, while unit testing focuses on its components, and regression testing checks whether things that used to work still do.

- Unit tests should operate independently so that an error in one will not affect the results reported for the rest.

- The most cost-effective way to test is to focus on boundary cases. It's also important to test that software fails when it's supposed to.

- Test-driven development consists of writing unit tests first and then writing code to make those tests pass. TDD helps programmers be more efficient by getting them to focus on what code is supposed to before worrying about how it is going to work.

- To debug software, you have to know what it is supposed to do and be able to repeat the failure. Simplifying the conditions that make the program fail is an effective way to narrow down the set of possible causes.

- Most variables in programs are used in one of a small number of stereotyped ways. Knowing these patterns helps with design, debugging, and communication.

12.7 Exercises

Here are some exercises for you to try on your own:

1. Python allows programmers to pass values to functions in any order they like, provided they specify the parameters' names. For example:

```
>>> def byName(red, green, blue):
...     print red, green blue
...
>>> byName(green=0.1, blue=0.5, red=0.4)
0.4 0.1 0.5
```

Why is this useful? Why is it dangerous? Explain why you do or don't think that Python (or any other programming language) should allow this or not.

2. The total function in Section 12.1, *Default Parameter Values*, on page 233 uses None as a default value for end. Why is this more sensible than using an integer like -1?

3. Python actually provides two ways to create variable parameter lists. The first, discussed in Section 12.1, *Variable Parameter Lists*, on page 235, takes all the "extra" values passed to the function call, puts them into a tuple, and assigns that tuple to a parameter with a star (*) in front of its name. The second takes any extra *named* parameters, puts them in a dictionary, and assigns it to a parameter with two stars (**) in front of its name.

   a) Find the description of this feature in the official Python documentation at http://www.python.org and give its URL.

   b) Write a short example to show how this feature works, along with 100–150 words of explanation.

   c) When should you use this feature, and why?

4. Your job is to come up with tests for a function called line_intersect, which takes two lines as input and returns their intersection. More specifically:

   - Lines are represented as pairs of distinct points, such as [[0.0, 0.0], [1.0, 3.0]].

   - If the lines do not intersect, line_intersect returns None.

   - If the lines intersect in one point, line_intersect returns the point of intersection, such as [0.5, 0.75].

   - If the lines are coincident (that is, lie on top of one another), the function returns its first argument (that is, a line).

   What are the six most informative test cases you can think of? (That is, if you were allowed to run only six tests, which would tell you the most about whether the function was implemented correctly?) Write out the inputs and expected output of these six tests, and explain why you would choose them. Do not worry about error handling (yet).

5. Your next job is to test whether line_intersect handles errors correctly. You have been told that it is supposed to raise a ValueError exception if either argument is not a pair or pairs of floating-point numbers and that it is supposed to raise a GeometryError exception if the two points used to define a line are not distinct (that is, if something like [1.0, 1.0], [1.0, 1.0]] is given as an input). What six tests would you write first to check that line_intersect was handling errors correctly? In a sentence or two, explain whether you think that testing error handling is more important than testing that the function gives the correct answer for valid input, or vice versa.

6. A friend of yours has written a function called common_name that takes two strings as input. The first is the one- or two-letter symbol for a chemical element, such as "He" or "Fe". The second is the two-letter international code for a language, such as "EN" (English) or "DE" (Deutsch, that is, German). You have been told that the function handles 106 elements and 26 languages. If you don't want to test every element with every language, then how many different inputs do you have to give it to feel confident that it works correctly? What assumptions are you making about those inputs in doing your calculation?

7. Another friend of yours has written a function called *average*, which returns the average of a list of floating-point numbers. She has tested it as follows:

```
from math import abs
from mylibrary import average

test_cases = [
    [0.0, [ 0.0]],
    [0.0, [-1.0,  1.0]],
    [1.0, [ 0.0,  2.0]],
    [2.0, [ 0.0,  1.0, 2.0, 3.0, 4.0]],
    ....
]

passes = failures = 0
for (expected, values) in test_cases:
    actual = average(values)
    if actual == expected:
        passes += 1
    else:
        failures += 1

print 'passes:', passes
print 'failures:', failures
```

She has implemented *average* correctly, but several of her test cases are failing. Explain why; identify which single line of code she should change, and how to change it, to improve her tests.

8. A function called is_salt takes the chemical symbols of two elements as input and returns True if the combination of those two elements is a salt (in other words, a combination of an acid and a base). You happened to know that the symbols for the elements that are considered acids and bases are contained in sets called Acids and Bases, respectively. A friend of yours thinks that an easy way to test is_salt would be to simplify the Acids and Bases sets and then run the tests:

```
Bases = set(["Mg"]) # nothing but magnesium
Acids = set(["Cl"]) # nothing but chlorine

def test_MgCl():
    '''Works if the base is a base, and the acid is an acid.'''

    assert is_salt("Mg", "Cl")
```

```
def test_ArCl():
    '''Doesn't work because the 'base' isn't a base.'''

    assert not is_salt("Ar", "Cl")

def test_MgO():
    '''Doesn't work because the 'acid' isn't an acid.'''

    assert not is_salt("Mg", "O")

def test_neither():
    '''Doesn't work because neither is right.'''

    assert not is_salt("Ar", "O")
```

There are (at least) two things wrong with this idea. Briefly explain what they are.

9. Using Nose, write four tests for a function called all_prefixes in a module called testprefixes.py that takes a string as its input and returns the set of all nonempty substrings that start with the first character. For example, given the string "lead" as input, all_prefixes would return the set {"l", "le", "lea", "lead"}.

10. Using Nose, write the ten most informative tests you can think of for a function called is_sorted in a module called testsorting.py that takes a list of integers as input and returns True if they are sorted in nondecreasing order, and False otherwise. If the argument is not a list or if any of the values are not integers, the function should raise a ValueError exception. Include a short comment justifying the number of tests you chose to write.

11. The function remove_all takes two arguments: a list and an item you want to completely remove from the list. If the item occurs in the list multiple times, every instance of it is removed. If the item does not occur in the list, the list remains unmodified.

Explain what is wrong with the following tests for the function remove_all:

`construct/remove_all.py`

```
empty_list = []
one_item_list = ['He']
multi_item_list = ['Ne', 'Ar', 'He', 'He']

def test_remove_from_empty():
    remove_all(empty_list, 'He')
    assert len(empty_list) == 0
```

```
def test_remove_from_one_item_list():
    remove_all(one_item_list, 'He')
    assert len(one_item_list) == 0

def test_remove_something_else():
    remove_all(one_item_list, 'Pb')
    assert len(one_item_list) == 1

def test_remove_multiple():
    remove_all(multi_item_list, 'He')
    assert len(multi_item_list) == 2
```

12. At first glance, it seems that the only way to test a function that reads from a file is to store some sample files on disk and have the function open and read those files. However, the standard Python library includes a module called StringIO (and a faster version called cStringIO) that makes file I/O easier to test. Explain how in one short paragraph, and then use cStringIO to test a function called count_lines (taken from a module called file_util).

13. The following function is broken. The docstring describes what it's supposed to do:

construct/minmaxexercise.py

```
def find_min_max(values):
    '''Print the minimum and maximum value from the given collection of
    values.'''

    min = None
    max = None

    for value in values:
        if value > max:
            max = value
        if value < min:
            min = value

    print 'The minimum value is %s' % min
    print 'The maximum value is %s' % max
```

What does it actually do? Use a debugger to verify. What line do you need to change to fix it?

14. The following function is also broken but only under certain circumstances:

construct/summationexercise.py

```python
def summation(limit):
    '''Return the sum of the numbers from 0 to limit.'''

    total = 0
    current = limit
    while current != 0:
        total += current
        current -= 1
    return total
```

a) What type of input causes the function to fail?

b) How does the function behave during a failure? Use a debugger to step through what happens.

c) What do you need to change to fix it?

15. Under what circumstances will the following function throw an exception? Use try and except to ensure the function returns the correct value even when an exception occurs.

construct/reciprocalexercise.py

```python
def compute_reciprocals(values):
    '''Return a list of the reciprocals of the given list of values.
    If a value has no reciprocal, it will be assigned a value of
    None in the returned list.'''

    reciprocals = []
    for value in values:
        reciprocals.append(1 / value)
    return reciprocals
```

16. For each function, identify the role of the variables v0, v1, and so on. Also, give each poorly named variable a better name.

construct/roleexercise1.py

```python
def find_last(filename, string):
    v0 = 0
    v1 = [None, None]
    v2 = open(filename, "r")
    for v3 in v2:
        v0 += 1
        if string in v3:
            v1 = [v0, v3]
    return v1
```

```
from math import sqrt

def standard_deviation(values):
    v0 = 0.0
    for v1 in values:
        v0 += v1
    v2 = v0 / len(values)
    v3 = 0.0
    for v4 in values:
        v3 += (v4 - v2) ** 2
    v5 = v3 / len(values)
    return sqrt(v5)
```

17. Write three functions that compute the mean, median, and mode, respectively, of a list of values. For each local variable you use, indicate its role using comments. Don't forget to identify the role of variables you use in loops. Use the following to get started:

```
def mean(values):
    '''Return the arithmetic mean of the list of values; i.e. the
    sum of all the values divided by the total number of values.
    If the list contains non-numeric elements, this function throws
    a ValueError.'''

def median(values):
    '''Return the median of the list of values. For an odd number
    of values, if the numbers are sorted, the median occurs at the
    center of the list. For an even number of values, the median is
    the mean of the two middle values in the sorted list of values.'''

def mode(values):
    '''Return a list containing the mode of the list of values. The
    mode is the most frequently occurring values in the list. For example,
    the mode of [0, 1, 0, 3, 2, 4, 1] is [0, 1].'''
```

18. Occasionally programmers don't close files that they have opened. This is bad style. The computer's operating system allows a running program to have only a limited number of files open at any time, so if programs don't close files they're done with, they will eventually not be able to open new ones. Modify the following function so that it *always* closes the file it has opened, even if something goes wrong while the file's contents are being read.

construct/add_error_handling.py

```python
def process_file(filename):
    '''Read and print the contents of a file.'''

    f = open(filename, 'r')
    for line in f:
        line = line.strip()
        print line
```

19. Take another look at the function we wrote in Section 8.4, *Multiline Records*, on page 170 to read molecule descriptions from a file:

fileproc/multimol_2.py

```python
def read_molecule(r):
    '''Read a single molecule from reader r and return it,
    or return None to signal end of file.'''

    # If there isn't another line, we're at the end of the file.
    line = r.readline()
    if not line:
        return None

    # Name of the molecule: "COMPND    name"
    key, name = line.split()

    # Other lines are either "END" or "ATOM num type x y z"
    molecule = [name]
    reading = True

    while reading:
        line = r.readline()
        if line.startswith('END'):
            reading = False
        else:
            key, num, type, x, y, z = line.split()
            molecule.append((type, x, y, z))

    return molecule
```

This function assumes that every file is correctly formatted. In the real world, data files often aren't. Lines may be missing or in the wrong order, values may be out of order on a line, and so on. In keeping with the philosophy of defensive programming, add assertions to this function so that it fails with appropriate error messages for badly formatted input.

20. Consider the following function:

```
def findButNotAfter(source, prefix, pattern):
    '''Return the index of the first occurrence of 'pattern' in
    'source' that is NOT immediately after an occurrence of
    'prefix'.  For example, findButNotAfter('abcdcd', 'ab', 'cd')
    returns 4, since the first occurrence of 'cd' comes immediately
    after an 'ab', but findButNotAfter('abxcdcd', 'ab', 'cd')
    returns 3.'''
```

a) What ambiguities or omissions are there in this specification?

b) Rewrite the function's docstring to address the shortcomings you identified earlier.

c) Write at least ten Nose tests to check that the function meets your revised specification.

d) Write a body for findButNotAfter that passes all of your tests.

## Chapter 13

Object-Oriented Programming

As you learned in Section 2.3, *What Is a Type?*, on page 12, a type is a set of values along with the operations that can be performed on those values. For example, the type bool consists of the values True and False, plus the operations and, or, and not, while the type int has approximately 2^{32} values and a wide range of operations, such as addition and subtraction.

Types like bool and int are built into programming languages because they are useful in almost every program. Thousands of other types, from File to Nematode, are just as useful, but not to as many people; trying to include all of them would be a never-ending task and would make the language so large that it would be practically impossible to work with.

One of the greatest advances in computer science was the realization that allowing programmers to define new types of their own can make programs easier to write and understand. In almost all modern languages, including Python, programmers do this by defining a *class* and then creating objects that are *instances* of the class. You can think of a class as being like a species, like *Pygoscelis antarctica* (the chinstrap penguin); its instances are then particular penguins.

Languages working this way are (unsurprisingly) called *object-oriented*. This chapter will show you how to create object-oriented programs in Python and why you would want to write programs that way. We will start by showing how to create a simple class, then look at some of the theory behind object-oriented programming, and finally examine some of the "extras" Python provides to make programmers' lives easier.

13.1 Class Color

To explain classes, over the next few sections we will build a Color class of our own that does the same things as the RGB model described in Section 4.4, *Pixels and Colors*, on page 59. Let's start with a very simple (but not very useful) class definition:

`oop/color_simple.py`

```python
class Color(object):
    '''An RGB color, with red, green and blue components.'''

    pass
```

Just as the keyword def tells Python that we're defining a new function, the keyword class signals that we're defining a new type. The (object) part says that class Color is a kind of object;[1] the docstring describes the features of a Color object, while pass says that the object is blank— that is, it doesn't store any data and doesn't offer any new operations.

The following sections will add data and operations to Color to make it more useful. Even without that, though, we can make a new Color object and assign it to a variable called black:

`oop/color_obj.cmd`

```python
>>> black = Color()
```

Using the name of the class as if it were a function tells Python to find the class and build one instance of it. We can check that this has worked by printing the value of black:

`oop/color_show_raw.cmd`

```python
>>> black
<__main__.Color object at 0xb7dbd24c>
```

That tells us that an object has been created (and where it happens to be in memory), but nothing more. To make the object more useful, we need to attach some red, green, and blue values to it. One way to do this—a very bad way, which we will clean up in a couple of sections—is simply to assign the values we want:

`oop/color_add_values.cmd`

```python
>>> black.red = 0
>>> black.green = 0
>>> black.blue = 0
```

---

1. This is needed for historical reasons, since early versions of Python did things a slightly different way.

The variable black now refers to a Color object that has three *instance variables* called red, green, and blue. To prove that they're there, we can examine their values:

`oop/color_print_parts.cmd`

```
>>> black.red
0
>>> black.green
0
>>> black.blue
0
```

An object's instance variables are like the local variables in a function call. Just as local variables can be accessed only inside their function and last only as long as the function call, instance variables can be accessed (using dot notation) only through the object that contains them and live only as long as that object.

Another way to think about objects is to compare them to dictionaries. We could store these same RGB values using this:

```
black = {"red" : 0, "green" : 0, "blue" : 0}
```

and then access them using black["red"] instead of black.red. As we'll see, though, objects allow us to do things that dictionaries can't.

Methods

Before showing how instance variables *ought* to be created, let's take a look at how we can add operations to a class. Suppose, for example, that we want to calculate the lightness of a color, that is, how close it is to being pure white. By definition, a color's lightness is the average of its strongest and weakest RGB values scaled to lie between 0 and 1. As a function, this is as follows:

`oop/color_lightness_func.py`

```python
def lightness(color):
    '''Return the lightness of color.'''

    strongest = max(color.red, color.green, color.blue)
    weakest   = min(color.red, color.green, color.blue)
    return 0.5 * (strongest + weakest) / 255
```

If we want to make the calculation a method of the class Color, we simply move its definition into the class.

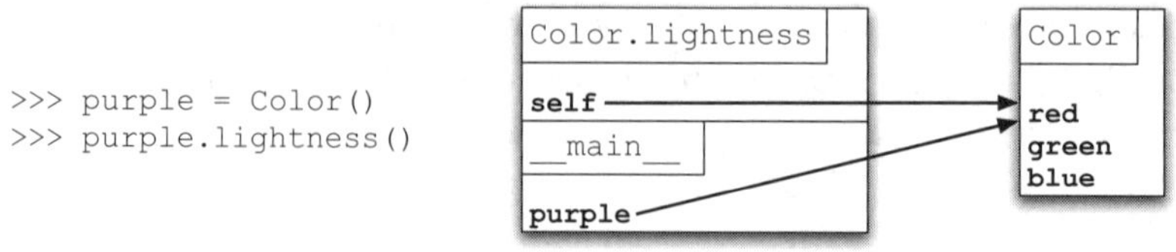

```
>>> purple = Color()
>>> purple.lightness()
```

Runtime stack after
calling `purple.lightness()`

Figure 13.1: AUTOMATIC SELF

---

oop/color_lightness_method.py

```python
class Color(object):
    '''An RGB color, with red, green and blue components.'''

    def lightness(self):
        '''Calculate the lightness of this color.'''

        strongest = max(self.red, self.green, self.blue)
        weakest   = min(self.red, self.green, self.blue)
        return 0.5 * (strongest + weakest) / 255
```

Actually, we do one other thing as well. We take out the parameter color and replace it with one called self. Whenever Python called a method for an object, it automatically passes a reference to that object as the method's first argument (see Figure 13.1). This means that when we call lightness, we don't need to give it any arguments—Python supplies the object itself for us. Inside the method, we can then access the object's instance variables using the usual dot notation on that variable:

oop/color_lightness_call.cmd

```python
>>> purple = Color()
>>> purple.red = 255
>>> purple.green = 0
>>> purple.blue = 255
>>> purple.lightness()
0.5
```

The rule about self means that when you define a method, you must include one more parameter than you're actually going to pass in. Alternatively, when you call a method, you provide one less parameter than the method's definition seems to require. Forgetting this is a very common beginner's mistake. Forgetting to put self in front of something that you intended to be a member variable is another common beginner's mistake.

For example, if the class was defined this way:

`oop/broken_color_self.py`

```python
class Color(object):
    '''An RGB color, with red, green and blue components.'''

    def lightness(self):
        '''Return the lightness of this color.'''

        # Fails: no such variables 'red', 'green', and 'blue'
        strongest = max(red, green, blue)
        weakest   = min(red, green, blue)
        return 0.5 * (strongest + weakest) / 255
```

then purple.lightness() would produce an error, because the variables red, green, and blue don't exist in lightness, even though purple.red, purple.green, and purple.blue have been assigned values.

Constructors

Let's take another look at the color purple:

`oop/color_purple.cmd`

```
>>> purple = Color()
>>> purple.red = 128
>>> purple.green = 0
>>> purple.blue = 128
```

We could create more colors this way, but it requires us to type in the name of the same variable over and over. What is worse—far worse—is that if the user forgets to add all the right instance variables, then the object's methods will probably fail. For example, suppose we created the color yellow:

`oop/yellow_create_error.cmd`

```
>>> yellow = Color()
>>> yellow.red = 128
>>> yellow.green = 128
```

That looks all right. Yellow is equal parts red and green, and both values have been set. However, if we try to call lightness for this color, we get an error, because we didn't specify a value for yellow.blue:

`oop/yellow_lightness_fail.cmd`

```
>>> yellow.lightness()
Traceback (most recent call last):
  File "<stdin>", line 1, in <module>
  File "<stdin>", line 3, in lightness
AttributeError: 'Color' object has no attribute 'blue'
```

The solution to all of these problems is to allow users to provide values for instance variables when new objects are created, like this:

oop/color_purple_init.cmd

```
>>> purple = Color(128, 0, 128)
```

We have already seen this with classes like str, which can be constructed with parameters (for example, str(45)). In order to make it work, we need to add a method to the class Color that will be run whenever a new Color is created. Such a method is called a *constructor*, and the way to create one in Python is to call it __init__:

oop/color.py

```
class Color(object):
    '''An RGB color, with red, green and blue components.'''

    def __init__(self, r, g, b):
        '''A new color with red value r, green value g, and blue value b.  All
        components are integers in the range 0-255.'''

        self.red = r
        self.green = g
        self.blue = b
```

The double underscores around the name signal that this method has a special meaning to Python—in this case, that the method is to be called when a new object is being created. There are other special methods, some of which we'll see later in this chapter. As with other methods, Python automatically passes a reference to the object itself—in this case, the one that is being created—as __init__'s first argument. It is then up to __init__ to set up the object. For example, the expression Color(128, 0, 128) actually means the following:

- Create an object with no instance variables.

- Call Color's __init__ method with that blank object as the first argument and the three color values as the second, third, and fourth arguments.

- Return a reference to that object—which, thanks to __init__, now has three instance variables—to whoever made the call.

With constructors, methods, and instance variables in hand, we can now create classes that look and work like those that come with Python itself.

13.2 Special Methods

When we introduced __init__ earlier, we said that Python provided other special methods with underscores around their names as well. We can use these special methods to make our types look and act more like Python's built-in types, which in turn can make our programs easier to understand.

For example, the output Python produces when we print a Color isn't particularly useful:

oop/color_purple_no_str.cmd

```
>>> purple = Color(128, 0, 128)
>>> print purple
<color.Color object at 0x6b150>
```

This is behavior that object defines for converting objects to strings. Since object can't know anything about the meaning of the classes we will derive from it, it just shows us where the object is in memory. If we want to present a more useful string, we need to explore two more special methods, __str__ and __repr__. __str__ is called when an informal, human-readable version of an object is needed, and __repr__ is called when more precise, but possibly less-readable, output is desired. In particular, __str__ is called when print is used.

Let's define Color.__str__ to provide useful output:

oop/color_str.py

```python
class Color(object):
    '''An RGB color, with red, green and blue components.'''

    def __init__(self, r, g, b):
        '''A new color with red value r, green value g, and blue value b.  All
        components are integers in the range 0-255.'''

        self.red = r
        self.green = g
        self.blue = b

    def __str__(self):
        '''Return a string representation of this Color in the form of an RGB
        tuple.'''

        return '(%s, %s, %s)' % (self.red, self.green, self.blue)
```

Printing Color now gives more useful information:

`oop/color_print.cmd`

```
>>> purple = Color(128, 0, 128)
>>> print purple
(128, 0, 128)
```

Python has lots of other special methods; the official Python website gives a full list. Among them are __add__, __sub__, and __eq__, which are called when we add objects with +, subtract them with -, or compare them with ==:

`oop/color_full.py`

```python
class Color(object):
    '''An RGB color, with red, green and blue components.'''

    def __init__(self, r, g, b):
        '''A new color with red value r, green value g, and blue value b.
        All components are integers in the range 0-255.'''

        self.red = r
        self.green = g
        self.blue = b

    def __str__(self):
        '''Return a string representation of this Color in the form
          Color(red, green, blue).'''

        return 'Color(%s, %s, %s)' % (self.red, self.green, self.blue)

    def __add__(self, other_color):
        '''Return a new Color made from adding the red, green, and blue
        components of this Color to Color other_color's components.  If the
        sum is greater than 255, then the color is set to 255.'''

        return Color(min(self.red + other_color.red, 255),
                     min(self.green + other_color.green, 255),
                     min(self.blue + other_color.blue, 255))

    def __sub__(self, other_color):
        '''Return a new Color made from subtracting the red, green, and blue
        components of this Color from Color other_color's components.  If
        the difference is less than 0, then the color is set to 0.'''

        return Color(max(self.red - other_color.red, 0),
                     max(self.green - other_color.green, 0),
                     max(self.blue - other_color.blue, 0))

    def __eq__(self, other_color):
        '''Return True if this Color's components are equal to Color
        other_color's components.'''
```

```
    return self.red == other_color.red and self.green == \
        other_color.green and self.blue == other_color.blue
```

This example shows these methods in action:

oop/color_full_use.cmd

```
>>> purple = Color(128, 0, 128)
>>> white = Color(255, 255, 255)
>>> dark_grey = Color(50, 50, 50)
>>> print purple + dark_grey
Color(178, 50, 178)
>>> print white - dark_grey
Color(205, 205, 205)
>>> print white == Color(255, 255, 255)
True
```

As you can see, if bright and dark are both colors, then Python interprets the expression bright+dark to mean bright.__add__(dark). This is called *operator overloading*, since we are overloading (that is, giving new meaning to) Python's built-in operators.

Operator overloading is a powerful tool but should be used very carefully. Take addition—we could easily define __add__ so that it modified the object it was being called on, instead of creating a new one:

oop/color_add_bad.py

```
class Color(object):
    ...other definitions as before...

    def __add__(self, other_color):
        '''This is a bad way to define this method.'''

        self.red += other_color.red
        self.green += other_color.green
        self.blue += other_color.blue
        return self
```

Python won't stop us from doing this—it doesn't understand the intended meaning, or *semantics*, of our code. However, just as nobody would expect adding the integers i and j to change the value of i, nobody would expect adding colors to change the colors being added. If our definitions of operators don't meet people's expectations, it is our fault, not theirs, when they use those operators incorrectly.

13.3 More About dir and help

We discussed functions help and dir in Section 4.1, *Importing Modules*, on page 41 and the sidebar on page 46. Notice that the contents of a Color object include the instance variables and all the Color methods.

`oop/color_dir.cmd`

```
>>> black = Color(0, 0, 0)
>>> dir(black)
['__add__', '__class__', '__delattr__', '__dict__', '__doc__', '__eq__',
 '__getattribute__', '__hash__', '__init__', '__module__', '__new__',
 '__reduce__', '__reduce_ex__', '__repr__', '__setattr__', '__str__',
 '__sub__', '__weakref__', 'blue', 'distance', 'green', 'red']
```

Since we have written docstrings, we can get help on class Color:

`oop/color_help.cmd`

```
>>> help(Color)
Help on class Color in module color_full_distance:

class Color(__builtin__.object)
 |  An RGB color, with red, green and blue components.
 |
 |  Methods defined here:
 |
 |  __add__(self, other_color)
 |      Return a new Color made from adding the red, green, and blue
 |      components of this Color to Color other_color's components.
 |      If the sum is greater than 255, then the color is set to 255.
 |
 |  __eq__(self, other_color)
 |      Return True if this Color's components are equal to Color
 |      other_color's components.
 |
 |  __init__(self, r, g, b)
 |      A new color with red value r, green value g, and blue value b.  All
 |      components are integers in the range 0-255.
 |
 |  __str__(self)
 |      Return a string representation of this Color in the form
 |      Color(red, green, blue).
 |
 |  __sub__(self, other_color)
 |      Return a new Color made from subtracting the red, green, and blue
 |      components of this Color from Color other_color's components.
 |      If the difference is less than 0, then the color is set to 0.
 |
 |  lightness(self)
 |      Return the lightness of this color.
 |  ----------------------------------------------------------------------
 |  Data descriptors defined here:
 |
 |  __dict__
 |      dictionary for instance variables (if defined)
 |
 |  __weakref__
 |      list of weak references to the object (if defined)
```

Toward the end of the help text, there is a __dict__ item described, and it says "dictionary for instance variables." Python implements instance variables using dictionaries, and you can inspect this variable:

`oop/color_dict.cmd`

```
>>> black.__dict__
{'blue': 0, 'green': 0, 'red': 0}
```

Whenever you assign to an instance variable, it changes the contents of the object's dictionary. You can even change it yourself directly, although we don't recommend it.

Before looking at another class example, let's take a short detour and look at some of the theory behind object-oriented programming.

13.4 A Little Bit of OO Theory

Classes and objects are programming's power tools. They let good programmers do a lot in very little time, but with them, bad programmers can create a real mess. This section will introduce some underlying theory that will help you design reliable, reusable object-oriented software.

Encapsulation

To *encapsulate* something means to enclose it in some kind of container. In programming, *encapsulation* means keeping data and the code that uses it in one place and hiding the details of exactly how they work together. For example, each instance of class file keeps track of what file on disk it is reading or writing and where it currently is in that file. The class hides the details of how this is done so that programmers can use it without needing to know the details of how it was implemented.

One of the biggest benefits of encapsulation is that it allows programmers to change their minds about one part of a program without having to rewrite other parts. For example, suppose we want to represent rectangular sections of images.

Our first attempt might store the XY coordinates of the rectangle's bottom-left and upper-right corners, like this:

oop/rectangle_corners.py

```python
class Rectangle(object):
    '''Represent a rectangular section of an image.'''

    def __init__(self, x0, y0, x1, y1):
        '''Create a rectangle with non-zero area. (x0,y0) is the
        lower left corner, (x1,y1) the upper right corner.'''

        self.x0 = x0
        self.y0 = y0
        self.x1 = x1
        self.y1 = y1

    def area(self):
        '''Return the area of the rectangle.'''

        return (self.x1 - self.x0) * (self.y1 - self.y0)

    def contains(self, x, y):
        '''Return True is (x,y) point is inside a rectangle,
        and False otherwise.'''

        return (self.x0 <= x <= self.x1) and \
               (self.y0 <= y <= self.y1)
```

Later, we might decide that it would be better to store the rectangle's lower-left corner and XY size, like this:

oop/rectangle_size.py

```python
class Rectangle(object):
    '''Represent a rectangular section of an image.'''

    def __init__(self, x0, y0, width, height):
        '''Create a rectangle with non-zero area. (x0,y0) is the
        lower left corner, width and height the X and Y extent.'''

        self.x0 = x0
        self.y0 = y0
        self.width = width
        self.height = height

    def area(self):
        '''Return the area of the rectangle.'''

        return self.width * self.height
```

```
def contains(self, x, y):
    '''Return True if (x,y) point is inside a rectangle,
    and False otherwise.'''

    return (self.x0 <= x) and (x <= self.x0 + width) and \
           (self.y0 <= y) and (y <= self.y0 + height)
```

If we made this change, we would obviously also have to change every piece of software that created new rectangles. However, we wouldn't have to change code that used the area or contains methods—since they hide the details of *how* they calculate their results, we can change their operation without affecting anything else.

Polymorphism

Polymorphism means "having more than one form." In programming, it means that an expression involving a variable can do different things depending on the type of the object to which the variable refers. For example, if obj refers to a string, then obj[1:3] produces a two-character string. If obj refers to a list, on the other hand, the same expression produces a two-element list. Similarly, the operator left + right can produce a number, a string, or a list, depending on the types of left and right.

Polymorphism is used throughout modern programs to cut down on the amount of code programmers need to write and test. It lets us write a generic function to count nonblank lines:

`oop/line_counter.py`
```
def non_blank_lines(thing):
    '''Return the number of non-blank lines in thing.'''

    count = 0
    for line in thing:
        if line.strip():
            count += 1
    return count
```

and then apply it to a list of strings, a file, a web page on a site halfway around the world (see Section 8.1, *Files Over the Internet*, on page 154), or a single string wrapped up in the StringIO class to look like a file. Each of those four types knows how to be the subject of a loop; in other words, each one knows how to produce its "next" element as long as there is one and then say "all done." That means that instead of writing four functions to count interesting lines or copying the lines into a list and then applying one function to that list, we can apply one function to all those types directly.

Languages like Java and C++ require programmers to declare in advance that classes are polymorphic to one another (usually by using inheritance, which is described in a moment). Python has a more relaxed approach. If the classes provide methods with the same names and the same number of arguments, then instances of one can be substituted for instances of the other without any extra work. This means that if you want to create something that can be used in place of a file, all you have to do is give it methods like read and readlines. Similarly, if someone else wants to create their own kind of rectangles for your code to use, all they have to do is provide the right kind of constructor and the methods area and contains.

At least, that's all they *should* have to do. Right now, though, the class Rectangle isn't properly encapsulated, so it would actually be harder for someone to write a replacement than it ought to be. The reason is that right now, users of the class have to deal with the rectangle's implementation to get its corner points. In our first implementation, for example, a user would write r.x1 to get the rectangle's maximum X extent, while in the second case, she would write r.x0 + r.width.

The way to make polymorphism easier is to encapsulate *all* of the implementation details by only ever talking to class instances through methods. If we do this, our first implementation becomes as follows:

`oop/rectangle_corners_enc.py`

```python
class Rectangle(object):
    '''Represent a rectangular section of an image.'''

    def __init__(self, x0, y0, x1, y1):
        ...as before...

    def area(self):
        ...as before...

    def contains(self, x, y):
        ...as before...

    def get_min_x(self):
        '''Return the minimum X coordinate.'''

        return self.x0

    def get_min_y(self):
        '''Return the minimum Y coordinate.'''

        return self.y0
```

```
    def get_max_x(self):
        '''Return the maximum X coordinate.'''

        return self.x1

    def get_max_y(self):
        '''Return the maximum Y coordinate.'''

        return self.y1
```

while our second becomes the following:

`oop/rectangle_size_enc.py`

```
class Rectangle(object):
    '''Represent a rectangular section of an image.'''

    def __init__(self, x0, y0, width, height):
        ...as before...

    def area(self):
        ...as before...

    def contains(self, x, y):
        ...as before...

    def get_min_x(self):
        '''Return the minimum X coordinate.'''

        return self.x0

    def get_min_y(self):
        '''Return the minimum Y coordinate.'''

        return self.y0

    def get_max_x(self):
        '''Return the maximum X coordinate.'''

        return self.x0 + width

    def get_max_y(self):
        '''Return the maximum Y coordinate.'''

        return self.y0 + height
```

More advanced programmers usually take advantage of a built-in function in Python called property to do some of the work that we're doing by hand in these examples; see the Python library documentation for details and examples.

Inheritance

Giving one class the same methods as another is one way to make them polymorphic, but it suffers from the same flaw as initializing an object's instance variables from outside the object. If a programmer forgets just one line of code, the whole program can fail for reasons that will be difficult to track down. A better approach is to use a third fundamental feature of object-oriented programming called *inheritance*, which allows you to recycle code in yet another way.

To explore how this is done, suppose we are trying to simulate the ecosystem of a tide pool. The pool contains all sorts of living things that float around and interact with their neighbors. Each critter moves around in its own special way and has its own favorite food. We define a class Organism that represents this living thing:

oop/organism.py

```
class Organism(object):
    '''A thing that lives in a tide pool.'''

    def __init__(self, name, x, y):
        '''A living thing that is at location (x,y) in the tide pool.'''

        self.name = name
        self.x = x
        self.y = y

    def __str__(self):
        '''Return a string representation of this Organism.'''

        return '(%s, [%s, %s])' % (self.name, self.x, self.y)

    def can_eat(self, food):
        '''Report whether this Organism can eat the given food.
        Since we don't know anything about what a generic organism
        eats, this always returns False.'''

        return False

    def move(self):
        '''Ask the organism to move.  By default, this does nothing,
        since we don't know anything about how fast or how far a
        generic organism would move.'''

        return
```

The class Organism has three instance variables: name, x, and y (the latter two representing its coordinates within the pool). It also has four methods: __init__, __str__, can_eat, and move. Since we don't know anything about the Organism, it never actually moves and doesn't eat anything.

Not all real organisms behave like our generic Organism. Crabs walk, green algae float, and mussels swim—though not the same way fish do. Some eat plants; some eat animals; green algae "eat" sunlight through photosynthesis.

We can define these specific types of organisms as new classes. Rather than defining each one from scratch, we start with our generic organism by replacing object with Organism in the class header:

`oop/arthropod_header.py`

```
class Arthropod(Organism):
    pass
```

Here, the keyword pass means "do nothing to the definitions inherited from Organism." We call Organism the *parent* or *superclass*, and we call Arthropod the *child* or *subclass*. Arthropod inherits instance variables and methods from its parent Organism, so an Arthropod object automatically has the instance variables name, x, and y and the methods __init__, __str__, can_eat, and move:

`oop/arthropod_basic.py`

```
>>> blue_crab = Arthropod('Callinectes sapidus', 0, 0)
>>> print blue_crab
(Callinectes sapidus, 0, 0)
```

However, we want the Arthropod class to be more than just a generic Organism, which means giving it its own instance variables, methods, or both. In this case, a leg_count instance variable is needed, which requires changing the definition of __init__:

`oop/arthropod_init.py`

```
class Arthropod(Organism):
    '''An arthropod that has a fixed number of legs.'''

    def __init__(self, name, x, y, legs):
        '''An arthropod with the given number of legs that exists at location
        (x, y) in the tide pool.'''

        Organism.__init__(self, name, x, y)
        self.legs = legs
```

In the first line of __init__, we call the constructor from class Organism to initialize the three instance variables, which are name, x, and y. The second line creates the leg_count instance variable and initializes it. Arthropod.__init__ *overrides* Organism __init__, so when an instance of Arthropod calls __init__, the version defined in that class is called, rather than the one in the parent class:

`oop/arthropod_init_result.py`

```
>>> lobster = Arthropod('Homarus gammarus', 0, 0)
Traceback (most recent call last):
  File "<stdin>", line 1, in <module>
TypeError: __init__() takes exactly 5 arguments (4 given)
>>> lobster = Arthropod('Homarus gammarus', 0, 0, 10)
```

The call to the Arthropod constructor with only three arguments results in an error. Once a function is overridden, the parent's version of the function cannot be called from outside the class definition.

Notice, though, that when we print an instance of Arthropod, the number of legs isn't reported:

`oop/arthropod_str.py`

```
>>> lobster = Arthropod('Homarus gammarus', 0, 0, 10)
>>> print lobster
(Homarus gammarus, 0, 0)
```

This happens because we haven't overridden the __str__ method, so Organism.__str__ is still being called. Fixing this is straightforward:

`oop/arthropod_str_override.py`

```
class Arthropod(Organism):
    '''An arthropod that has a fixed number of legs.'''

    def __init__(self, name, x, y, legs):
        '''An arthropod with the given number of legs that exists at location
        (x, y) in the tide pool.'''

        Organism.__init__(self, name, x, y)
        self.legs = legs

    def __str__(self):
        '''Return a string representation of this Arthropod.'''

        return '(%s, %s, [%s, %s])' % (self.name, self.legs, self.x, self.y)
```

Of course, a child class can also have methods that are not part of the parent class:

`oop/arthropod.py`

```
class Arthropod(Organism):
    '''An arthropod that has a fixed number of legs.'''
```

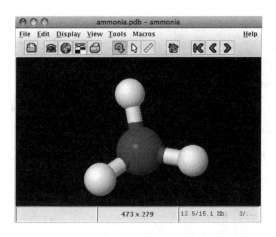

Figure 13.2: JMOL: AN OPEN SOURCE JAVA VIEWER FOR CHEMICAL STRUCTURES IN 3D

```python
    def __init__(self, name, x, y, legs):
        '''An arthropod with the given number of legs that exists at location
        (x, y) in the tide pool.'''

        Organism.__init__(self, name, x, y)
        self.legs = legs

    def __str__(self):
        '''Return a string representation of this Arthropod.'''

        return '(%s, %s, [%s, %s])' % (self.name, self.legs, self.x, self.y)

    def is_decapod(self):
        '''Return True if this Arthropod is a decapod.'''

        return self.legs == 10

    def leg_count(self):
        '''Return the number of legs this Arthropod possesses.'''

        return self.legs
```

13.5 A Longer Example

Molecular graphic visualization tools allow for interactive exploration of molecular structures. Most read PDB-formatted files, which we describe in Section 8.4, *Multiline Records*, on page 170.

In a molecular visualizer, every atom, molecule, bond, and so on, has a location in 3D space, usually defined as a *vector*, which is an arrow from the origin to where the structure is. All of these structures can be rotated and translated.

A vector is usually represented by x, y, and z coordinates that specify how far along the x-axis, y-axis, and z-axis the vector extends.

Here is how ammonia can be specified in PDB format:

fileproc/ammonia.pdb

```
COMPND      AMMONIA
ATOM      1 N  0.257  -0.363   0.000
ATOM      2 H  0.257   0.727   0.000
ATOM      3 H  0.771  -0.727   0.890
ATOM      4 H  0.771  -0.727  -0.890
END
```

In our simplified PDB format, a molecule is made up of numbered atoms. In addition to the number, an atom has a symbol and (x, y, z) coordinates. For example, in one of the atoms in ammonia is nitrogen with symbol N at coordinates (0.257, -0.363, 0.0). In the following sections, we will look at how we could translate these ideas into object-oriented Python.

Class Atom

We might want to create an atom like this, using information we read from the PDB file:

oop/atom.py

```
nitrogen = Atom(1, "N", 0.257, -0.363, 0.0)
```

To do this, we'll need a class called Atom with a constructor that creates all the appropriate instance variables:

oop/atom.py

```
class Atom(object):
    '''An atom with a number, symbol, and coordinates.'''

    def __init__(self, num, sym, x, y, z):
        '''Create an Atom with number num, string symbol sym, and float
        coordinates (x, y, z).'''

        self.number = num
        self.center = (x, y, z)
        self.symbol = sym
```

To inspect an Atom, we'll want to provide __repr__ and __str__ methods:

`oop/atom.py`

```python
def __str__(self):
    '''Return a string representation of this Atom in this format:

        (SYMBOL, X, Y, Z)
    '''

    return '(%s, %s, %s, %s)' % \
        (self.symbol, self.center[0], self.center[1], self.center[2])

def __repr__(self):
    '''Return a string representation of this Atom in this format:

        Atom("SYMBOL", X, Y, Z)
    '''

    return 'Atom(%s, "%s", %s, %s, %s)' % \
        (self.number, self.symbol, \
        self.center[0], self.center[1], self.center[2])
```

We'll use those later, when we define a class for molecules.

In visualizers, one common operation is translation: move an atom to a different location. We'd like to be able to write this in order to tell the nitrogen atom to move up by 0.2 units:

`oop/atom.py`

```python
nitrogen.translate(0, 0, 0.2)
```

This code works as expected if we add the following method to class Atom:

`oop/atom.py`

```python
def translate(self, x, y, z):
    '''Move this Atom by adding (x, y, z) to its coordinates.'''

    self.center = (self.center[0] + x,
                   self.center[1] + y,
                   self.center[2] + z)
```

Class Molecule

Remember that we read PDB files one line at a time. When we reach the line containing COMPND AMMONIA, we know that we're building a complex structure: a molecule with a name and a list of atoms.

Here's the start of a class for this, including an add method that adds an Atom to the molecule:

`oop/molecule.py`

```python
class Molecule(object):
    '''A molecule with a name and a list of Atoms.'''

    def __init__(self, name):
        '''Create a Compound named name with no Atoms.'''

        self.name = name
        self.atoms = []

    def add(self, a):
        '''Add Atom a to my list of Atoms.'''

        self.atoms.append(a)
```

As we read through the ammonia PDB information, we add atoms as we find them; here is the code from Section 8.4, *Multiline Records*, on page 170 rewritten to return a Molecule object instead of a list of tuples:

`oop/multimol_2.py`

```python
from molecule import Molecule
from atom import Atom

def read_molecule(r):
    '''Read a single molecule from reader r and return it,
    or return None to signal end of file.'''

    # If there isn't another line, we're at the end of the file.
    line = r.readline()
    if not line:
        return None

    # Name of the molecule: "COMPND    name"
    key, name = line.split()

    # Other lines are either "END" or "ATOM num kind x y z"
    molecule = Molecule(name)
    reading = True

    while reading:
        line = r.readline()
        if line.startswith('END'):
            reading = False
        else:
            key, num, kind, x, y, z = line.split()
            molecule.add(Atom(num, kind, float(x), float(y), float(z)))

    return molecule
```

If we compare the two versions, we can see the code is nearly identical. It's just as easy to read the new version as the old—more so even, because it includes type information. Here are the __str__ and __repr__ methods:

`oop/molecule.py`

```python
def __repr__(self):
    '''Return a string representation of this Molecule in this format:

    Molecule("NAME", (ATOM1, ATOM2, ...))
    '''

    res = ''
    for atom in self.atoms:
        res = res + repr(atom) + ', '

    # Strip off the last comma.
    res = res[:-2]
    return 'Molecule("%s", (%s))' % (self.name, res)

def __str__(self):
    '''Return a string representation of this Molecule in this format:

    (NAME, (ATOM1, ATOM2, ...))
    '''

    res = ''
    for atom in self.atoms:
        res = res + str(atom) + ', '

    # Strip off the last comma.
    res = res[:-2]
    return '(%s, (%s))' % (self.name, res)
```

We'll add a translate method to Molecule to make it easier to move:

`oop/molecule.py`

```python
def translate(self, x, y, z):
    '''Move this Compound, including all Atoms, by (x, y, z).'''

    for atom in self.atoms:
        atom.translate(x, y, z)
```

And here we call it:

`oop/molecule.py`

```python
ammonia = Molecule("AMMONIA")
ammonia.add(Atom(1, "N", 0.257, -0.363, 0.0))
ammonia.add(Atom(2, "H", 0.257, 0.727, 0.0))
ammonia.add(Atom(3, "H", 0.771, -0.727, 0.890))
ammonia.add(Atom(4, "H", 0.771, -0.727, -0.890))
ammonia.translate(0, 0, 0.2)
```

13.6 Summary

In this chapter, we learned the following:

- In object-oriented languages, new types are defined by creating classes. Classes support encapsulation; in other words, they combine data and the operations on it so that other parts of the program can ignore implementation details.

- Classes also support polymorphism. If two classes have methods that work the same way, instances of those classes can replace one another without the rest of the program being affected. This enables "plug-and-play" programming, in which one piece of code can perform different operations depending on the objects it is operating on.

- Finally, new classes can be defined by inheriting features from existing ones. The new class can override the features of its parent and/or add entirely new features.

- When a method is defined in a class, its first argument must be a variable that represents the object the method is being called on. By convention, this argument is called self.

- Some methods have special predefined meanings in Python; to signal this, their names begin and end with two underscores. Some of these methods are called when constructing objects (__init__) or converting them to strings (__str__ and __repr__); others, like __add__ and __sub__, are used to imitate arithmetic.

13.7 Exercises

The best way to learn how to do object-oriented programming is to go back through the examples and exercises of previous chapters and see which ones are easier or more naturally written using classes and objects. You can also create object-oriented programs that represent things in the real world. For example, what classes would you use to model the stars, planets, moons, rings, and comets that make up a solar system? What methods should each class have? How and where would you keep track of things like orbital parameters? How would you prevent programmers from accidentally putting a star in orbit around a comet or something equally silly?

## Chapter 14

Graphical User Interfaces

Most of the programs in previous chapters are not interactive. Once launched, they run to completion without giving us a chance to steer them or provide new input. The few that do communicate with us do so through the kind of text-only *command-line user interface*, or CLUI, that would have already been considered old-fashioned in the early 1980s.

As you already know, most modern programs interact with users via a *graphical user interface*, or GUI, which is made up of windows, menus, buttons, and so on. In this chapter, we will show you how to build simple GUIs using a Python module called Tkinter. Along the way, we will introduce a different way of structuring programs called *event-driven programming*. A traditionally structured program usually has control over what happens when, but an event-driven program must be able to respond to input at unpredictable moments. As we shall see, the easiest way to do this is to use some of Python's more advanced features.

Tkinter is one of several toolkits you can use to build GUIs in Python, and other languages have toolkits of their own. However, knowing how to put buttons and sliders on the screen is only part of knowing how to create an application that people will understand, use, and enjoy. To do the latter, you will also need to know something about graphic design and other aspects of human-computer interaction. Hundreds of books have been written on the subject (we particularly like [Joh07]), and you can find hundreds of tutorials and resources on the Web.

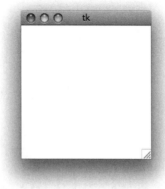

Figure 14.1: A ROOT WINDOW

14.1 The Tkinter Module

Tkinter comes with Python and allows us to create windows, buttons, menus, text areas, checkboxes, and many other *widgets*. We usually start by importing everything in the Tkinter module into our program:[1]

gui/import.py

```
from Tkinter import *
```

Every Tkinter GUI application starts by creating a *root window* and saving a reference to it in a variable:

gui/getwindow.py

```
window = Tk()
```

The root window is initially empty (see Figure 14.1). It acts as the outermost container for the application; all the other widgets we create will depend on it. If the window on the screen is closed, the window object is destroyed (though we can create a new root window by calling Tk() again). All of the applications we will create have only one main window, but additional windows can be created using the TopLevel widget (see Figure 14.2, on the next page).

---

1. We said in Section 4.1, *Importing Modules*, on page 41 that import * was bad style because of the risk of name collision. We are using it here because most online tutorials about Tkinter are written this way. In your applications, you should use import Tkinter as tk and then use tk.thing to refer to its elements.

Widget	Description
Button	A clickable button
Canvas	An area used for drawing or displaying images
Checkbutton	A clickable box that can be selected or unselected
Entry	A single-line text field that the user can type in
Frame	A container for widgets
Label	A single-line display for text
Listbox	A drop-down list that the user can select from
Menu	A drop-down menu
Message	A multiline display for text
Menubutton	An item in a drop-down menu
Text	A multiline text field that the user can type in
TopLevel	An additional window

Figure 14.2: Tkinter widgets

14.2 Basic GUI Construction

The next step in developing a GUI is to add widgets to the root window. The simplest widget is a Label, which is used to display short pieces of text. When we create one, we must specify its *parent widget*, which is the widget that the label is placed inside. In our case, the parent widget is the root window of the application. We also need to provide the text that is to be displayed, which can be done by setting the label's text attribute when we construct it. (By convention, we do not place spaces on either side of the equal sign when setting the value of attributes like text.)

gui/label.py

```python
from Tkinter import *
window = Tk()
label = Label(window, text="This is our label.")
label.pack()
```

The last line of this little program is crucial. Like other widgets, Label has a method called pack that places it in its parent and then tells the parent to resize itself as necessary. If we forget to call this method, the child widget (in this case, the label) won't be displayed or will be displayed improperly. After label.pack() is called, on the other hand, we see the GUI shown in Figure 14.3, on the following page.

Figure 14.3: A WINDOW WITH A LABEL

Labels are often used to display static text that never changes, such as copyright information. Often, though, applications will want to update a label's text as the program runs to show things like the currently open file or the time of day. One way to do this is simply to assign a new value to the widget's text using named parameters (Section 12.1, *Named Parameter*, on page 237):

gui/label-dict.py
```
from Tkinter import *
import time

window = Tk()
label = Label(window, text="First label.")
label.pack()
time.sleep(2)
label.config(text="Second label.")
```

Run the previous code one line at a time from the Python command prompt to see how the label changes. This code will not display the window at all if run all at once as a script or from within Wing 101. In those cases, the call to window.mainloop() is needed to tell the program to pay attention to the outside world.

Mutable Variables

There is a better way to manage the interactions between a program's GUI and its variables, and the reason it's better brings us face to face with the biggest difference between the applications we have seen in previous chapters and event-driven GUI applications. Suppose we want to display a string, such as the current time, in several places in a GUI—the application's status bar, some dialog boxes, and so on. Assigning a new value to each widget each time the string changes isn't

Immutable Type	Tkinter Mutable Type
int	IntVar
string	StringVar
bool	BooleanVar
double	DoubleVar

Figure 14.4: Tkinter mutable types

hard, but as the application grows, so too do the odds that we'll forget to update at least one of the widgets that's displaying the string. What we really want is a string that "knows" which widgets care about its value and can update them itself when that value changes.

Since Python's strings, integers, doubles, and Booleans are immutable, Tkinter provides types of its own that can be updated in place and that can notify widgets whenever their values change (see Figure 14.4). Rather than set the text of the label using an immutable type such as string, we can set it using the corresponding mutable type, such as StringVar. Whenever a new value is assigned to that StringVar, it tells the label, and any other widgets it has been assigned to, that it's time to update.

The values in Tkinter mutable types are set and retrieved using the set and get methods. To show how they work, the following code creates a Tkinter string variable called data and sets its value to "Data to display". It then creates a label to display the contents of data:

gui/label-variable.py

```python
from Tkinter import *
window = Tk()
data = StringVar()
data.set("Data to display")
label = Label(window, textvariable=data)
label.pack()
window.mainloop()
```

Notice that this time we set the textvariable attribute of the label rather than the text attribute. Any time the program changes the contents of data, the text the label is displaying will automatically change as well. The relationships between the three main variables in this program are shown in Figure 14.5, on the next page.

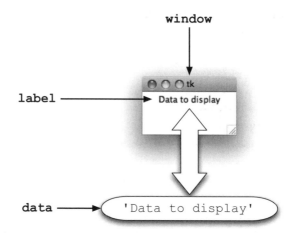

Figure 14.5: Widgets and mutable variables

There is one small trap here for newcomers: because of the way the Tkinter module is structured, you cannot create a StringVar or any other mutable variable until you have called the Tk() function to create the top-level window. This doesn't make much difference in this case, but as we'll see in a moment, it sometimes forces programmers to do things in an unintuitive order.

Frame

To show the real power of mutable variables, we need to create a GUI that has several widgets. We will use this as an opportunity to introduce another widget called Frame. A frame isn't directly visible on the screen; instead, its purpose is to organize other widgets. To create a GUI that displays three labels, for example, the following code puts a frame in the root window and then adds the labels to the frame one by one:

`gui/frame.py`

```
from Tkinter import *

window = Tk()
frame = Frame(window)
frame.pack()
first = Label(frame, text="First label")
first.pack()
second = Label(frame, text="Second label")
second.pack()
third = Label(frame, text="Third label")
third.pack()
window.mainloop()
```

Figure 14.6: A WINDOW WITH A FRAME AND THREE LABELS

The resulting GUI is shown in Figure 14.6, while in Figure 14.7, on the next page, we can see how the five widgets are organized. Note that we call pack on every widget; if we omit one of these calls, that widget will not be displayed.

Putting the three labels in the same frame is equivalent to putting the labels directly into the main window widget, but we can use multiple frames to format the window's layout. Here we use two frames containing the three labels and put a border around the second frame. We specify the border width using the borderwidth attribute (0 is the default) and the border style using relief (FLAT is the default). The other border styles are SUNKEN, RAISED, GROOVE, and RIDGE.

gui/frame2.py
```
window = Tk()
frame = Frame(window)
frame.pack()
frame2 = Frame(window, borderwidth=4, relief=GROOVE)
frame2.pack()
first = Label(frame, text="First label")
first.pack()
second = Label(frame2, text="Second label")
second.pack()
third = Label(frame2, text="Third label")
third.pack()
window.mainloop()
```

Entry

Two widgets let users enter text. The simplest one is Entry, which allows for a single line of text. If we associate a StringVar with the Entry, then

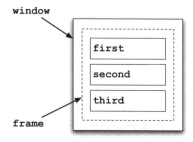

Figure 14.7: STRUCTURE OF A THREE-LABEL GUI

whenever a user types anything into that Entry, the StringVar's value will automatically be updated to the contents of the Entry. If that same String-Var is also bound to a label, then the label will display whatever is currently in the Entry without us doing any extra work. The following code shows how to set this up, and we can see what the GUI looks like in Figure 14.8, on the facing page:

`gui/entry.py`

```python
from Tkinter import *

window = Tk()

frame = Frame(window)
frame.pack()

var = StringVar()

label = Label(frame, textvariable=var)
label.pack()

entry = Entry(frame, textvariable=var)
entry.pack()

window.mainloop()
```

14.3 Models, Views, and Controllers

Using a StringVar to connect a text-entry box and a label is the first step toward separating *models*, *views*, and *controllers*, which is the key to building larger GUIs (and many other kinds of applications). As its name suggests, a view is something that displays information to the user, like Label.

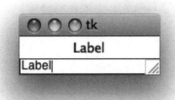

Figure 14.8: AN ENTRY AND A LABEL TIED TOGETHER

Many views, like Entry, also accept input, which they display immediately. The key is that they don't do anything else: they don't calculate average temperatures, move robot arms, or do any other calculations.

Models, on the other hand, just store data, like a piece of text or the current inclination of a telescope. They also don't do calculations; their job is simply to keep track of the application's current state (and, in some cases, to save that state to a file or database and reload it later).

Sitting beside an application's models and views are its controllers, implementing its intelligence. The controller is what decides whether two gene sequences match well enough to be colored green or whether someone is allowed to overwrite an old results file. Controllers may update an application's models, which in turn can trigger changes to its views.

The following code shows what all of this looks like in practice. Here, the model is a simple integer counter, which is implemented as an IntVar so that the view will update itself automatically. The controller is the function click, which updates the model whenever a button is clicked. Four objects make up the view: the root window, a Frame, a Label that shows the current value of counter, and a button that the user can click to increment counter's value:

`gui/mvc.py`

```
# Initialization.
from Tkinter import *

# The controller.
def click():
    counter.set(counter.get() + 1)
```

```
if __name__ == '__main__':
    # More initialization.
    window = Tk()

    # The model.
    counter = IntVar()
    counter.set(0)

    # The views.

    frame = Frame(window)
    frame.pack()

    button = Button(frame, text="Click", command=click)
    button.pack()

    label = Label(frame, textvariable=counter)
    label.pack()

    window.mainloop()
```

The first two arguments used to construct the Button should be familiar by now. The third, command=click, tells it to call the function click each time the user presses the button. This makes use of the fact that, in Python, a function is just another kind of object and can be passed as an argument like anything else.

The click function in the previous code does not have any parameters but uses the variable counter that is defined outside the function. Variables like this are called *global variables*, and their use should be avoided, since they make programs hard to understand. It would be better to pass any variables the function needs into it as parameters. We can't do this using the tools we have seen so far, because the functions that our buttons can call must not have any parameters. We will show you one way to avoid using global variables in the next section, and we'll show you another in Section 13.1, *Class Color*, on page 268.

Using Lambda

The simple counter GUI shown earlier does what it's supposed to, but there is room for improvement. For example, suppose we want to be able to lower the counter's value as well as raise it.

Using only the tools we have seen so far, we could add another button and another controller function like this:

```
gui/mvc2.py
```

```python
# Initialization.
from Tkinter import *
window = Tk()

# The model.
counter = IntVar()
counter.set(0)

# Two controllers
def click_up():
    counter.set(counter.get() + 1)

def click_down():
    counter.set(counter.get() - 1)

# The views.
frame = Frame(window)
frame.pack()

button = Button(frame, text="Up", command=click_up)
button.pack()

button = Button(frame, text="Down", command=click_down)
button.pack()

label = Label(frame, textvariable=counter)
label.pack()

window.mainloop()
```

This seems a little clumsy, though. The two functions click_up and click_down are doing almost the same thing; surely we ought to be able to combine them into one. While we're at it, we ought to pass counter into the function explicitly, rather than using it as a global variable:

```
gui/mvc_one_func.py
```

```python
# The model.
counter = IntVar()
counter.set(0)

# One controller with parameters.
def click(variable, value):
    variable.set(variable.get() + value)
```

The problem with this is figuring out what to pass into the buttons, since we can't provide any arguments for the functions assigned to the buttons' command attributes when creating those buttons.[2] Tkinter cannot read our minds—it can't magically know how many arguments our functions require or what values to pass in for them. For that reason, it requires that the controller functions triggered by buttons and other widgets take zero arguments so they can all be called the same way. It is our job to figure out how to take the two-argument function we want to use and turn it into one that needs no arguments at all.

We *could* do this by writing a couple of wrapper functions:

gui/mvc_wrapper_func.py
```
def click_up():
    click(counter, 1)

def click_down():
    click(counter, -1)
```

but this gets us back to two nearly identical functions that rely on global variables. A better way is to use a *lambda function*, which allows us to create a one-line function anywhere we want without giving it a name.[3] Here's a very simple example:

gui/lambda_1.py
```
>>> lambda: 3
<function <lambda> at 0x00A89B30>
>>> (lambda: 3)()
3
```

The expression lambda: 3 on the first line creates a nameless function that always returns the number 3. The second expression creates this function and immediately calls it, which has the same effect as this:

gui/lambda_2.py
```
>>> def f():
...     return 3
...
>>> f()
3
```

---

2. If we tried to pass parameters to click_up when creating the button, then Python would call click_up and assign the result of the call to the command parameter, instead of assigning the function itself to command.

3. The name *lambda function* comes from the Lambda Calculus, a mathematical system for investigating function definition and application that was developed in the 1930s by Alonzo Church and Stephen Kleene.

However, the lambda form does *not* create a new variable or change an existing one. Finally, lambda functions can take arguments, just like other functions:

gui/lambda_4.py

```
>>> (lambda x: 2 * x)(3)
6
```

So, how does this help us with GUIs? The answer is that it lets us write one controller function to handle different buttons in a general way and then wrap up calls to that function when and as needed. Here's the two-button GUI once again using lambda functions:

gui/mvc3.py

```
# Initialization.
from Tkinter import *
window = Tk()

# The model.
counter = IntVar()
counter.set(0)

# General controller
def click(var, value):
    var.set(var.get() + value)

# The views.
frame = Frame(window)
frame.pack()

button = Button(frame, text="Up", command=lambda: click(counter, 1))
button.pack()

button = Button(frame, text="Down", command=lambda: click(counter, -1))
button.pack()

label = Label(frame, textvariable=counter)
label.pack()

window.mainloop()
```

This code creates a zero-argument lambda function to pass into each button just where it's needed. Those lambda functions then pass the right values into click. This is cleaner than the preceding code because the function definitions are enclosed in the call that uses them—there is no need to clutter the GUI with little functions that are used only in one place.

Note, however, that it is a very bad idea to repeat the same function several times in different places—if you do that, the odds are very high that you will one day want to change them all but will miss one or two. If you find yourself wanting to do this, reorganize the code so that the function is defined only once.

14.4 Style

Every windowing system has its own *look and feel*—square or rounded corners, particular colors, and so on. In this section, we will see how to change the appearance of a GUI's widgets to make an application look more distinctive.

A note of caution before we begin: the default styles of most windowing systems have been chosen by experts trained in graphic design and human-computer interaction. The odds are that any radical changes on your part will make things worse, not better. In particular, be careful about colors (several percent of the male population has some degree of color blindness) and font sizes (many people, particularly the elderly, cannot read small text).

Fonts

Let's start by changing the size, weight, slant, and family of the font used to display text. To specify the size, we provide the height as an integer in points. We can set the weight to either bold or normal and the slant to either italic (slanted) or roman (not slanted).

The font families we can use depend on what system the program is running on. Common families include Times, Courier, and Verdana, but dozens of others are usually available. One note of caution, though: if you choose an unusual font, people running your program on other computers might not have it, so your GUI might appear different than you'd like for them.

The following sets the font of a button to be 14-point, bold, italic, and Courier. The result is shown in Figure 14.9, on the facing page.

`gui/font.py`

```
from Tkinter import *
window = Tk()
button = Button(window, text="Hello", font=("Courier", 14, "bold italic"))
button.pack()
window.mainloop()
```

Figure 14.9: A BUTTON WITH CUSTOMIZED TEXT FONT

Colors

Almost all widgets have background and foreground colors, which can be set using the bg and fg attributes, respectively. As the following code shows, we can set either of these to a standard color by specifying the color's name, such as white, black, red, green, blue, cyan, yellow, or magenta:

gui/color.py

```python
from Tkinter import *
window = Tk()
button = Label(window, text="Hello", bg="green", fg="white")
button.pack()
window.mainloop()
```

The result is shown in Figure 14.10, on the next page. As you can see, pure white text on a bright green background is *not* particularly readable.

We can choose more colors by specifying them using the RGB color model introduced in Section 4.4, *Pixels and Colors*, on page 59. As we said there, RGB values are conventionally written in hexadecimal (base-16) notation; the best way to understand them is to play with them.

Figure 14.10: A label with color

The following color picker does this by updating a piece of text to show the color specified by the red, green, and blue values entered in the text boxes:

`gui/colorpicker.py`

```python
from Tkinter import *

def change(widget, colors):
    '''Update the foreground color of a widget to show the RGB color value
    stored in a dictionary with keys 'red', 'green', and 'blue'.  Does
    *not* check the color value.
    '''
    new_val = '#'
    for name in ('red', 'green', 'blue'):
        new_val += colors[name].get()
    widget['bg'] = new_val

# Create the application.
window = Tk()
frame = Frame(window)
frame.pack()

# Set up text entry widgets for red, green, and blue, storing the
# associated variables in a dictionary for later use.
colors = {}
for (name, col) in (('red', '#FF0000'),
                    ('green', '#00FF00'),
                    ('blue', '#0000FF')):
    colors[name] = StringVar()
    colors[name].set('00')
    entry = Entry(frame, textvariable=colors[name], bg=col, fg="white")
    entry.pack()
```

```
# Display the current color.
current = Label(frame, text='      ', bg='#FFFFFF')
current.pack()

# Give the user a way to trigger a color update.
update = Button(frame, text='Update', command=lambda: change(current, colors))
update.pack()

# Run the application.
mainloop()
```

This is the most complicated GUI we have seen so far but can be understood by breaking it down into a model, some views, and a controller. The model is three StringVars that store the hexadecimal strings representing the current red, green, and blue components of the color to display. These three variables are kept in a dictionary indexed by name for easy access. The controller is the function change, which concatenates the strings to create an RGB color and applies that color to the background of a widget. The views are the text-entry boxes for the color components, the label that displays the current color, and the button that tells the GUI to update itself.

This program works, but neither the GUI nor the code is very attractive. It's annoying to have to click the update button, and if a user ever types anything that isn't a two-digit hexadecimal number into one of the text boxes, it results in an error. The exercises will ask you to redesign both the appearance and the structure of this program.

Layout

One of the things that makes the color picker GUI ugly is the fact that everything is arranged top to bottom. Tkinter uses this *layout* by default, but we can usually come up with something better.

To see how, let's revisit the example from Figure 14.8, on page 299, placing the label and button horizontally. We tell Tkinter to do this by providing a side argument to the pack method. The code to do this is shown here, and the result can be seen in Figure 14.11, on the following page:

gui/side.py

```
from Tkinter import *
window = Tk()
frame = Frame(window)
frame.pack()
```

Figure 14.11: A window with horizontal layout

```
label = Label(frame, text="Name")
label.pack(side="left")
entry = Entry(frame)
entry.pack(side="left")
window.mainloop()
```

Setting side to "left" tells Tkinter that the leftmost part of the label is to be placed next to the left edge of the frame, and then the leftmost part of the entry field is placed next to the right edge of the label—in short, that widgets are to be packed using their left edges. We could equally well pack according to the right, top, or bottom edges, or we could mix packings (though that can quickly become confusing).

For even more control of our window layout, we can use a different layout manager called grid. As its name implies, it treats windows and frames as grids of rows and columns. To add the widget to the window, we call grid instead of pack. Do not call both! The grid call can take several parameters, which are shown in Figure 14.12, on the next page.

In the following code, we place the label in the upper left (row 0, column 0) and the entry field in the lower right (row 1, column 1). As you can see in Figure 14.13, on page 310, this leaves the bottom-left and upper-right corners empty:

gui/grid.py

```
from Tkinter import *
window = Tk()
frame = Frame(window)
frame.pack()
label = Label(frame, text="Name:")
label.grid(row=0, column=0)
entry = Entry(frame)
entry.grid(row=1, column=1)
window.mainloop()
```

Parameter	Description
row	The number of the row to insert the widget into. Row numbers begin at 0.
column	The number of the column to insert the widget into. Column numbers begin at 0.
rowspan	The number of rows the widget occupies. The default is 1.
columnspan	The number of columns the widget occupies. The default is 1.

Figure 14.12: GRID() PARAMETERS

14.5 A Few More Widgets

To end this chapter, we will look at a few more commonly used widgets.

Text

The Entry widget that we have been using since the start of this chapter allows for only a single line of text. If we want multiple lines of text, we use the Text widget instead, as shown here:

`gui/text.py`
```
from Tkinter import *

def cross(text):
    text.insert(INSERT, 'X')

window = Tk()
frame = Frame(window)
frame.pack()

text = Text(frame, height=3, width=10)
text.pack()

button = Button(frame, text="Add", command=lambda: cross(text))
button.pack()

window.mainloop()
```

Text provides a much richer set of methods than the other widgets we have seen so far. We can embed images in the text area, put in tags, select particular lines, and so on. The exercises will give you a chance to explore its capabilities.

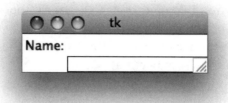

Figure 14.13: A WINDOW WITH GRID LAYOUT

Figure 14.14: A WINDOW WITH A TEXT FIELD

Figure 14.15: A CHECKBUTTON-BASED COLOR PICKER

Checkbutton

Checkbuttons, often called *checkboxes*, have two states, on and off. When a user clicks a checkbutton, the state changes (see Figure 14.15, on the preceding page). We use a Tkinter mutable variable to keep track of the user's selection. Typically, a VarInt variable is used, and the values 1 and 0 indicate on and off, respectively. In the following code, we use three checkbuttons to create a simpler color picker, and we use the config method to change the configuration of a widget after it has been created:

`gui/checkbutton.py`
```python
from Tkinter import *

window = Tk()
frame = Frame(window)
frame.pack()

red = IntVar()
green = IntVar()
blue = IntVar()

for (name, var) in (('R', red), ('G', green), ('B', blue)):
    check = Checkbutton(frame, text=name, variable=var)
    check.pack(side='left')

def recolor(widget, r, g, b):
    color = '#'
    for var in (r, g, b):
        color += 'FF' if var.get() else '00'
    widget.config(bg=color)

label = Label(frame, text='[        ]')
button = Button(frame, text='update',
                command=lambda: recolor(label, red, green, blue))

button.pack(side='left')
label.pack(side='left')

window.mainloop()
```

Menu

The last widget we will look at is Menu.

The following code uses this to create the simple text editor shown in Figure 14.16, on the facing page:

`gui/menu.py`

```python
from Tkinter import *
import tkFileDialog as dialog

def save(root, text):
    data = text.get('0.0', END)
    filename = dialog.asksaveasfilename(
        parent=root,
        filetypes=[('Text', '*.txt')],
        title='Save as...')
    writer = open(filename, 'w')
    writer.write(data)
    writer.close()

def quit(root):
    root.destroy()

window = Tk()
text = Text(window)
text.pack()

menubar = Menu(window)
filemenu = Menu(menubar)
filemenu.add_command(label='Save', command=lambda : save(window, text))
filemenu.add_command(label='Quit', command=lambda : quit(window))

menubar.add_cascade(label = 'File', menu=filemenu)
window.config(menu=menubar)

window.mainloop()
```

The program begins by defining two functions: save, which saves the contents of a text widget, and quit, which closes the application. The save function uses tkFileDialog to create a standard "Save as..." dialog box, which will prompt the user for the name of a text file.

After creating and packing the Text widget, the program creates a menubar, which is the horizontal bar into which we can put one or more menus. It then creates a File menu and adds two menu items to it called Save and Quit. We then add the File menu to the menu bar and run mainloop.

Figure 14.16: A WINDOW WITH A MENU

14.6 Object-Oriented GUIs

The GUIs we have built so far have not been particularly well structured. Most of the code to construct them has not been modularized in functions, and they have relied on global variables. We can get away with this for very small examples, but if we try to build larger applications this way, they will be difficult to understand and debug.

For this reason, almost all real GUIs are built using classes and objects that tie models, views, and controllers together in one tidy package. In the counter shown next, for example, the application's model is a member variable of the class Counter called self.state, and its controllers are the methods upClick and quitClick.

gui/oogui.py

```python
from Tkinter import *

class Counter:
    '''A simple counter GUI using object-oriented programming.'''

    def __init__(self, parent):
        '''Create the GUI.'''

        # Framework.
        self.parent = parent
        self.frame = Frame(parent)
        self.frame.pack()

        # Model.
        self.state = IntVar()
        self.state.set(1)

        # Label displaying current state.
        self.label = Label(self.frame, textvariable=self.state)
        self.label.pack()

        # Buttons to control application.
        self.up = Button(self.frame, text='up', command=self.upClick)
        self.up.pack(side='left')

        self.right = Button(self.frame, text='quit', command=self.quitClick)
        self.right.pack(side='left')

    def upClick(self):
        '''Handle click on 'up' button.'''
        self.state.set(self.state.get() + 1)

    def quitClick(self):
        '''Handle click on 'quit' button.'''
        self.parent.destroy()

if __name__ == '__main__':
    window = Tk()
    myapp = Counter(window)
    window.mainloop()
```

14.7 Summary

In this chapter, we learned the following:

- Most modern programs provide a graphical user interface (GUI) for displaying information and interacting with users. GUIs are built out of widgets, such as buttons, sliders, and text panels; all modern programming languages provide at least one GUI toolkit.

- Unlike command-line programs, GUI applications are usually event-driven. In other words, they react to events such as keystrokes and mouse clicks when and as they occur.

- Experience shows that GUIs should be built using the Model-View-Controller pattern. The model is the data being manipulated; the view displays the current state of the data and gathers input from the user, while the controller decides what to do next.

- Lambda expressions create functions that have no names. These are often used to define the actions that widgets should take when users provide input, without requiring global variables.

- Designing usable GUIs is as challenging a craft as designing software. Being good at the latter doesn't guarantee that you can do the former, but dozens of good books can help you get started.

14.8 Exercises

Here are some exercises for you to try on your own:

1. Write a GUI application with a button labeled "Good-bye." When the button is clicked, the window closes.

2. Write a GUI application with a single button. Initially, the button is labeled 0, but each time it is clicked, the value on the button increases by 1.

3. What is a more readable way to write the following?

   ```
   x = lambda: y
   ```

4. A DNA sequence is a string made up of As, Ts, Cs, and Gs. Write a GUI application in which a DNA sequence is entered, and when the Count button is clicked, the number of As, Ts, Cs and Gs are counted and displayed in the window (see Figure 14.17, on the following page).

5. In Section 2.6, *Local Variables*, on page 22, we wrote a function to convert degrees Fahrenheit to Celsius. Write a GUI application that looks like Figure 14.18, on the following page.

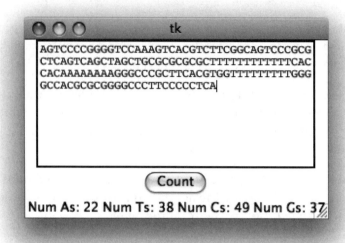

Figure 14.17: OCCURRENCE OF LETTERS IN A DNA SEQUENCE

Figure 14.18: A TEMPERATURE CONVERSION GUI

Figure 14.19: TEMPERATURE CONVERSION RESULTS

When a value is entered in the text field and the Convert button is clicked, the value should be converted from Fahrenheit to Celsius and displayed in the window, as shown in Figure 14.19.

Chapter 15

Databases

In earlier chapters, we used files to store data. This is fine for small problems, but as our data sets become larger and more complex, we need something that will let us search for data in many different ways, control who can view and modify the data, and ensure that the data is correctly formatted. In short, we need a *database*.

Many different kinds of databases exist. Some are like a dictionary that automatically saves itself on disk, while others store backup copies of the objects in a program. The most popular by far, however, are *relational databases*, which are at the heart of most large commercial and scientific software systems. In this chapter, we will introduce the key concepts behind relational databases and then show you how to perform a few common operations. If you would like to know more, there are thousands of books to turn to; [Feh03] is a good place for newcomers to start.

15.1 The Big Picture

A relational database is a collection of *tables*, each of which has a fixed number of columns and a variable number of rows. Each column in a table has a name and contains values of the same data type, such as integer or string. Each row, or *record*, contains values that are related to each other, such as a particular patient's name, age, and blood type. Superficially, each table looks like a spreadsheet or a file with one record per line (see Section 8.1, *One Record per Line*, on page 154), but behind the scenes, the database does a lot of work to keep track of which values are where and how the tables relate to one another.

There are many different brands of database to choose from, including commercial systems like Oracle, IBM's DB2, and Microsoft Access, and open source databases like MySQL and PostgreSQL. Our examples use one called SQLite. It isn't fast enough to handle the heavy loads that sites like Amazon.com experience, but it is free, it is simple to use, and as of Python 2.5 the standard library includes a module called sqlite3 for working with it.

A database is usually stored in a file, or in a collection of files. These files are not formatted as plain text—if you open them in an editor, they will look like garbage, and any changes you make will probably corrupt the data and make the database unusable. Instead, you must interact with the database in one of two ways:

- By typing commands into a GUI, just as you type commands into a Python interpreter. This is good for simple tasks but not for writing applications of your own.

- By writing programs in Python (or some other language). These programs import a library that knows how to work with the kind of database you are using and use that library to create tables, insert records, and fetch the data you want. Your code can then format the results in a web page, calculate statistics, or do whatever else you want.

As shown in Figure 15.1, on the facing page, database libraries can work in two different ways. The simplest is to manipulate the database directly, just as a program would manipulate a file. In most cases, though, the library never actually touches the database itself. Instead, it communicates with a separate program called a *database management system*, or DBMS, which may run on a separate machine and which is designed to manage connections from dozens or hundreds of programs at once. Setting up a DBMS isn't hard, but it isn't trivial either; the fact that SQLite takes the "direct" approach is another reason we chose to use it in this chapter.

Python and other languages do their best to hide the disparity between these two approaches, and between different DBMSs, by having every database-specific library implement the same *application programming interface*, or API. A library's API is just the set of functions it provides for programs to call. If two libraries provide the same API, then programs can switch from one to the other without any code having to be rewritten. We have already seen this idea in the picture module introduced

Figure 15.1: DATABASE ARCHITECTURE

in Section 4.3, *Objects and Methods*, on page 51, which treated GIF, JPEG, and PNG images the same way. In the examples in this chapter, our programs all start with this line:

`db/db_import.cmd`

```
>>> import sqlite3 as dbapi
```

which means, "Find version 3 of the SQLite library, and import version 2 of the database API from it using the name dbapi." If we change our minds later and want to use MySQL as a database, we would just change this line to this:

`db/db_mysql.cmd`

```
>>> import MySQLdb as dbapi
```

and leave the rest of our code alone.

Python's database API hides some of the differences between different database systems, but not all of them. To put data into a database or get information out, we must write commands in a special-purpose language called SQL, which stands for Structured Query Language and is pronounced either as "sequel" or as the three letters "S-Q-L." There are international standards for SQL, but unfortunately, every database interprets those standards differently or adds a few "improvements" that no other database provides. As a result, SQL that works for one database system may work differently, or not at all, for another. Tools like SQLAlchemy (http://www.sqlalchemy.org/ and [Cop08]) have been built to hide the differences between SQL dialects, but they are beyond the scope of this course.

15.2 First Steps

That's enough theory; let's create a database and start doing things with it. As a running example, we will use the predictions for regional

Region	Population
Central Africa	330993
Southeastern Africa	743112
Northern Africa	1037463
Southern Asia	2051941
Asia Pacific	785468
Middle East	687630
Eastern Asia	1362955
South America	593121
Eastern Europe	223427
North America	661157
Western Europe	387933
Japan	100562

Figure 15.2: ESTIMATED WORLD POPULATION IN 2300

populations in the year 2300 shown in Figure 15.2, which is taken from http://www.worldmapper.org. (These values are shown graphically in Figure 15.3, on the next page.)

As promised earlier, we start by telling Python that we want to use sqlite3 by importing the database API:

db/db_import.cmd

```
>>> import sqlite3 as dbapi
```

Next we must make a connection to our database by calling the database module's connect method. This method takes one string as a parameter, which identifies the database we want to connect to. Since SQLite stores each entire database in a single file on disk, this is just the path to the file. If the database does not exist, it will be created.

db/db_connect.cmd

```
>>> con = dbapi.connect('population.db')
```

Once we have a connection, we need to get a *cursor*. Like the cursor in your editor, this keeps track of where we are in the database so that if several programs are accessing the database at the same time, the database can keep track of who is trying to do what:

db/db_cursor.cmd

```
>>> cur = con.cursor()
```

Figure 15.3: World populations in 2300 shown graphically

We can now actually start working with the database. The first step is to create a table to store the population data. To do this, we have to describe the operation we want in SQL, put that SQL in a string, and tell the database to execute that string. The general form of the SQL statement for table creation is as follows:

```
CREATE TABLE TableName(ColumnName Type, ColumnName Type, ...)
```

where the names of tables and columns are like the names of variables in a program and the types are chosen from the types the database supports (which we will talk about in a couple of paragraph). To create a two-column table to store region names as strings and projected populations as integers, we use this:

`db/db_create.cmd`

```
>>> cur.execute('CREATE TABLE PopByRegion(Region TEXT, Population INTEGER)')
<sqlite3.dbapi2.Cursor object at 0x00AEEC50>
```

Our table is called PopByRegion; as you can see, executing the command returns a cursor object, which in this case we don't actually need.

The most commonly used data types in SQLite databases are listed in Figure 15.4, on the following page, along with the corresponding Python data types. A few of these deserve some more explanation:

- Python stores integers using a single 32-bit word of memory if the value will fit into it or a more complex multiword structure if it will not. When fetching values from a database, the sqlite3 library decides which to use based on the size of those values.

Type	Python Equivalent	Use
NULL	NoneType	Means "know nothing about it"
INTEGER	int or long	Integers
REAL	float	8-byte floating-point numbers
TEXT	unicode or str	Strings of characters
BLOB	buffer	Binary data

Figure 15.4: SQLITE DATA TYPES

- As we said way back in Section 3.1, *Strings*, on page 29, Python normally stores strings using ASCII, which represents each character using a single byte and includes only those characters common in English. Python and other (programming) languages use another scheme called Unicode to represent characters from other alphabets like Cyrillic, Arabic, Devanagari, and Thai. By default, sqlite3 represents strings taken from databases as Unicode; we will see in a moment how to get it to use the more familiar str.

- The term BLOB stands for Binary Large OBject, which to a database means a picture, an MP3, or any other lump of bytes that isn't of a more specific type. The Python equivalent is a type we have not seen before called buffer, which also stores a sequence of bytes that have no particular predefined meaning. We will not use BLOBs in our examples, but the exercises will give you a chance to experiment with them.

After we create a table, our next task is to insert data into it. We do this one record at a time using the INSERT command, whose general form is as follows:

```
INSERT INTO TableName VALUES(Value1, Value2, ...)
```

As with the parameters to a function call, the values are matched left to right against the columns. For example, we insert data into the PopByRegion table like this:

db/db_insert.cmd

```
>>> cur.execute('INSERT INTO PopByRegion VALUES("Central Africa", 330993)')
>>> cur.execute('INSERT INTO PopByRegion VALUES("Southeastern Africa", 743112)')
...
>>> cur.execute('INSERT INTO PopByRegion VALUES("Japan", 100562)')
```

Notice that the number and type of values in the INSERT statements matches the number and type of columns in the database table. If we try to insert a value of a different type than the one declared for the column, the library will try to convert it, just as it converts the integer 5 to a floating-point number when we do 1.2 + 5. For example, if we insert the integer 32 into a TEXT column, it will automatically be converted to "32"; similarly, if we insert a string into an INTEGER column, it is parsed to see whether it represents a number. If so, the number is inserted.

If the number of values being inserted does not match the number of columns in the table, the database reports an error, and the data is not inserted. Surprisingly, though, if we try to insert a value that cannot be converted to the correct type, such as the string "string" into an INTEGER field, SQLite will actually do it (though other databases will not).

Saving Changes

After we've inserted data into the database or made any other changes, we must *commit* those changes using the connection's commit method:

db/db_commit.cmd

```
>>> con.commit()
```

Committing to a database is like saving the changes made to a file in a text editor. Until we do it, our changes are not actually stored and are not visible to anyone else who is using the database at the same time. Requiring programs to commit is a form of insurance. If a program crashes partway through a long sequence of database operations and commit is never called, then the database will appear as it did before any of those operations was executed.

15.3 Retrieving Data

Now that we have data in our database, we can start to run *queries* to search for data that meets specified criteria. The general form of a query is as follows:

```
SELECT ColumnName, ColumnName, ... FROM Table
```

where TABLE is the name of the table we want to get data from and the column names specify which values we want. For example, this query retrieves all the data in the table PopByRegion:

db/db_query_allYear2300.cmd

```
>>> cur.execute('SELECT Region, Population FROM PopByRegion')
```

Once the database has executed this query for us, we can access the results one record at a time by calling the cursor's fetchone method, just as we can read one line at a time from a file using readline:

db/db_fetchone.cmd

```
>>> print cur.fetchone()
(u'Central Africa', 330993)
```

The fetchone method returns each record as a tuple (Section 5.9, *Other Kinds of Sequences*, on page 91) whose elements are in the order specified in the query. If there are no more records, fetchone returns None.

By default, TEXT values in the database are returned as Unicode strings (as indicated by the u prefix in front of the string 'Central Africa'). We can tell sqlite3 to return strings as type str instead by assigning the type str to the cursor's text_factory member:

db/db_fetchone_2.cmd

```
con.text_factory = str
>>> print cur.fetchone()
('Northern Africa', 1037163)
```

Just as files have a readlines method to get all the lines in a file at once, database cursors have a fetchall method that returns all the data produced by a query as a list of tuples:

db/db_query_allYear2300_2.cmd

```
>>> print cur.fetchall()
[('Souteastern Africa', 743112), ('Asia Pacific', 785468), ('Middle East',
687630), ('Eastern Asia', 1362955), ('South America', 593121), ('Eastern
 Europe', 223427), ('North America', 661157), ('Western Europe', 387933),
 ('Japan', 100562)]
```

Notice that the tuples are *not* sorted in any way. Like a dictionary or a set (Chapter 9, *Sets and Dictionaries*, on page 179), a database store records in whatever order it think is most efficient. To put the data in a particular order, we could sort the list returned by fetchall. However, it is more efficient to get the database to do the sorting for us by adding an ORDER BY clause to the query like this:

db/db_query_sort.cmd

```
>>> cur.execute('SELECT Region, Population FROM PopByRegion ORDER BY Region')
>>> cur.fetchall()
[('Asia Pacific', 785468), ('Central Africa', 330993), ('Eastern
Asia', 1362955), ('Eastern Europe', 223427), ('Japan', 100562),
('Middle East', 687630), ('North America', 661157), ('Northern
Africa', 1037463), ('South America', 593121), ('Southeastern Africa',
743112), ('Southern Asia', 2051941), ('Western Europe', 387933)]
```

By changing the column name after the phrase ORDER BY, we can change the way the database sorts. As the following code shows, we can also specify whether we want values sorted in ascending (ASC) or descending (DESC) order:

```
>>> cur.execute('SELECT Region, Population FROM PopByRegion
                ORDER BY Population DESC')
>>> cur.fetchall()
[('Southern Asia', 2051941), ('Eastern Asia', 1362955), ('Northern
Africa', 1037463), ('Asia Pacific', 785468), ('Southeastern Africa',
743112), ('Middle East', 687630), ('North America', 661157), ('South
America', 593121), ('Western Europe', 387933), ('Central Africa',
330993), ('Eastern Europe', 223427), ('Japan', 100562)]
```

Rather than getting all columns, we can specify one or more columns by name. We can also use * to indicate that we want all columns, just as we would use import * to import all of the contents of a module:

```
>>> cur.execute('SELECT Region FROM PopByRegion')
[('Central Africa',), ('Southeastern Africa',), ('Northern Africa',),
('Southern Asia',), ('Asia Pacific',), ('Middle East',), ('Eastern
Asia',), ('South America',), ('Eastern Europe',), ('North America',),
('Western Europe',), ('Japan',)]
>>> cur.execute('SELECT * FROM PopByRegion')
[('Central Africa', 330993), ('Southeastern Africa', 743112),
('Northern Africa', 1037463), ('Southern Asia', 2051941), ('Asia
Pacific', 785468), ('Middle East', 687630), ('Eastern Asia', 1362955),
('South America', 593121), ('Eastern Europe', 223427), ('North
America', 661157), ('Western Europe', 387933), ('Japan', 100562)]
```

Query Conditions

Much of the time, we want only some of the data in the database. (Think about what would happen if you asked Google for all of the web pages it had stored.) We can select a subset of the data by using the keyword WHERE to specify conditions that the rows we want must satisfy. For example, we can get the regions with populations greater than 1 million using the greater-than operator:

```
>>> cur.execute('SELECT Region FROM PopByRegion WHERE Population > 1000000')
>>> print cur.fetchall()
[('Northern Africa',), ('Southern Asia',), ('Eastern Asia',))]
```

Operator	Description
=	Equal to
!=	Not equal to
>	Greater than
<	Less than
>=	Greater than or equal to
<=	Less than or equal to

Figure 15.5: SQL RELATIONAL OPERATORS

The relational operators that may be used with WHERE are listed in Figure 15.5. Not surprisingly, they are the same as the ones that Python and other programming languages provide.

As well as these relational operators, we can also use the Boolean operators AND, OR, and NOT. To get a list of regions with populations greater than 1 million that have names that come before the letter *L* in the alphabet, we would use this:

`db/db_where_2.cmd`

```
>>> cur.execute('SELECT Region FROM PopByRegion
                 WHERE Population > 1000000 AND Region < "L"')
>>> print cur.fetchall()
[('Eastern Asia',))]
```

WHERE conditions are always applied row by row—they cannot be used to compare two or more rows. We will see how to do that in Section 15.7, *Using Joins to Combine Tables*, on page 332.

15.4 Updating and Deleting

Data often changes over time, so we need to be able to change the information stored in databases. To do that, we use the UPDATE command, as shown here:

`db/db_update.cmd`

```
>>> cur.execute('SELECT * FROM PopByRegion WHERE Region = "Japan"')
>>> cur.fetchone()
('Japan', 100562)
>>> cur.execute('UPDATE PopByRegion SET Population = 100600
                 WHERE Region = "Japan"')
>>> cur.execute('SELECT * FROM PopByRegion WHERE Region = "Japan"')
>>> cur.fetchone()
('Japan', 100600)
```

We can also delete records from the database:

`db/db_delete.cmd`

```
>>> cur.execute('DELETE FROM PopByRegion WHERE Region < "L"')
>>> cur.execute('SELECT * FROM PopByRegion');
>>> cur.fetchall()
[('Southeastern Africa', 743112), ('Northern Africa', 1037463),
('Southern Asia', 2051941), ('Middle East', 687630), ('South America',
593121), ('North America', 661157), ('Western Europe', 387933)]
```

In both cases, all records that meet the WHERE condition are affected. If we do not include a WHERE condition, then all rows in the database are updated or removed. Of course, we can always put records back into the database:

`db/db_delete_2.cmd`

```
>>> cur.execute('INSERT INTO PopByRegion VALUES ("Japan", 100562)')
```

To remove an entire table from the database, we can use the DROP command:

```
DROP TABLE TableName
```

For example, if we no longer want the table PopByRegion, we would execute this:

`db/db_drop.cmd`

```
>>> cur.execute('DROP TABLE PopByRegion');
```

When a table is dropped, all the data it contained is lost. You should be very, very sure you want to do this (and even then, it's probably a good idea to make a backup copy of the database before deleting any sizable tables).

15.5 Transactions

Database operations are almost always grouped into a *transaction*. No operation in a transaction can be committed unless every single one can be successfully committed in sequence. If an operations fails, the transaction must be *rolled back*. That causes all the operations in the transaction to be undone. Using transactions ensures the database doesn't contain half-baked results. Databases create transactions automatically. As soon as you try to start an operation, it becomes part of a transaction. When you commit the transaction successfully, the changes becomes permanent, and the database creates a new one.

Imagine a library that may have multiple copies of the same book. It uses a computerized system to track its books by their ISBN number. Whenever a patron signs out a book, the following code is executed by one of the library computers:

db/db_transaction_1.cmd

```
cur.execute('SELECT SignedOut FROM Books WHERE ISBN = "%s"' % isbn)
signedOut = cur.fetchone()[0]
cur.execute('UPDATE Books SET SignedOut = %d
            WHERE ISBN = "%s"' % (signedOut + 1, isbn))
cur.commit()
```

When a patron returns a book, the reverse happens:

db/db_transaction_2.cmd

```
cur.execute('SELECT SignedOut FROM Books WHERE ISBN = "%s"' % isbn)
signedOut = cur.fetchone()[0]
cur.execute('UPDATE Books SET SignedOut = %d
            WHERE ISBN = "%s"' % (signedOut - 1, isbn))
cur.commit()
```

What if the library had two computers that handled book signouts and returns? Both computers connect to the same database. What would happen if one patron tried to return a copy of *Gray's Anatomy*, while another was signing out a different copy of the same book at the exact same time? Here's one possibility:

db/db_transaction_3.cmd

```
Computer A: cur.execute('SELECT SignedOut FROM Books WHERE ISBN = "%s"' % isbn)
Computer A: signedOut = cur.fetchone()[0]

Computer B: cur.execute('SELECT SignedOut FROM Books WHERE ISBN = "%s"' % isbn)
Computer B: signedOut = cur.fetchone()[0]

Computer A: cur.execute('UPDATE Books SET SignedOut = %d
                        WHERE ISBN = "%s"' % (signedOut + 1, isbn))
Computer A: cur.commit()

Computer B: cur.execute('UPDATE Books SET SignedOut = %d
                        WHERE ISBN = "%s"' % (signedOut - 1, isbn))
Computer B: cur.commit()
```

Notice that Computer B counts the number of signed-out copies before Computer A updates the database. After Computer A commits its changes, the value that Computer B fetched is no longer accurate. If Computer B were allowed to commit its changes, the library database would account for more books than the library actually has!

Fortunately, databases can detect such a situation and would prevent Computer B from committing its transaction.

15.6   Using NULL for Missing Data

In the real world, we often don't have all the data we want. We might be missing the time at which an experiment was performed or the postal code of a patient being given a new kind of treatment. Rather than leave what we *do* know out of the database, we may choose to insert it and use the value NULL to represent the missing values. For example, if there is a region whose population we don't know, we could insert this into our database:

`db/db_null.cmd`

```
>>> cur.execute('INSERT INTO PopByRegion VALUES ("Mars", NULL)')
```

On the other hand, we probably don't ever want a record in the database that has a NULL region name. We can prevent this from ever happening, stating that the column is NOT NULL when the table is created:

`db/db_null_2.cmd`

```
>>> cur.execute('CREATE TABLE Test (Region TEXT NOT NULL, Population INTEGER)')
```

Now when we try to insert a NULL region into our new Test table, we get an error message:

`db/db_null_3.cmd`

```
>>> cur.execute('INSERT INTO Test VALUES (NULL, 456789)')
Traceback (most recent call last):
  File "<string>", line 1, in <string>
sqlite3.dbapi2.IntegrityError: Test.Region may not be NULL
```

Stating that the value must not be NULL is not always necessary, and imposing such a constraint may not be reasonable in some cases. Rather than using NULL, it may sometimes be more appropriate to use the value zero, an empty string, or false. You should do so in cases where you know something about the data and use NULL only in cases where you know nothing at all about it.

In fact, some experts recommend not using NULL at all because its behavior is counterintuitive (at least until you've retrained your intuition). The general rule is that operations involving NULL produce NULL as a result; the reasoning is that if the computer doesn't know what one of the operation's inputs is, it can't know what the output is either.

Adding a number to NULL therefore produces NULL, no matter what the number was, and multiplying by NULL also produces NULL.

Things are more complicated with logical operations. The expression NULL OR 1 produces 1, rather than NULL, because of the following:

- If the first argument was false (or 0, or the empty string, or some equivalent value), the result would be 1.

- If the first argument was true (or nonzero, or a nonempty string) the result would also be 1.

The technical term for this is *three-valued logic*. In SQL's view of the world, things aren't just true or false—they can be true, false, or unknown, and NULL represents the latter. Unfortunately, different databases interpret ambiguities in the SQL standard in different ways, so their handling of NULL is not consistent. NULL should therefore be used with caution and only when other approaches won't work.

15.7 Using Joins to Combine Tables

When designing a database, it often makes sense to divide data between two or more tables. For example, if we are maintaining a database of patient records, we would probably want at least four tables: one for the patient's personal information (such as their name date of birth), a second to keep track of their appointments, a third for information about the doctors who are treating them, and a fourth for information about the hospitals those doctors work in (see Figure 15.6, on the facing page). We could store all of this in one table, as shown Figure 15.7, on the next page, but then a lot of information would be needlessly duplicated.

If we divide information between tables, though, we need some way to pull that information back together. For example, if we want to know the hospitals at which a patient has had appointments, we need to combine data from all four tables to find out:

- What appointments the patient has had

- Which doctor each appointment was with

- Which hospital that doctor works at

The right way to do this in a relational database is to use a *join*. As the name suggests, a join combines information from two or more tables to

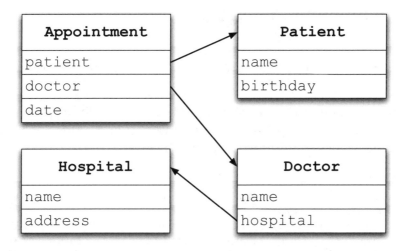

Figure 15.6: Dividing data between tables

Patient-Doctor-Appointment-Hospital					
patient	birthday	doctor	date	hospital	address
Alice	1978/04/02	Rajani	2008/09/01	Central	52 Walnut St.
Alice	1978/04/02	Nianiaris	2008/10/04	Central	52 Walnut St.
Alice	1978/04/02	Newton	2008/09/14	East	8 Elm St.
Zack	1964/12/15	Newton	2008/09/18	East	8 Elm St.
Zack	1964/12/15	Vaz	2008/11/01	East	8 Elm St.

Figure 15.7: A bad database design

create a new set of records, each of which can contain some or all of the information in the tables involved.

To begin, let's add another table that contains the names of countries, the regions that they are in, and their populations:

db/db_add_tables.cmd

```
>>> cur.execute('CREATE TABLE PopByCountry(Region TEXT, Country TEXT,
                Population INTEGER)')
```

and then insert data into the new table:

db/db_insert_2.cmd

```
>>> cur.execute('INSERT INTO PopByCountry VALUES("Eastern Asia", "China",
                1285238)')
```

Inserting data one row at a time like this requires a lot of typing. It is simpler to make a list of tuples to be inserted and write a loop that inserts the values from these tuples one by one:

db/db_insert_3.cmd

```
>>> countries = [("Eastern Asia", "DPR Korea", 24056), ("Eastern Asia",
"Hong Kong (China)", 8764), ("Eastern Asia", "Mongolia", 3407), ("Eastern
Asia", "Republic of Korea", 41491), ("Eastern Asia", "Taiwan", 1433),
("North America", "Bahamas", 368), ("North America", "Canada", 40876),
("North America", "Greenland", 43), ("North America", "Mexico", 126875),
("North America", "United States", 493038)]
>>> for c in countries:
...     cur.execute('INSERT INTO PopByCountry VALUES (?, ?, ?)', (c[0], c[1], c[2]))
...
>>> con.commit()
```

This time, the call to execute has two arguments. The first is the SQL command with question marks as placeholders for the values we want to insert. The second is a tuple of values, which the database matches up against the question marks from left to right when it executes the command.

Now that we have two tables in our database, we can use joins to combine the information they contain. There are several types of joins; we will begin with *inner joins*, which involve the following:

1. Constructing the *cross product* of the tables

2. Discarding rows that do not meet the selection criteria

3. Selecting columns from the remaining rows

These steps are shown graphically in Figure 15.8, on the facing page. First, all combinations of all rows in the tables are combined, which makes the cross product. Second, the selection criteria specified by WHERE is applied, and rows that don't match are removed. Finally, the selected columns are kept, and all others are discarded.

In an earlier query, we retrieved the names of regions with projected populations greater than 1 million. Using an inner join, we can get the names of the countries that are in those regions.

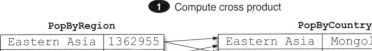

1 Compute cross product

PopByRegion			PopByCountry		
Eastern Asia	1362955		Eastern Asia	Mongolia	3407
North America	661157		North America	Greenland	43

2a Keep rows where `PopByRegion.Region = PopByCountry.Region`

Eastern Asia	1362955	**Eastern Asia**	Mongolia	3407
North America	661157	**North America**	Greenland	43
Eastern Asia	1362955	North America	Greenland	43
North America	661157	Eastern Asia	Mongolia	3407

2b Keep rows where `PopByRegion.Population > 1000000`

Eastern Asia	**1362955**	Eastern Asia	Mongolia	3407
North America	661157	North America	Greenland	43

3 Keep columns `PopByRegion.Region` and `PopByCountry.Country`

Eastern Asia	1362955	Eastern Asia	**Mongolia**	3407

Figure 15.8: INNER JOINS IN ACTION

The query and its result look like this:

`db/db_inner_join.cmd`

```
>>> cur.execute('''
SELECT PopByRegion.Region, PopByCountry.Country
FROM    PopByRegion INNER JOIN PopByCountry
WHERE   (PopByRegion.Region = PopByCountry.Region)
AND     (PopByRegion.Population > 1000000)
''')
>>> print cur.fetchall()
[('Eastern Asia', 'China'), ('Eastern Asia', 'DPR Korea'),
('Eastern Asia', 'Hong Kong (China)'), ('Eastern Asia', 'Mongolia'),
('Eastern Asia', 'Republic of Korea'), ('Eastern Asia', 'Taiwan')]
```

To understand what this query is doing, we can analyze it in terms of the three steps outlined earlier:

1. Combine every row of PopByRegion with every row of PopByCountry. PopByRegion has two columns and twelve rows, while PopByCountry has three columns and eleven rows, so this produces a temporary table with five columns and 132 rows (see Figure 15.9, on the next page).

Central Africa	330993	Eastern Asia	DPR Korea	24056
Southeastern Africa	743112	Eastern Asia	DPR Korea	24056
Northern Africa	1037463	Eastern Asia	DPR Korea	24056
Southern Asia	2051941	Eastern Asia	DPR Korea	24056
Asia Pacific	785468	Eastern Asia	DPR Korea	24056
Middle East	687630	Eastern Asia	DPR Korea	24056
Eastern Asia	1362955	Eastern Asia	DPR Korea	24056
South America	593121	Eastern Asia	DPR Korea	24056
Eastern Europe	223427	Eastern Asia	DPR Korea	24056
North America	661157	Eastern Asia	DPR Korea	24056
Western Europe	387933	Eastern Asia	DPR Korea	24056
Japan	100562	Eastern Asia	DPR Korea	24056
Central Africa	330993	Eastern Asia	Hong Kong (China)	8764
Southeastern Africa	743112	Eastern Asia	Hong Kong (China)	8764
Northern Africa	1037463	Eastern Asia	Hong Kong (China)	8764
Southern Asia	2051941	Eastern Asia	Hong Kong (China)	8764
Asia Pacific	785468	Eastern Asia	Hong Kong (China)	8764
Middle East	687630	Eastern Asia	Hong Kong (China)	8764
Eastern Asia	1362955	Eastern Asia	Hong Kong (China)	8764
South America	593121	Eastern Asia	Hong Kong (China)	8764
Eastern Europe	223427	Eastern Asia	Hong Kong (China)	8764
North America	661157	Eastern Asia	Hong Kong (China)	8764
Western Europe	387933	Eastern Asia	Hong Kong (China)	8764
Japan	100562	Eastern Asia	Hong Kong (China)	8764
...	...	...	...	...

Figure 15.9: AN INNER JOIN IN PROGRESS

2. Discard rows that do not meet the selection criteria. The join's WHERE clause specifies two of these: the region taken from PopByRegion must be the same as the region taken from PopByCountry, and the region's population must be greater than 1 million. The first criterion ensures that we don't look at records that combine countries in North America with regional populations in East Asia; the second filters out information about countries in region whose populations are less than our threshold.

3. Finally, we select the region and country names from the rows that have survived.

To find the regions where one country accounts for more than 10 percent of the region's overall population, we would also need to join the two tables.

db/db_duplicates.cmd

```
>>> cur.execute('''
SELECT PopByRegion.Region
FROM PopByRegion INNER JOIN PopByCountry
WHERE (PopByRegion.Region = PopByCountry.Region)
AND ((PopByCountry.Population * 1.0) / PopByRegion.Population > 0.10)''')
>>> print cur.fetchall()
[('Eastern Asia',), ('North America',), ('North America',)]
```

We use multiplication and division in our WHERE condition to calculate the percentage of the region's population by country as a floating-point number. The resulting list contains duplicates, since more than one North American country accounts for more than 10 percent of the region's population. To remove the duplicates, we add the keyword DISTINCT to the query:

db/db_distinct.cmd

```
>>> cur.execute('''
SELECT DISTINCT PopByRegion.Region
FROM PopByRegion INNER JOIN PopByCountry
WHERE (PopByRegion.Region = PopByCountry.Region)
AND ((PopByCountry.Population * 1.0) / PopByRegion.Population > 0.10)''')
>>> print cur.fetchall()
[('Eastern Asia',), ('North America',)]
```

15.8 Keys and Constraints

Our query in the previous section relied on the fact that our regions and countries were uniquely identified by their names. A column in a table that is used this way is called a *key*. Ideally, a key's values should be unique, just like the keys in a dictionary. We can tell the database to enforce this constraint by adding a PRIMARY KEY clause when we create the table. For example, when we created the PopByRegion table, we should have specified the primary key:

db/db_primary_key.cmd

```
>>> cur.execute('CREATE TABLE PopByRegion (Region TEXT NOT NULL,
                 Population INTEGER NOT NULL, PRIMARY KEY (Region))');
```

Just as a key in a dictionary can be made up of multiple values, the primary key for a database table can consist of multiple columns.

The following code uses the CONSTRAINT keyword to specify that no two entries in the table being created will ever have the same values for region *and* country:

`db/db_constraint.cmd`

```
>>> cur.execute('''
CREATE TABLE PopByCountry(
    Region TEXT NOT NULL,
    Country TEXT NOT NULL,
    Population INTEGER NOT NULL,
    CONSTRAINT Country_Key PRIMARY KEY (Region, Country))
''')
```

A table can also contain one or more *foreign keys*. As the name suggests, these are values that aren't guaranteed to be unique in that table but that are (unique) keys in another table. Going back to the example of patients, appointments, doctors, and hospitals, suppose the hospital's name is the primary key in the HOSPITAL table. The DOCTOR table could then have a column called HOSPITAL_NAME to identify where the doctor worked. This column would be a foreign key, since its values wouldn't be unique in DOCTOR (many doctors could work at the same hospital) but would be unique in the HOSPITAL table.

In practice, most database designers do not use real names as primary keys. Instead, they usually create a unique integer ID for each "thing" in the database, such as a driver's license number or a patient ID. This is partly done for efficiency's sake—integers are faster to sort and compare than strings—but the real reason is that it is a simple way to deal with hospitals (or people) that have the same name. There are a lot of Jane Smiths in the world; using that name as a primary key in a database is almost guaranteed to lead to confusion. Giving each person a unique ID, on the other hand, ensures that they can be told apart.

Using unique IDs in this way also makes some operations much easier to implement. For example, imagine what would happen in a database using a hospital's name as a primary key if the hospital changed its name. Someone would have to write code that found every use of that hospital's name and changed it to the new value. If the hospital was identified by an integer hospital ID, then renaming the hospital would be as simple as replacing one string with another—the doctor records that referred to the hospital would not have to be updated.

Aggregate Function	Description
AVG	Average of the values
MIN	Minimum value
MAX	Maximum value
COUNT	Number of non-null values
SUM	Sum of the values

Figure 15.10: AGGREGATE FUNCTIONS

15.9   Advanced Features

The SQL we have seen so far is powerful enough for many everyday tasks, but other questions require more powerful tools. This chapter introduces a handful and shows when and how they are useful. If you need to do things that are even more complicated, you may want to add [Bea05] and [VH07] to your reading list.

Aggregation

Our next task is to calculate the total projected world population for the year 2300. We will do this by adding up the values in PopByRegion's Population column using the SQL *aggregating* function SUM:

`db/db_aggregate.cmd`

```
>>> cur.execute('SELECT SUM (Population) FROM PopByRegion')
>>> cur.fetchone()
(8965762,)
```

SQL provides many other aggregation functions (see Figure 15.10). All of these are *associative*; that is, the result doesn't depend on the order of operations.[1] This ensures that the result doesn't depend on the order in which records are pulled out of tables, which is something that only the database knows.

Grouping

What if we only had the table PopByCountry and wanted to find the projected population for each region? We could get the table's contents into a Python program using SELECT * and then loop over them to add them

---

1. Addition and multiplication are associative, since 1 + (2 + 3) produces the same results as (1 + 2) + 3, and 4 * (5 * 6) produces the same result as (4 * 5) * 6. By contrast, subtraction is not: 1 - (2 - 3) is not the same thing as (1 - 2) - 3.

up by region, but again, it is simpler and more efficient to have the database do the work for us. In this case, we use SQL's GROUP BY to collect results into subsets:

db/db_group.cmd

```
>>> cur.execute('SELECT SUM (Population) FROM PopByCountry GROUP BY Region')
>>> cur.fetchall()
[(1364389,), (661200,)]
```

Since we have asked the database to construct groups by Region and there are two distinct values in this column in the table, the database divides the records into two subsets. It then applies the SUM function to each group separately to give us the projected populations of Eastern Asia and North America (see Figure 15.11, on the next page).

Self-Joins

SQL is powerful, but it isn't always obvious how to translate a simple question into selects, joins, and Boolean conditions. Once you have seen a few examples of common cases, though, it is easy to apply the pattern in other situations.

A common example is the problem of comparing a table's values to themselves. Suppose that we want to find pairs of countries whose populations are close to one another—say, within 1,000 of one another. Our first attempt might look like this:

db/db_self1.cmd

```
>>> cur.execute('SELECT Country FROM PopByCountry
                    WHERE (ABS(Population - Population) < 1000)')
>>> cur.fetchall()
[('China',), ('DPR Korea',), ('Hong Kong (China)',), ('Mongolia',),
('Republic of Korea',), ('Taiwan',), ('Bahamas',), ('Canada',),
('Greenland',), ('Mexico',), ('United States',)]
```

The output is definitely not what we want, and there are two reasons why. First, the phrase SELECT Country is going to return only one country per record, but we want pairs of countries. Second, the expression ABS(Population - Population) is always going to return zero; since we're subtracting each country's population from itself, every results will be less than 1,000, so the names of all the countries in the table will be returned.

What we actually want to do is compare the population in one row with the populations in the other rows. To do this, we need to join PopByCountry with itself (see Figure 15.12, on page 342) using an INNER JOIN.

PopByCountry

North America	Bahamas	368
North America	Mexico	126875
Eastern Asia	Mongolia	3407
Eastern Asia	Republic of Korea	41491

1 Group by `Region` and compute SUM of `Population`

North America	Bahamas	368
North America	Mexico	126875
		127243

Eastern Asia	Mongolia	3407
Eastern Asia	Republic of Korea	41491
		44898

2 Keep selected columns

North America	127243
Eastern Asia	44898

Figure 15.11: SUMMATION

PopByCountry

North America	Canada	40876
North America	United States	493038
Eastern Asia	Taiwan	1433

PopByCountry cross joined with itself

North America	Canada	40876	North America	Canada	40876
North America	United States	493038	North America	United States	493038
Eastern Asia	Taiwan	1433	Eastern Asia	Taiwan	1433
North America	Canada	40876	North America	United States	493038
North America	United States	493038	Eastern Asia	Taiwan	1433
Eastern Asia	Taiwan	1433	North America	Canada	40876
North America	Canada	40876	Eastern Asia	Taiwan	1433
North America	United States	493038	North America	Canada	40876
Eastern Asia	Taiwan	1433	North America	United States	493038

Figure 15.12: JOINING A TABLE TO ITSELF

This will result in the rows for each pair of countries being combined into a single row with six columns: two regions, two countries, and two populations. To tell them apart, we have to give the two instances of the PopByCountry table temporary names (in this case A and B) to each table:

`db/db_self_join.cmd`

```
>>> cur.execute('''
SELECT A.Country, B.Country
FROM    PopByCountry A INNER JOIN PopByCountry B
WHERE   (ABS(A.Population - B.Population) <= 1000)
AND     (A.Country != B.Country)''')
>>> cur.fetchall()
[('Republic of Korea', 'Canada'), ('Bahamas', 'Greenland'), ('Canada',
'Republic of Korea'), ('Greenland', 'Bahamas')]
```

Notice that we have used ABS to get the absolute value of the population difference. If we simply wrote this:

```
(A.Population - B.Population) <= 1000
```

then our results would have included pairs like ('Greenland', 'China'), because every negative difference is less than 1,000. If we want each pair of countries to appear only once, we could rewrite the second half of the condition as follows:

```
A.Country < B.Country
```

which would rule out half of each duplicated pair of countries.

Nested Queries

Up to now, our queries have involved only one SELECT command. Since the result of every query looks exactly like a table with a fixed number of columns and some number of rows, we can run a second query on the result, that is, run a SELECT on the result of another SELECT, rather than directly on the database's tables. Such queries are called *nested queries* and are analogous to having one function call another, which might in turn call a third.

To see why we would want to do this, let's try to write a query on the PopByCountry table to get the regions that do *not* have a country with a population of exactly 8,764. Our first attempt looks like this:

```
db/db_nested_1.cmd
>>> cur.execute('''
SELECT DISTINCT Region
FROM            PopByCountry
WHERE           (PopByCountry.Population != 8764)
''')
>>> cur.fetchall()
[('Eastern Asia',), ('North America',)]
```

This result is wrong—Hong Kong has a projected population of 8,764, so Eastern Asia should not have been returned. Because there are other countries in Eastern Asia whose populations are not 8,764, though, Eastern Asia was included in the final results.

Let's rethink our strategy. What we have to do is to find out which regions include countries with a population 8,764 and then exclude those regions from our final result—basically, find the regions that *fail* our condition and subtract them from the set of all countries (see Figure 15.13, on the next page). The first step is to get those regions that have countries with a population of 8,764:

```
db/db_nested_2.cmd
>>> cur.execute('''
SELECT DISTINCT Region
FROM            PopByCountry
WHERE           (PopByCountry.Population = 8764)
''')
>>> cur.fetchall()
[('Eastern Asia',)
```

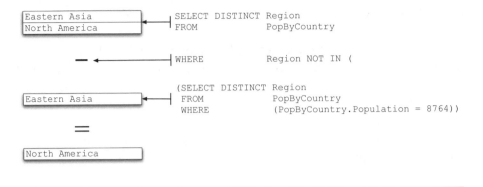

Figure 15.13: NESTED NEGATION

Now we want to get the names of regions that were not in the results of our first query. To do this, we will use a WHERE condition and NOT IN:

`db/db_nested_3.cmd`

```
>>> cur.execute('''
SELECT DISTINCT Region
FROM            PopByCountry
WHERE           Region NOT IN
    (SELECT DISTINCT Region
      FROM            PopByCountry
      WHERE           (PopByCountry.Population = 8764))
''')
>>> cur.fetchall()
[('North America',)]
```

This time we got what we were looking for. Nested queries are often used for situations like this one where negation is involved.

15.10 Summary

In this chapter, we learned the following:

- Most large applications store information in relational databases. A database is made up of tables, each of which stores logically related information. A table has one or more columns, each of which has a name and a type, and zero or more rows, or records. In most tables, each row can be identified by a unique key, which consists or one or more of the values in the row.

- Commands to put data into databases, or get data out, are written in a specialized language called SQL. SQL is supposed to be a standard, but there are significant differences in how different databases implement it.

- SQL commands can be sent to databases interactively from GUIs or command-line tools, but for larger jobs, it is more common to write programs that create SQL and process the results. Since SQL's data types are not always exactly the same as those in the language used to write the program, it may be necessary to translate from one to the other.

- Changes made to a database do not actually take effect until they are committed. This ensures that if two or more programs are working with a database at the same time, it will always be in a consistent state. However, it also means that operations in one program can fail because of something that another program is doing.

- SQL queries must specify the table(s) and column(s) that values are to be taken from. They may also specify Boolean conditions those values must satisfy and the ordering of results.

- Simple queries work on one row at a time, but programs can join tables to combine values from different rows. Queries can also group and aggregate rows to calculate sums, averages, and other values.

- Databases can use the special value NULL to represent missing information. However, it must be used with caution, since operations on NULL values do not behave in the same way as operations on "real" values.

15.11 Exercises

Here are some exercises for you to try on your own:

1. In this exercise, you will create a table to store the population and land area of the Canadian provinces and territories according to the 2001 Census. Our data is taken from http://www12.statcan.ca/english/census01/home/index.cfm.

    a) Create a new database called census.db.

    b) Make a database table called Density that will hold the name of the province or territory (TEXT), the population (INTEGER), and the land area (REAL).

Province/Territory	Population	Land Area
Newfoundland and Labrador	512930	370501.69
Prince Edward Island	135294	5684.39
Nova Scotia	908007	52917.43
New Brunswick	729498	71355.67
Quebec	7237479	1357743.08
Ontario	11410046	907655.59
Manitoba	1119583	551937.87
Saskatchewan	978933	586561.35
Alberta	2974807	639987.12
British Columbia	3907738	926492.48
Yukon Territory	28674	474706.97
Northwest Territories	37360	1141108.37
Nunavut	26745	1925460.18

Figure 15.14: 2001 CANADIAN CENSUS DATA

c) Insert the data from Figure 15.14.

d) Display the contents of the table.

e) Display the populations.

f) Display the provinces that have populations of less than 1 million.

g) Display the provinces that have populations less than 1 million or greater than 5 million.

h) Display the provinces that do not have populations less than 1 million or greater than 5 million.

i) Display the populations of provinces that have a land area greater than 200,000 square kilometers.

j) Display the provinces along with their population densities (population divided by land area).

2. For this exercise, add a new table called Capitals to the database. Capitals has three columns—province/territory (TEXT), capital (TEXT), and population (INTEGER)—and it holds the data shown in Figure 15.15, on the facing page. Provide the SQL to do the following:

a) Retrieve the contents of the table.

Province/Territory	Capital	Population
Newfoundland and Labrador	St. John's	172918
Prince Edward Island	Charlottetown	58358
Nova Scotia	Halifax	359183
New Brunswick	Fredericton	81346
Quebec	Quebec	682757
Ontario	Toronto	4682897
Manitoba	Winnipeg	671274
Saskatchewan	Regina	192800
Alberta	Edmonton	937845
British Columbia	Victoria	311902
Yukon Territory	Whitehorse	21405
Northwest Territories	Yellowknife	16541
Nunavut	Iqaluit	5236

Figure 15.15: 2001 CANADIAN CENSUS DATA: CAPITAL CITY POPULATIONS

b) Retrieve the populations of the provinces and capitals (in a list of tuples of the form (province population, capital population)).

c) Retrieve the land area of the provinces whose capitals have populations greater than 100,000.

d) Retrieve the provinces with land densities less than 2 people per square kilometer and capital city populations more than 500,000.

e) Retrieve the total land area of Canada.

f) Retrieve the average capital city population.

g) Retrieve the lowest capital city population.

h) Retrieve the highest province/territory population.

i) Retrieve the provinces that have land densities within 0.5 of each other. Report each pair of provinces only once.

3. Write a Python program that creates a new database and executes the following SQL statements. How do the results of the SELECT statements differ from what you would expect Python itself to do? Why?

```
CREATE TABLE Numbers(Val INTEGER)
INSERT INTO Numbers Values(1)
INSERT INTO Numbers Values(2)
SELECT * FROM Numbers WHERE 1/0
SELECT * FROM Numbers WHERE 1/0 AND Val > 0
SELECT * FROM Numbers WHERE Val > 0 AND 1/0
```

4. A friend of yours has written a run_query function that will execute a single SQL query against a database and return the results, doing all of the required setup and teardown automatically:

```
import sqlite3 as dbapi

def run_query(db, query):
    '''Return the results of running the given query on database db.'''

    con = dbapi.connect(db)
    cur =  con.cursor()
    cur.execute(query)
    data = cur.fetchall()
    cur.close()
    con.close()
    return data

# Example of use.
run_query(db, 'SELECT * FROM Precipitation')
```

Modify this function so that it will use a tuple of arguments if one is provided so that both the previous call and the following one will work:

```
run_query(db, 'SELECT City, Temp, Snow FROM Precipitation
            WHERE Snow >= (?) and Temp > (?)', (s,t))
```

Appendix A

Bibliography

[AW06]   Mike Andrews and James A. Whittaker. *How to Break Web Software*. Addison-Wesley, Boston, MA, 2006.

[Bea05]   Alan Beaulieu. *Learning SQL*. O'Reilly & Associates, Inc, Sebastopol, CA, 2005.

[Cop08]   Rick Copeland. *Essential SQLAlchemy*. O'Reilly & Associates, Inc, Sebastopol, CA, 2008.

[DEM02]   Allen Downey, Jeff Elkner, and Chris Meyers. *How to Think Like a Computer Scientist: Learning with Python*. Green Tea Press, Needham, MA, 2002.

[Feh03]   Chris Fehily. *SQL: Visual QuickStart Guide*. Peachpit Press, Berkeley, CA, 2003.

[GL07]   Michael H. Goldwasser and David Letscher. *Object-Oriented Programming in Python*. Prentice Hall, Englewood Cliffs, NJ, 2007.

[Guz04]   Mark Guzdial. *Introduction to Computing and Programming in Python: A Multimedia Approach*. Prentice Hall, Englewood Cliffs, NJ, 2004.

[Hoc04]   Roger R. Hock. *Forty Studies That Changed Psychology*. Prentice Hall, Englewood Cliffs, NJ, 2004.

[Hynnd]   R. J. Hyndman. Time series data library. http://www.robjhyndman.com/TSDL, n.d. Accessed on 19 September 2006.

[Joh07]   Jeff Johnson. *GUI Bloopers 2.0: Common User Interface Design Don'ts and Dos.* Morgan Kaufmann Publishers, San Francisco, 2007.

[KS04]   Marja Kuittinen and Jorma Sajaniemi. Teaching roles of variables in elementary programming courses. In *ITiCSE 9*, pages 57–61, 2004.

[LA03]   Mark Lutz and David Ascher. *Learning Python.* O'Reilly & Associates, Inc, Sebastopol, CA, 2003.

[Lak76]   Imre Lakatos. *Proofs and Refutations.* Cambridge University Press, Cambridge, United Kingdom, 1976.

[McC04]   Steve McConnell. *Code Complete: A Practical Handbook of Software Construction.* Microsoft Press, Redmond, WA, 2004.

[Pyt]   Python education special interest group (edu-sig). http://www.python.org/community/sigs/current/edu-sig/.

[VH07]   John L. Viescas and Michael J. Hernandez. *SQL Queries for Mere Mortals: A Hands-On Guide to Data Manipulation in SQL.* Addison-Wesley, Reading, MA, 2007.

[Whi03]   James A. Whittaker. *How to Break Software.* Addison-Wesley, Reading, MA, 2003.

[Wil05]   Greg Wilson. *Data Crunching: Solve Everyday Problems using Java, Python, and More.* The Pragmatic Programmers, LLC, Raleigh, NC, and Dallas, TX, 2005.

[Win06]   Jeannette M. Wing. Computational thinking. *Communications of the ACM*, 49(3):33–35, 2006.

[WT04]   James A. Whittaker and Herbert H. Thompson. *How to Break Software Security.* Addison-Wesley, Reading, MA, 2004.

[Zel03]   John Zelle. *Python Programming: An Introduction to Computer Science.* Franklin Beedle & Associates, Wilsonville, OR, 2003.

Index

The Pragmatic Bookshelf

Available in paperback and DRM-free PDF, our titles are here to help you stay on top of your game. The following are in print as of April 2009; be sure to check our website at pragprog.com for newer titles.

Title	Year	ISBN	Pages
Advanced Rails Recipes: 84 New Ways to Build Stunning Rails Apps	2008	9780978739225	464
Agile Retrospectives: Making Good Teams Great	2006	9780977616640	200
Agile Web Development with Rails: Second Edition	2006	9780977616633	719
Agile Web Development with Rails, Third Edition	2009	9781934356166	784
Augmented Reality: A Practical Guide	2008	9781934356036	328
Behind Closed Doors: Secrets of Great Management	2005	9780976694021	192
Best of Ruby Quiz	2006	9780976694076	304
Core Animation for Mac OS X and the iPhone: Creating Compelling Dynamic User Interfaces	2008	9781934356104	200
Data Crunching: Solve Everyday Problems using Java, Python, and More	2005	9780974514079	208
Deploying Rails Applications: A Step-by-Step Guide	2008	9780978739201	280
Design Accessible Web Sites: 36 Keys to Creating Content for All Audiences and Platforms	2007	9781934356029	336
Desktop GIS: Mapping the Planet with Open Source Tools	2008	9781934356067	368
Developing Facebook Platform Applications with Rails	2008	9781934356128	200
Enterprise Integration with Ruby	2006	9780976694069	360
Enterprise Recipes with Ruby and Rails	2008	9781934356234	416
Everyday Scripting with Ruby: for Teams, Testers, and You	2007	9780977616619	320
FXRuby: Create Lean and Mean GUIs with Ruby	2008	9781934356074	240
From Java To Ruby: Things Every Manager Should Know	2006	9780976694090	160
GIS for Web Developers: Adding Where to Your Web Applications	2007	9780974514093	275
Google Maps API, V2: Adding Where to Your Applications	2006	PDF-Only	83
Groovy Recipes: Greasing the Wheels of Java	2008	9780978739294	264
Hello, Android: Introducing Google's Mobile Development Platform	2008	9781934356173	200
Interface Oriented Design	2006	9780976694052	240

Continued on next page

Title	Year	ISBN	Pages
Learn to Program, 2nd Edition	2009	9781934356364	230
Manage It! Your Guide to Modern Pragmatic Project Management	2007	9780978739249	360
Mastering Dojo: JavaScript and Ajax Tools for Great Web Experiences	2008	9781934356111	568
My Job Went to India: 52 Ways to Save Your Job	2005	9780976694014	208
No Fluff Just Stuff 2006 Anthology	2006	9780977616664	240
No Fluff Just Stuff 2007 Anthology	2007	9780978739287	320
Practices of an Agile Developer	2006	9780974514086	208
Pragmatic Project Automation: How to Build, Deploy, and Monitor Java Applications	2004	9780974514031	176
Pragmatic Thinking and Learning: Refactor Your Wetware	2008	9781934356050	288
Pragmatic Unit Testing in C# with NUnit	2007	9780977616671	176
Pragmatic Unit Testing in Java with JUnit	2003	9780974514017	160
Pragmatic Version Control Using Git	2008	9781934356159	200
Pragmatic Version Control using CVS	2003	9780974514000	176
Pragmatic Version Control using Subversion	2006	9780977616657	248
Programming Erlang: Software for a Concurrent World	2007	9781934356005	536
Programming Groovy: Dynamic Productivity for the Java Developer	2008	9781934356098	320
Programming Ruby: The Pragmatic Programmers' Guide, Second Edition	2004	9780974514055	864
Prototype and script.aculo.us: You Never Knew JavaScript Could Do This!	2007	9781934356012	448
Rails Recipes	2006	9780977616602	350
Rails for .NET Developers	2008	9781934356203	300
Rails for Java Developers	2007	9780977616695	336
Rails for PHP Developers	2008	9781934356043	432
Rapid GUI Development with QtRuby	2005	PDF-Only	83
Release It! Design and Deploy Production-Ready Software	2007	9780978739218	368
Scripted GUI Testing with Ruby	2008	9781934356180	192
Ship it! A Practical Guide to Successful Software Projects	2005	9780974514048	224
Stripes ...And Java Web Development Is Fun Again	2008	9781934356210	375
TextMate: Power Editing for the Mac	2007	9780978739232	208
The Definitive ANTLR Reference: Building Domain-Specific Languages	2007	9780978739256	384
ThoughtWorks Anthology	2008	9781934356142	240
Ubuntu Kung Fu: Tips, Tricks, Hints, and Hacks	2008	9781934356227	400

The Pragmatic Bookshelf

The Pragmatic Bookshelf features books written by developers for developers. The titles continue the well-known Pragmatic Programmer style and continue to garner awards and rave reviews. As development gets more and more difficult, the Pragmatic Programmers will be there with more titles and products to help you stay on top of your game.

Visit Us Online

Practical Programming's Home Page
http://pragprog.com/titles/gwpy
Source code from this book, errata, and other resources. Come give us feedback, too!

Register for Updates
http://pragprog.com/updates
Be notified when updates and new books become available.

Join the Community
http://pragprog.com/community
Read our weblogs, join our online discussions, participate in our mailing list, interact with our wiki, and benefit from the experience of other Pragmatic Programmers.

New and Noteworthy
http://pragprog.com/news
Check out the latest pragmatic developments, new titles and other offerings.

Save on the eBook

Save on the eBook versions of this title. Owning the paper version of this book entitles you to purchase the electronic versions at a terrific discount.

PDF's are great for carrying around on your laptop—they are hyperlinked, have color, and are fully searchable. Most titles are also available for the iPhone and iPod touch, Amazon Kindle, and other popular e-book readers.

Buy now at pragprog.com/coupon.

Contact Us

Online Orders:	www.pragprog.com/catalog
Customer Service:	support@pragprog.com
Non-English Versions:	translations@pragprog.com
Pragmatic Teaching:	academic@pragprog.com
Author Proposals:	proposals@pragprog.com
Contact us:	1-800-699-PROG (+1 919 847 3884)